Norman

Norman Corwin

His Early Life and Radio Career, 1910–1950

WAYNE SOINI

McFarland & Company, Inc., Publishers

Jefferson, North Carolina

ISBN (print) 978-1-4766-8641-7
ISBN (ebook) 978-1-4766-4378-6

LIBRARY OF CONGRESS AND BRITISH LIBRARY
CATALOGUING DATA ARE AVAILABLE

Library of Congress Control Number 2021036243

Front cover image: Norman Corwin during the 1940s (Photofest)

Printed in the United States of America

McFarland & Company, Inc., Publishers
Box 611, Jefferson, North Carolina 28640
www.mcfarlandpub.com

Dedicated to all of the Corwins

[T]he resolves aborted, opportunities missed, works released too soon, scripts, speeches, scenes, words irrevocably printed or spoken, blunders in my personal life, stupidities, obstinacies, neglects of education, impetuous decisions, excesses of brashness and caution, all came together like a tweedy TV pattern, blurred and blobbed, a hail of dried bird-shit.

—Norman Corwin, Radio's Prince Hamlet, recalling himself at age 38, exhausted, staring out of a train window, on the first page of *RE ME*, his unpublished autobiography, ca. 1980 (abandoned due to "I-strain").

Table of Contents

Preface and Acknowledgments

I would like to share a story with you. You will not imitate it, at least not closely. You will not follow Norman Corwin to become a star of the first magnitude on wartime radio. But because Norman made many little decisions that turned out, very surprisingly, to matter later, reading his story will probably make you feel good not only about him but also about your own chance of making little decisions that impact others' lives favorably. In that spirit, the unlikely story of Norman's rise, improbable and unforeseeable even by him, is offered. You never know what might be just around the corner.

Though he was the best radio writer ever, Norman Corwin is not widely remembered today. Norman was denied a permanent place in the pantheon of American writers because the horse he was riding died under him. Television replaced radio. The technical skills he arduously accrued became obsolete. Simultaneously, escapist fare overwhelmed Norman's thoughtful and relevant work. Out of the public ear, by 1950 Norman had vanished from magazine covers. During the decades since, his name has fallen from headlines to footnotes. As of this writing, Norman stands, no longer distinctly, among forgotten figures of World War II.[1]

This is unfair. A case may be made that, beyond world leaders, his words were heard by more people more often during World War II than anybody's. It was not unusual for tens of millions to hear Norman's shows. People arranged their lives not to miss one.

His popularity was a consequence of content. And Norman knew how to write for sound alone. His sonorous lines thrilled not only in his time but, in some of his best shows, survive as thrilling to this day. Not surprisingly, his most popular shows were literally poetry. Called "The Poet Laureate of Radio," Norman won awards and critical praise as well as huge audiences. Out of every hundred letters, he might get one complaint.[2]

His popularity was also a consequence of context. In shows about universal themes, in turn inspiring, thrilling, funny, moving, Norman's poetry or poetic prose was frequently the choice of *most* listeners across

1

the country. By unique circumstances in 1942, Norman's was the *only* show on the air for an hour on thirteen consecutive Saturday nights. He also addressed the *entire* country over all networks at the beginning and at the end of the war, in 1941 a week after Pearl Harbor and in 1945 on the nights of V-E and V-J Days.[3]

Norman earned his place at the head table. From years of appearing in person before audiences, chiefly by lecturing and reciting poetry, often for free, and after over a year of writing up and delivering nightly news over the air, Norman, came to divine what caught people's attention. He exemplified how love's labors last. Before he turned thirty, Norman could craft powerful and enduring scripts. Self-taught, without a high school diploma, Norman in his twenties generated original phrases and lines that would snag any listener's ear and made up ripping yarns that beguiled the worldly and the artless alike.

Although he would be famous by age thirty, Norman spent eighty per cent of his youth obscure, awaiting a chance and wondering if he had what it took to succeed. He was never sure. Hired by CBS in 1938, at age 28, without pushing and shoving, without stealing credit, this self-doubting American Prince Hamlet climbed until he broke through as the first radio writer to reach "box office" stature. Crowds gathered at the drop of his name. Although he declined *The Norman Corwin Show* title when it was offered, his CBS series included *Norman Corwin's Words Without Music*, *26 by Corwin* and *Columbia Presents Corwin*.

Norman looked like a movie star but never was one. Friends thought that he should act but Norman, a handsome, dark-haired man who sported a neat moustache, and moved an Adonis-like body with fluid grace, never became a screen idol. The closest Norman came to being in a movie was, however, documented. One of the classic books about Hollywood, *Picture* by Lillian Ross, described MGM's million-dollar movie *The Red Badge of Courage* as dying before its release. Director John Huston asked a selected group of advisors to tell him how to save the project. When a narrator was suggested, they wanted his voice. Huston asked, "Is Norman Corwin in town?"[4]

The poetic Prince became a hyperbolized figure. Unquestionably the top writer at CBS when CBS reigned supreme and radio itself dominated all American media, Norman experienced the glaring spotlight of fame. Critics bestowed upon him the honorific "The Poet Laureate of Radio" and the superlative "Mr. Radio." Photos of Norman directing his shows or at his typewriter appeared in publications all over the world. *Life* magazine devoted an article to him. Items appeared in *TIME* and in daily newspapers everywhere.[5]

What about the man behind the screen? Some people are beloved by the masses while they repulse those closest to them. In fact, Norman's peers adored him. Norman's family idolized him. Friendships he started were made for life. Women pursued him until he found it "logical" to marry a Broadway star. The country's best actors vied to take part in his radio shows. (As chronicled here in detail, one young scriptwriter left his promising career in Hollywood for the chance merely to be Norman's assistant.) What else ought one think of a person who wrote in a letter, "We can never have too much peace, or good government, or Beethoven"?[6]

He was a *mensch* who, inside, dwelled not on his fame but upon his faults. Self-distrust accompanied him. Although his career demonstrated that talent mattered, he saw his life as "a whole series of serendipities." He forever came short of meeting his standard, which was perfection.[7]

Witness his response to the ecstatic praise of one listener in 1941:

> I wish I could be a party to your suspicion that I am going to be the greatest writer in America, but when I read such works as *The People, Yes* and certain sections of *Leaves of Grass*, and read the little bejeweled lyrics of Emily Dickinson, I could weep for the beauty and strength in them, and for the lacks of my own writing. I shall die a happy man if I have written ten lines that can move a stranger living a century hence … or if I shall have contributed one jot of one tittle of one iota to the advancement of a universal brotherhood of man or to the establishment of a brave and clean and working peace, for all men, for all time.[8]

With such lofty goals, one wonders *what if*—what if radio had continued to be the dominant media into the fifties and sixties? Would Norman, the only writer ever to produce an original script every week for six months, have continued to be so prolific—and so good? Probably. Probably, he would have prospered as "a radiowright" for decades more because, as he finally expressed in his mellowing seventies, he was "the best of the breed."[9]

This book recounts Norman Corwin's earliest and possibly his best story, one he did not write but lived, a heroic battle against the odds. Although his name has long lost its ready recognition, Norman's stunning progress to the top of his profession endures as a terrific tale to be told. Norman lived to be 101. This book covers his emergence from the wrong side of the tracks in East Boston to the height of celebrity in Manhattan, all before he turned 40. Because it is simultaneously the story of a man who did the human race proud in the darkest hours of its bloodiest worldwide struggle, finding the words needed then, to read of and to remember Norman is to be inspired—and fascinated.

Some notes on structure: Norman's shows are but summarized in passing for two reasons. One is changing public tastes. Nursery rhymes cleverly modified and recited with sound effects, Emperor Nero's cackling laugh in Hades and Curley the caterpillar who tap danced to the tune of "Yes, sir, that's my baby" tend to puzzle modern ears. In general, also, shows dealing with contemporary concerns customarily fade along with their context, and much of Norman's work was topical. Scenes of children singing over Hitler's grave, a British dad's poignant letter to his son, a tense bomber, and a shattering crash, all of which once held the country in thrall, have lost their hook.

Besides this, many other books already cover Norman's works in great detail and many of his radio scripts themselves were published and, although now out of print, remain accessible in used bookstores and libraries.

Finally, Norman's best shows, which embodied scenes of universal human conflict dramatically or, more rarely, satirically or comedically, are available to *hear*. An exemplary selection was issued in 2010 in a centennial CD edition, a collection that readers are definitely encouraged to seek out.[10]

Accordingly, the works of Norman Corwin are not treated in detail in this book. After a vignette focused on just one of his shows, "We Hold These Truths," broadcast in December 1941, Norman's life story is arranged chronologically by decade.

Part One tracks a street urchin weaving words for tiny but appreciative audiences before he could read, and on up to local prominence as a reporter in print media who went on the air when he was but 19.

Part Two follows Norman in his twenties through several hardships, some self-inflicted, some unlucky, until he reached the threshold of choosing between New York radio *or* scripting movies in Hollywood before he turned thirty.

Finally, **Part Three** pursues Norman through his thirties, when, despite the expiration of his contract with CBS, as a government worker, by historical accident, he won instant fame and meteoric prominence as the country's leading wartime radio writer. After exploring the subsequent most active and most widely known years of his life, this part hits a high note with his courtship and marriage to a Broadway star, Kate Locke.

After formally concluding on his fortieth birthday in 1950, this book summarizes Norman's later years by way of a brief epilogue. (Future biographers are alerted and invited to take up the untold but dramatic story of a family man and patriot blacklisted in Hollywood who successfully defended his name.)

Acknowledgments

The Brookline Public Library must be noted first. One day in 2011 a staffer (whose name I do not know) put together a collection of books by

Norman Corwin, as they traditionally do at the Coolidge Corner Branch when one of their authors dies. When I saw, "Norman Corwin, 1910–2011," though, I thought that this must be incorrect. I checked. He *had* lived to 101, and I also saw how much he had done. I wanted to read his biography. After reading Leroy Bannerman's book, my appetite was only whetted. I decided to research Norman's life, to visit his old homesteads in Massachusetts, to go to his California archives, to find out more after I retired. Then, I fell down the slippery slope of writing a biography of Norman Corwin myself, the first since Bannerman's noble effort.

I was assisted at various times by many people. A biographer's work is always a cooperative endeavor, or it fails. To begin with, I wish to thank the late Professor Bannerman (may he somehow know!) for very graciously encouraging me, and not only by way of his pioneering book. When we spoke by phone, it was Professor Bannerman who pointed me emphatically in the direction of archives at Thousand Oaks, California. There he, Norman and others had deposited largely unpublished documents of all phases of Norman's life. When I followed through and visited the impressive Norman Corwin Collection of the amazingly varied American Radio Archives at the Thousand Oaks Library, Thousand Oaks, California, the library's well-informed and friendly staff including Jeanette M. Berard and Klaudia Englund, helped me to explore its truly enormous collection. My friend, Gloucester High School classmate, and California resident, Bob Bosselman, later made a trek to take photos of some of these materials.

Brilliant and affable Professor Donna Halpern of Emerson College— whose own radio work enviably began alongside the legendary Arne "Woo Woo" Ginsburg on old WMEX's "Night Train"—was generous with her time and spent a lot of it hunting up items I would never have found but could (and did) use to enrich my text. In amongst other kindness of strangers on which I depended, Professor Jeff Porter of the University of Iowa instantly placed his recent panoramic book *Lost Sound: The Forgotten Art of Radio Storytelling* (Chapel Hill: The University of North Carolina Press, 2016) at my disposal. It was a great boon that I could quote from it several times. Thanks, similarly, to Mr. and Mrs. John Dunning for phone encouragement and permission to quote from their comprehensive *On the Air: The Encyclopedia of Old-Time Radio* (1998) A great teacher of narrative history, and the author of many classics of psychobiography including *Lincoln's Quest for Union, A Psychological Portrait*, Dr. Charles B. Strozier helped me toe the mark in interpreting what Norman said upon awakening from his appendectomy operation in 1927.

Local writing group colleagues who helped me with useful feedback include Robin Jean Hubbard, who called my many sprawling first-draft pages to order. As the final draft came inching closer, Arley Pett, Professor George Rosen, Elizabeth Ann Maney, Laura Ventimiglia, and others who shrewdly chose anonymity commented and some went over and weeded, trimming my most awkward and diffuse lines. They all claimed that the task was a pleasure, a white lie that God in Her infinite goodness will surely forgive.

BIO, the Biographers' International Organization, is another world of resources for biographers. It works simply by putting biographers together. Nobody exceeded Professor Patti Bender's capacity as an editor or kindness as a friend. She is destined for fame as the author of the definitive biography of her own beloved author, Emilie Loring. From Patti I received both encouragement and critical feedback—the "breakfast of champions"—and likewise from BIO's regional chapter, which meets monthly in Cambridge, Massachusetts. I salute its long-time leaders Ray Shepard, Melinda Ponder and Nigel Hamilton but omit to name many others for fear I forget any.

Another kind and generous soul, Michael James Kacey, Norman's friend and still one of his biggest fans, is the volunteer who maintains a terrific online website in Norman's honor. He also produced a remarkable documentary about Norman during Norman's life, *The Poet Laureate of Radio*. Mike not only helped me directly but also enabled me to link up with Norman's children, of whom Diane Corwin Okarski is Norman's literary executor. It is hard to overstate Ms. Okarski's kind assistance. She blessed my biographical project without conditions. She helped me with letters and by granting rights to use photographs and other materials. Some of these were unique and unpublished. She and her husband made leaps of faith in sending me rare and priceless materials which overcame several research obstacles. The ancient phrase *sine qua non* comes to mind as apt. Every biographer should experience such encouragement. Few do!

Others who granted me interviews, often at substantial inconvenience to themselves, include Allan Broverman (thanks, Shelby!), and John Tranghese, who gave me an extended guided tour of Springfield sights that were important in Norman's life. Truly, few human beings have grown up enduring greater hardships than John, remained standing and then moved forward to become the Gibraltar of their families. *Per cento anno!*

David Alff and others at McFarland & Company served as the cavalry to rescue a book that was on its way to a lower drawer in my file cabinet.

Not least, let me thank my patient family. They all accepted this book over spending more time with me, not necessarily a bad exchange. Thanks, son Eric and his wife, Mai, daughter Heather, son Kevin (who also spent many hours making accurate transcripts of vital taped interviews) and grandchildren Derek, Hannah, and Jayden. Finally, my partner, Anne Brodeur, deserves not only acknowledgment but accolades.

—Wayne Soini

Author's Note

Family letters, books and interviews quoted herein have been edited for capitalization, spelling, punctuation, grammar, and flow. However, in each instance substantive content was preserved. No words were added without being bracketed. All words quoted from books appear in those books. All words quoted from interviews were, indeed, spoken by the subjects of the interviews.

Broadcast dates not otherwise footnoted are drawn from Professor Leroy Bannerman's magnum opus, *Norman Corwin and Radio: The Golden Years* (University of Alabama Press, 1986). Few books justify rereading. Bannerman's humane, warm, and perceptive chronicle is one of them.

Professor Bannerman as donor is likewise the ultimate source of the American Radio Archive's irreplaceable collection of some 24 compact disc recordings of interviews with Norman, his family, one of his high school teachers, the man who hired him at CBS, etc.

Photographs herein were received from several generous sources. However, the wording and accuracy of the captions were exclusively my responsibility. Blame no one else.

Norman's December Surprise

"We Hold These Truths"

> [P]eople often asked me, some in a friendly, others in a
> hostile spirit, why I felt it necessary to plug so constantly
> at social and war themes. The answer was not that I was
> asked to do it, or ordered to do it, or paid to do it, or talked
> into doing it. It was a matter of my personal conscience—
> an apparatus that, for good or bad, would let me do noth-
> ing else.
> —Norman Corwin, Preface to "There Will Be Time Later,"
> in *Untitled and Other Radio Plays* (1947), 428.

An exception sometimes proves the rule and "We Hold These Truths,"
Norman's masterpiece, exceptional in so many other ways, *was* a project
that he was asked to do, and had to be talked into doing after his initially
firm rejection. Though not ordered to do it, Norman wrote and directed
"We Hold These Truths" for the Office of Facts and Figures (later, the
"Office of War Information") and finished it because President Franklin D.
Roosevelt told him to do so when Norman had doubts.

It was not his idea. It was not his dream project. The idea for this show,
alternately known in radio history as Norman's "Bill of Rights show," came
out of Washington as an unwelcome challenge to an exhausted writer.

Just before Thanksgiving, he was asked to travel. This script could not
be written in a cottage on the Hudson. Besides shuttling between New York
and Washington for research, with lots of overnights in the capital, working at the Library of Congress, finally, there would be California. He would
have to book a train to Los Angeles and stay there for a week because Hollywood stars, on loan for this special show, would rehearse at and broadcast
from the CBS studio in Los Angeles. The job involved so much travel that it
was hard for Norman to accept.

Besides, Norman had just lost his job at CBS. He was not only beyond
tired but, given short notice, Norman would have to cancel everything to

Norman (center) with Hollywood star Jimmy Stewart (right) in the NBC control room in December 1941. The legendary actor's narration began and helped hold together Norman's first huge national hit, "We Hold These Truths" (courtesy American Radio Archives and Museum).

concentrate. It meant no recreation or socializing. The dry stretch would eliminate from his calendar the testimonial dinner of his close friend and CBS colleague, Ed Murrow, the foreign correspondent on his homecoming from covering the London Blitz.

Norman allowed himself to be persuaded and was busily at work on the script on Tuesday, December 2, 1941, rather than seated at a front table among the those who greeted Murrow as the CBS-sponsored-and-broadcast dinner took place at the Waldorf Astoria without Norman.

Although President Roosevelt missed the shindig, too, he could make up for it. FDR asked Murrow to come to *him*. Exemplifying the high place occupied by radio in American society at that time, Murrow was invited to dine with President and Mrs. Roosevelt at the White House. That dinner meant a private meal shared in the family quarters. Murrow was scheduled to appear on the evening of Sunday, December 7.[1]

Not so Norman. On that Sunday, Norman began his trek West, making the run from Washington to Chicago on the "Twentieth Century Limited."

In Chicago, he transferred to be ensconced in a private compartment on the "Super Chief" luxury train. Rocking and rolling with a clipboard on his knees, his papers spread out around him, Norman aimed to modify, to expand and to chop his fourth draft into a tight, final script.

The words were up to him. Norman was writing everything but the President's speech at the end. (FDR's short remarks were being crafted in Washington by the President's friend and frequent ghostwriter, Archibald MacLeish.)[2]

At least, the cast awaiting Norman and his final script in Los Angeles included few strangers. Almost all of the actors had been in Norman's last CBS series, *26 by Corwin*. They all knew the deadline. The show would be broadcast live on the evening of December 15, the 150th anniversary of the ratification of the Bill of Rights.

Facing down that deadline, sacrificing three weeks of normal life, working alone, Norman was traveling in style. The train was not only a limited express but its amenities embraced a dining car, sleeping compartments, and squads of porters and maids. Though born and raised in modest circumstances, Norman was not averse to spending money when his services were gratuitous and only his expenses were being covered.

Moreover, the fourth script in hand was not the final script. Norman had booked a compartment not for sleep but for surface space. While creating, Norman liked to shuffle whatever he wrote, to lay out his writing, placing his pages first in one sequence, then another. Keeping everything in sight also helped him spot pieces that did not fit, which he relentlessly discarded.

He planned only one extended break. In mid-afternoon, he would rent a radio. A portable set could be rented from the porter. It was one amenity that he especially valued. Norman hardly ever took a trip without tuning in on selected shows, classical music, or news. Tonight it was to be "The Gulf Screen Guild Theater," starring Orson Welles. Welles went on the air at 7:30 performing "Between Americans." This show, written by Norman, who had produced and directed it five months earlier for his *26 by Corwin* series, was a relatively lively and light-hearted play about being an American.[3]

Ceasing work as the sun began to sink, having culled rejected lines, modified others, and jotted down new ideas while they were hot, having had a productive day, Norman was well into the completion of his final draft before he rang for the porter. To his surprise, the porter said, "There are no radios. Ain't you heard?" He then succinctly summarized for his most isolated traveler, "The Japs just bombed Pearl Harbor. We're at war."

In confusion now, Norman joined the rush of passengers who swamped the Western Union office at the next stop, in Kansas City. When the harried agent read Norman's draft, being in no mood for levity, he asked, "This a joke? Franklin D. Roosevelt?" Norman simply pointed to his own name. For years, his CBS series had broadcast under it. "Oh, that Corwin," the agent said, his expression changing. He solemnly assured Norman that his wire would receive priority transmission.

Back on the train, Norman knocked on the door of the next compartment, occupied by Edna Best, a British actress married to Norman's agent, Nat Wolff. He begged pardon, asked if she had a radio and would mind a fellow listener. She and he thereafter listened as bulletins continued for hours before normal programming resumed—coincidentally with the Orson Welles' show, promptly at 7:30. As they listened to Norman's words, he judged the live audience's hearty laughter (implying that he joined in it) and prolonged applause to be "cathartic." Maybe he could laugh, but a Draconian sword remained over his head: Would FDR think that the Bill of Rights show was needed now?[4]

Norman got his answer. The next morning, as soon as the train stopped in Albuquerque, a Western Republican messenger came through first-class shouting, "Passenger Corwin! Passenger Corwin!" Faithful to good grammar from rote classes in East Boston, Norman said, "I am he." The word from Washington was: the show must go on.[5]

Carried by all four networks, on every radio station on the dial, the broadcast would conclude with the President of the United States speaking. But now a commemorative program that nobody had expected to set the world on fire was going out reframed. By a new context, it was thrown into a national moment of attention as a world war began.

Norman suddenly had a lot more work to do. He faced heavy revision from page one. He had another full day before he would reach Los Angeles, but the anniversary loomed closer by the minute and the country's leading actors were looking to him for dynamite. The President expected as much. The country needed moral succor from Norman's words. He did not freeze up, but neither did ink flow swiftly. Norman cobbled away on the moving train, he said later, with what seemed to him to be "the speed of a glacier."[6]

As the Super Chief rolled to a stop early Tuesday morning in Los Angeles, sleepless Norman held on tight to a finished and final draft that could be copied and distributed to his cast. He scheduled their rehearsals. He molded them into a group for live broadcast.

On Monday night, December 15, 1941, the studio's red light lit up and for an hour Norman's show *was* American radio. His "We Hold These Truths," no longer a nostalgic retrospective, aired as the opening gun of American radio in World War II.

"We Hold These Truths" rocked the country as no radio show had since Orson Welles' "The War of the Worlds" broadcast of 1938. After the surprise attack on Pearl Harbor on December 7, 1941, recruiting stations had been jammed and Americans at large bought newspapers and listened, starved for orientation on what was happening and why. Broadcast just ahead of the President's first wartime address to the public, "We Hold These Truths" implicitly communicated what we were taking up arms to defend.

In a chin-up, defiant script, Norman dramatized the Bill of Rights in operation. Everybody's favorite "good guy," Jimmy Stewart, the honest and polite but firm reporter chasing the Bill of Rights story, encountered Edward G. Robinson, everybody's favorite "bad guy," in jail but coming out on bail, entitled to a jury trial and confident of beating back false charges brought against him by a political machine. "No Gestapo tactics in this country," Robinson snarled in his distinctive voice and manner. Germany, with whom the United States was now at war, was in Norman's sights. Lionel Barrymore, Marjorie Main, Walter Brennan, still-the-*Wunderkind* Orson Welles, and others starred and stirred millions in a dramatized debate over American ideals. Listening to the show, people trying to understand why the country was going to war felt that they were hearing answers.

At this distance, objective criticism is difficult. It is only by hindsight (or "hindhearing") that missing voices are obvious. For example, an all-white cast represented American history. Although "We Hold These Truths" was about all men being created equal, those men who originally enacted the Bill of Rights were white. The absence of Blacks or Native Americans (or Asians, given war against the Empire of Japan) is arguably historical and understandable but nonetheless glaring these many years later. The program is most fairly judged by 1940s standards.

The country's response was uniformly positive. Excitement carried over to the next day. To gauge the show's success, Norman phoned his youngest brother for help. Al, in the Army and stationed in New York, whose wife worked in the city, was ideally positioned to gather data. Although his letter to Norman itself was lost, Al's simultaneous letter to Ma and Pa Corwin in Winthrop, Massachusetts, survived. Much the same wording must have raised Norman's spirits and discounted any doubts. To their parents, Al wrote:

> I haven't heard an adverse comment. It's all praise of the grandest sort. I wish I had a dictaphone near my desk so's I could recapture on a record, just what they said and how they said it. Had lunch with Em today and he confirms the fact that superlatives for the broadcast is (*sic*) something overwhelming.[7]

Al reported people talking about the show "in elevators, in restaurants and on the streets" while his wife, Sarita, told him "that she even heard raves on the show in the ladies' toilet." The show was praised in all media. Al told his parents that he sent a letter "air mail" to Norman with "all the printed and spoken reactions" that he could "get ahold of."[8]

The show unavoidably illuminated its author like a lightning bolt. By historical accident, this program, never planned to be a wartime show at all and written mostly in peacetime, became its author's beachhead landing. Norman the poet was, after this single broadcast, branded as radio's leading *wartime* writer. Norman's interrupted network radio career instantly restarted. Norman, the target of a truckload of job offers, selected the one from CBS. He marched back to New York as the network's conquering hero.[9]

Unaware of Norman's CBS negotiations, Al wrote within two weeks of a serious discussion with his own new boss, Hans Christian Adamson, the head of the Army Air Force public relations bureau. Al said that Adamson "has nothing but admiration for you. He took your address and means to write you, I think, about joining his bureau. He would give his eye-tooth to have you head his radio division. Your title would be Major."[10]

As things happened, the Army Air Force would have to win the war without Major Norman Corwin. Norman had his old job back.

"We Hold These Truths" formed the climax of an unlikely story, a story that began in a triple-decker tenement in East Boston, Massachusetts, in 1910, a story not acted by Hollywood stars on all stations but lived day to day by real and ordinary people, often under inauspicious circumstances, in places both small and large, a story of grit, persistence and broad shoulders, the story that this book was written to tell.

PART ONE

Norman to Nineteen
(1910–1929)

A "Tough Kid" in Eastie

The Corwin brothers, from left: Emil ("Em"), born 1900; Norman, born 1910; and Alfred ("Al"), born 1906, lived in an East Boston triple-decker across from the railroad yard, and enjoyed their immersive visits in the country (courtesy Diane Corwin Okarski).

Reminiscing during a taped interview with his first biographer, Leroy Bannerman, Norman described himself in East Boston, known as "Eastie." He was, he said, in those days a "tough kid." He said that he took "himself and the world personally and grouchily." Without neatening the mess, he summed up his screwed-up youth in three words: "chronic refractory behavior."[1]

Anecdotes support Norman's bleak view of his boyhood. Others interviewed told Bannerman more details. Norman carried a large chip on his shoulder. His outspoken, oldest brother, Emil or "Em," recalled, "At a store to get some oranges or apples, when he came up with a bagful and the proprietor said something like 'Are you sure you have a dozen in there? you don't have any more?' Norman emptied the bag and said, 'You count it yourself,' and walked out."[2]

Norman could provoke his normally gentle middle brother, bespectacled bookworm Al, until fists flew. Al recalled vividly that Norman had to win in anything he took on. Al was tall and lithe, a track star used to competition himself, but the ferocity that his youngest brother displayed in games took him aback. Em, athletic but smallish, said of Norman, who was in grade school when Em was in college, "He was a hard loser. He lost very hard. And if he felt that a play was called unfairly, he'd just as soon quit the game if he didn't get his way."[3]

Such a boy might have grown up to become one of the many violent gangsters of his time. That tragic narrative was averted. Among other early influences was Sam Corwin, Norman's easy-going father ("Pa"). He dubbed Norman "Peck's Bad Boy" after a mischievous stage character. Em said that Norman was his parents' "problem child." He admitted overall, "My father had a difficult time with him." Whatever he did, Pa's intervention was firm and enough to precipitate a painful reaction. Again during his interview with Bannerman, without any context, Norman offered the searing image of himself as a street kid who "sat on the curb, head in hands."[4]

Pa smoked but tried to keep his sons from bad habits. Em recalled Pa showing them "what would happen" to their lungs if they smoked by "blowing a mouthful of cigarette smoke through his handkerchief" and displaying the resulting smudge.[5]

Norman grew up in Eastie, not in nearby Boston. With his family, Norman spent his first fifteen years on gritty Bremen Street, not on lace curtained Beacon Hill. Norman was a world away from mansions that front the green expanse of the Boston Common, beside the golden domed State House and within sight of the famous swan boats and the elegant Parker House, where Charles Dickens once stayed, and Boston cream pie was invented.

Eastie could grate the ears of its residents. Up on the top floor apartment of a triple-decker tenement, Norman heard bells, whistles and bangs as cargo cars slammed into place day and night. Em recalled the regular "terrible crash that used to wake us up in the middle of the night." It was the noise of "coupling and uncoupling and this kind of thing" of the Boston & Maine Railroad. "We'd all be sleeping and suddenly we'd hear these freight trains collide and crash and make the house rumble. After you lived there long enough, I suppose you slept through these things." Norman said that the freight yards and their freight trains were "the cyclorama of (his) boyhood."[6]

Across the street from the railroad yard, the Corwins were enmired in dirt and noise. Em said it was "an awful place to live." He recalled how "dust used to rise up on the streets when wagons rumbled by."

It was also noisy. The Corwins lived within earshot of fire alarms and clanging fire-engines. Nearby Maverick Square was Dickensian. Boys hawked morning and afternoon editions of five competing newspapers there, bursting their young lungs screaming headlines, often invented them to lure pennies out of passersby. Hard-helmeted policemen blew their whistles as pushcart dealers touted their fruits and shouted out prices for attention. Teams of horses pulled wagons through neighborhoods, drivers yelling for old rags as they passed. Immigrants found their footing here. Diverse dialects and voices swirled about in the air in the Eastie. Norman's parents were immersed in Jewish culture on both sides. He would have heard raucous klezmer bands and attended Temple ceremonies. He and his brothers came to understand Yiddish from many common phrases shared in their home and neighborhood.[7]

Three Arts and a Boy

As a boy, "tough kid" Norman found himself drawn to poetry, story-telling and classical music. Nothing Norman said or wrote ever explained this. His motivation is lost but nothing could be clearer than the facts that Norman in turn fell hard for poetry first, then charmed neighboring street kids with stories of his own spinning and, finally, he found inexhaustibly interesting and came to know classical music better than many professional musicians. Neither Pa nor Ma ever claimed a role in inviting Norman's attention to these fields. His brothers may have encouraged him, likely inadvertently or after Norman was already hooked. The veil over this aspect of his boyhood is most opaque.

Norman's brothers were older than Norman and they left him before he was in high school. In 1920, when Norman was ten, Em went off to college a hundred miles away in western Massachusetts. Al matriculated at Harvard in 1922. They may have had an impact earlier because, before he

was ten years old, Norman discovered the three arts that later enabled him
to excel in radio.

First, Norman closely encountered poetry. It is a baffling fascination
basically because Norman knew no poets. Nor was anybody in his family
a writer. However it happened, Norman at age four memorized and then
recited a poem to his family. The source of Norman's first poem may have
been his oldest brother. Repetition was the first rule of learning in public schools. Teachers of those days routinely assigned pupils texts to learn
by heart. By this speculative scenario, Em had to memorize and recite a
poem and Norman imitated him, his idol and mentor. Although this
is no story that Norman ever told, circumstantially, Norman could not
read. Thus, he needed some patient and tolerant reciter to whom he could
repeatedly listen. One is without a clue who this may have been other than
Em.[8]

Norman debuted live in the family's front parlor. At age four, he delivered a romantic vision of war, Robert Browning's *Incident of the French
Camp*. To the drumbeat of the rhythmic poem, line by line, Norman
unfurled a maudlin melodrama until its boy hero lay dead at Napoleon's
feet. It was a powder keg in words. Norman learned how explosively and
emotionally powerful a poem could be.

Norman took his show on the road. On a triumphant tour in relatives'
homes in the fall or winter of 1914, the poetic prodigy recited the *Incident
of the French Camp* before appreciative audiences for an ever-extended
run. Dramatic effects were added beyond any schoolroom standards. At
the poem's conclusion—after the cue line, "Smiling the boy fell dead"—and
after a doubtless wan smile, Norman threw himself to the floor.

A moment after his death, however, Norman rose and bowed.
Applause and praise came to the resurrected boy from his parents, his
grandmother, his aunt, his cousins and his brothers, some of whom gave
him hugs or offered sweets or tossed a rare penny or two—possibly the first
money he ever made.

Ever after, Norman associated poetry with pleasure. But that was not
the only lesson he drew from the experience of recitation. He may also
have learned that, in show business, timing is everything. It was current
events that generated an audience for patriotic war poems in 1914. Countries all over Europe had mobilized. Millions of men were marching into
a world war in August. Browning's dusty old 1895 poem acquired new
relevance.

Lastly, he realized that the spoken arts were a way to attract attention
and to bond with other people in a fun way. One imagines a tour along Bremen Street's row of tenements. For example, the large and poor but gen-
teel and cultured Hoffman family, which likewise included several boys,

lived just next door. Because, as Em recalled of Bremen Street, "there were no such things as any lawns or terraces, there was a brick sidewalk and the flats themselves," little Norman would have performed in the coziness of the Hoffmans' parlor.[9]

After poetry came storytelling. At six or seven, Norman's imagination found an outlet: telling stories to neighborhood classmates. Essentially in opposition to his "tough guy" rebel exterior, on the run from the streets, Norman again found in language a path to a more social self.

Norman the storyteller worked the streets. Em witnessed the phenomenon. Coming home from high school, Em spotted a crowd of kids in front of the family's tenement. Worried that something bad had happened, he picked up his pace. Among other things, Norman had a hair-trigger temper and was known for fighting. Although Em found Norman the center of attention, Norman was not fighting that afternoon. As cool and confident as Scheherazade, the youngest of the three Corwin brothers sat atop the building's three-step granite block stoop, occupying his own niche, telling stories that he made up to a half-dozen attentive peers.

What Em caught was the first show that Norman composed, produced, directed, and acted—and he marveled. His kid brother on the stoop, no costume, props, or music, held an audience of urchins in the palm of his hand. Even decades later, Em could not get over his surprise.

"He was a little boy, he was only about six or eight years old. And the kids were fascinated by these stories he told. He had a marvelous imagination," Em told Bannerman.

Plainly, Em joined the bunch himself. He listened until a near-professional twist: the story became a serial. Em reported to Bannerman that when Norman "used to get to the most important part, the cliff hanger, he would stop and say 'Well, I'll finish it tomorrow.'"[10]

Em showed his wonder by repeating, restating in different words, "When it came to the most exciting part, the kids would be listening with their mouths open, he'd tell them these long stories then he'd tell them, 'That's the end of the story, I'll finish tomorrow,' and the next day he'd start telling them again, finish telling that story."

Em's astonishment is our own. Norman had nobody to emulate as an entertainer. His accomplishment seems to be his own. No Corwin had been even a stagehand or a ticket-seller. His father was a plate maker, his mother was a housewife who did watercolors. Without acting classes or any known example, Norman found his calling on Bremen Street between the front door and the sidewalk. He was a storyteller, and the friends that telling stories brought him kept coming back.[11]

Besides poetry and serial storytelling, Norman fell in love with classical music. By a chronology now impossible to reconstruct, but probably as

Norman was turning 8 or 10, he somehow was pointed to or browsed inde-
pendently and discovered treasures. He found that the nearby East Boston
branch of the great Boston Public Library system possessed not only books
but phonograph records, long playing albums. He later declared public
libraries to be "the greatest institution of all" and "the preserver of civilization's dearest values." But in his boyhood on Bremen Street he craved
not only books but something else, incredibly available via his library card,
sounds that were of another world than his.

To mine auditory gold, he literally had to do heavy lifting. The boy
awkwardly toted home thick, heavy albums of 78 rpm phonograph records.
These records comprised the best versions of classical music performed by
world-class musicians. Norman played them continuously for hours on his
family's Victrola. Concerts at home became his chief pleasure. He heard
and memorized the world's greatest music. The repertoire in his head was
prodigious. He came to know Beethoven, to distinguish Verdi from Puc-
cini, and to love Mozart. Few adults in the country carried as much great
music inside of their heads as Norman.

Em noticed and Em acted. He shelled out for concert tickets. Nor-
man never forgot that, through his older brother's generosity, he heard
the Boston Symphony Orchestra. The BSO went back to 1881, Symphony
Hall to 1900. His brother's beneficence was a break, as was Norman's proximity to Symphony Hall. Only a handful of spaces existed in the United
States in which a boy could be introduced so grandly to classical music.
When Norman attended his first concert, the BSO was at the start of its
"French-directed" era under Henry Rabaud and Pierre Monteux. Its acous-
tics are famously excellent. He wasn't in Eastie anymore. Instead, at the corner of Huntington and Massachusetts Avenue, to his already sophisticated
ears, the music of the spheres magically manifested.[12]

As his oldest brother's grateful guest—and mindful that his ticket
cost Em the then-unimaginably large sum of $2.50—Norman's behav-
ior was one of complete attention. Among some 2,500 other people, the
self-conscious, sensitive boy might have been overwhelmed. The great Beethoven's name was inscribed over the stage. Despite so much to see, something kicked in before the orchestra began to play: *Norman shut his eyes.*
However it happened, whether by Em's suggestion or spontaneously, Norman, his eyes closed, found himself in pure sound and entranced by fine
music. That first concert experience molded him for life. Silent listening,
eyes closed, was Norman's exclusive way of attending concerts. Ears rather
than eyes advanced as his preferred organs of perception.[13]

The acute importance of sound to Norman resurfaced after his
first published book of radio scripts. In its preface, Carl Van Doren had
commented:

The blind who can hear are more often happy than the deaf who can see. Let persons who have both senses try an easy experiment. They will find, at a play or motion picture, that if they close their eyes and listen they do not miss as much as they think they are missing when they stop their ears and look."[14]

Van Doren's thesis struck Norman as right. He wrote Van Doren, heartily endorsing his take. Norman declared that Van Doren had "summed up in a few words what exhaustive analytical treatises have never succeeded in making plain."[15]

Of his three youthful passions, occupying first place in Norman's heart was music. He realized his limits at the same time, however. For one thing, he had nagged his parents to buy him a violin. However, as he put it, "When Emil one night took me to a concert at Symphony Hall, and I heard a master perform a violin concerto, I knew at once that if I studied hard for the rest of my life I would never begin to approach such quality; why then scrape away?"[16]

Norman not only stopped "scraping away," he never took up another instrument. (He did hold a violin in the yearbook picture of his high school co-ed orchestra, but at the time he was the new kid in school and wanted friends, especially girls. One wonders how many times he played the violin.)

Another musical skill likewise fell to his unmet desire for perfection. What he could not do well, he chose not to do at all. He taught himself to read music and to compose scores but he did not compose music to his satisfaction. He tossed away score sheets he wrote. He also never wrote a song.

Norman was left with his personal pleasure and, professionally, he collaborated in radio shows with a studio orchestra. Once, a radio script he wrote became the libretto for an award-winning opera. But, above all, Norman was a gifted listener. Lifelong, what Norman did musically was to listen to classical music, his eyes closed, all ears.

Overall, Norman pursued classical music, storytelling, and poetry with a passion and with an industry unusual for any child. These art forms stirred something deep within him. Browning's poem enabled him to be another boy, a glorious one, of another place and time. Possibly, telling stories likewise offered a safe outlet to identify with invented characters and their intense emotions. And music may have relieved him from otherwise overpoweringly dark moods. The intensity and constancy of the boy's reaction to these three arts is documented. The motivation, his own, is completely absent from the record. The early causes behind the "tough kid's" sustained and dazzling devotion to poetry, story-telling and classical music must be at best suggested and left undefined, honored as the Holy Grail of Norman Corwin studies.

One must nonetheless not minimize the apparent contemporary

triviality of the boy's chief interests. At the time, Norman was walking a short plank to nowhere. The combination of a love of poetry, a tongue for stories and an ear for music ought not to have changed his life. Had he been born twenty years earlier or even twenty years later, these talents could at most have provided him with pleasant hobbies. In the early 1920s, no job existed for a poet-storyteller with a fine taste in music. Commercial radio, half-hour dramatic radio shows and radio networks were unimaginable. Norman did not pursue poetry, stories and music for a career. There then existed no such career.

As often, timing was everything. Suddenly blossoming in the mid–1920s, radio not only existed but grew. By the 1930s, network radio covered the country. In the early 1940s, radio was the dominant media. Accidently born at the right time, Norman was blessedly buoyed up above earlier (and later) generations of boys and girls whose bliss was poetry, stories, or Beethoven, Mozart, and others. Norman's unlikely rise became a tiny bit more possible because the time that American radio would exist and reach "Mr. and Mrs. North and South America, and all the ships at sea" was just over the horizon.[17]

His Father's Business

For a time, Sam Corwin realized the American dream. He arrived in America at the right time, ahead of the Turn of the Century rush of immigrants. He arrived already speaking English, from years in London, and could go into business midway between the major depressions of 1893 and 1907. At 21, he was a successful entrepreneur who owned and operated a small but lucrative printing and engraving company on the edge of Beacon Hill, a few blocks from Boston's City Hall and the golden-domed, Bulfinch-designed State House. His future seemed secure. Printing was a sound industry and Boston was prime territory. Throughout the country, Boston was synonymous with quality plate printing. If timing was everything, Sam's clock was set on too good to be true. Orders came pouring into the Hub and Sam got his share, or more.

He got so busy that he needed help with the harvest. He somehow found an older man, a part-time minister, to fill the bill. Thereafter, Sam contentedly oversaw his busy two-machine shop on Somerset Street while his new partner took the orders, made the collections, cashed the checks, and kept the books—until the day he ran off with all of the company's money.[18]

Norman either closed his ears or never heard this story. Norman claimed only vague knowledge of his father's business. "I know almost nothing at all of his career as a businessman," Norman told Bannerman. "What I think of is a rather short-lived career because he became sick, my mother became sick, and I think the thing collapsed not long after he began the business."

But this dramatic version was simply not so. Sam's loss was sadder. Norman's father did not lose his business to illness nor was he married at the time. The business did not, in fact, collapse. Printing was not going away. A savvy new entrepreneur named McKenzie stepped in and snapped up the machines that Sam had to sell in order to pay his dunning creditors. McKenzie simultaneously, and very shrewdly, offered Sam a job. Trained, talented,

Sam "Pa" Corwin, c. 1900. The nattily dressed immigrant was then realizing the American Dream. He owned and ran a job print shop with two machines in then-booming Boston (courtesy Diane Corwin Okarski.)

hard-working Sam promptly accepted and by that quirk became an employee instead of the owner of a profitable and growing company.

Sam thereafter worked for 41 years at the ever-expanding McKenzie Company. Sam, who had guessed right about the industry, the city, his talents, and future trends, from one bad guess about one man's integrity became a witness rather than a winner. It was upon his shoulders—Sam trained all of the engravers and printers and was handy in fixing and adjusting the machinery—that the McKenzie company operated so well. Only war-time paper shortages, which crippled production lines everywhere, presented an obstacle that Sam could not fix or work around. Only then, McKenzie had to shut down the company that Sam had founded and had in actuality largely kept going for decades.[19]

One wonders if Norman really did not know. Norman may have preferred not to describe his guileless father as first the hapless victim of a swindler and then the foil of a rapacious entrepreneur. His father was McKenzie's employee when Norman was born. When his father, and then his mother, were severely sick, McKenzie floated loans or "advances" to the family. It was peonage. Norman may have had mixed feelings about the generosity of Mr. McKenzie, whose desire to get Sam back to work again—for him—was his major motive.

Interviewed by Bannerman, Norman obscured any awareness that McKenzie ran the business that Sam ought by rights to have owned. Although Norman probably viewed McKenzie as an exploiter rather than—as ever in his father's eyes—the Corwin family's chief benefactor, he said nothing of that, or of his intense feelings. It was Em, not Norman, who told Bannerman that Norman hated McKenzie.[20]

Norman's knowledge of his father's business may have been far greater than "almost nothing." The boy seethed. The Corwins lived in a tenement in working-class Eastie for twenty years while Mr. McKenzie owned a comfortable home in seaside Winthrop, where he was a proud and prominent member of the Boston Rotary Club.

(Only by counting pennies, stinting, and saving could the Corwins afford to move to Winthrop. Even then, it took ingenuity. In a Rube Goldberg machine of many moving parts, they made a down payment, got a mortgage and for two more years stayed on in Eastie while they rented out all of their new four-family home for the income to pay for it.)

Before Winthrop, within Bremen Street's constant cacophony, Sam and Rose Corwin, "Pa" and "Ma," raised their children. Early life had toughened up both of them. Rose, as the oldest of thirteen children, served as their second mother, while Sam, the oldest boy of a bed-ridden disabled father, left school to help support the family of seven as soon as they arrived in Boston, when he was ten. It was common then for the oldest child in immigrant families to pick up English rather than their parents. The oldest child often became, in effect and involuntarily, translators in the middle and mediators at an early age, dealing with landlords, teachers and bill collectors.

Pa was an originally Yiddish-speaking streetwise child of Russian Jews who retained a strong accent although he grew up in the largest English-speaking city in the world, London. Pa, an incorrigible user of the double negative, was gabby and an extrovert. As a boy in Boston, Sam sold newspapers in the street, fruitlessly asking customers about any other jobs. Then, one day, he saw a "help wanted" sign outside a store.[21]

Sam broke into making "plate" in two steps. He left selling newspapers in the street for an indoor job downstairs in a fine stationery company's shipping room. This was the advertised position. As soon as he learned that better jobs existed in the building, he moved upstairs. A happy match ensued. The small but wiry young man with muscles and fine motor skills took on plate making. This was an art that took a diamond-cutter's eyesight and steady hands. As they scratched with surgeon's tools, plate makers worked with magnifying lenses on eye loops, but they also needed brute strength to lift and set completed heavy plates exactly into place for printing. Patience was its main psychological prerequisite. Sam discovered that he could persist for hours making a manually operated ink-seeping machine turn out delicate engravings without a single smudge.

Although Sam technically had a boss, he basically worked autonomously. Burned once as a business owner, he never tried it again. As a "plate man" or engraver, Pa was like an artist assigned to individual projects. McKenzie might tell him what to do, but not how. Fine engraving involved judgment calls and creativity. None of his sons became engravers, but they all duplicated their father's workplace. Neither Em, Al nor Norman ever chose to earn their livings by running their own businesses. They also worked on their own projects as semi-autonomous but loyal employees of large companies.

The Corwin boys' father was a skilled tradesman, a straw boss and the best trainer McKenzie had. As a teacher, Pa proudly kept track of students who went on from him to the most prized jobs of all, those at the Bureau of Printing & Engraving in Washington, where the plates for currency and Treasury bonds were made. Em boasted to Bannerman of the number of men (over 20) whom Pa trained who worked for the Bureau of Printing & Engraving.

This was how they saw him, except after hours, when one deficit haunted him. Pa found arithmetic difficult. He abhorred one foreman duty in particular, computing the pay due to the printers. He was never sure that he did correctly. He used to bring the paperwork home, "long pink slips that were ruled to designate the various hours of the day," time clock readings from when the printers punched in and out. It was a weekly struggle for Pa to compute the hours for each one. Norman said years later, his antipathy still obvious, "It drove my mother crazy because on Saturdays and Sundays and nights, that's all he would be doing, pouring over these damn things."[22]

In addition, as the boys also knew and closely monitored, Pa may have hindered himself from achieving accurate calculations. Norman recalled that Pa "drank well, smoked, and he drank too well as a matter of fact and he had to curtail this," although Norman did not precisely date either the instances of inebriation or the curtailment.[23]

When he courted Rose Ober, Sam Corwin presented himself as a skilled tradesman with a steady job. Em probably heard the story at his mother's knee of how, when Sam came calling, Rose was already engaged. He laid siege nonetheless to Rose, a beautiful woman then called by some "the 'Belle of East Boston.'" Rose, earnest and serious by nature, was quiet while Sam was comparatively a force of nature. She was obviously overwhelmed by a dashing man who was *never* at a loss for words.

Besides, Sam was handsome. By promoting his good looks, presenting Rose with photos of himself, coupled with his lively personality, Sam
swayed Rose to break her engagement. As Em reported, "My father was a
very handsome man. We have pictures of him in a very handsome mustache, he was a very active man with interest in sports and in good company. I would say that he was the only extrovert we had in our family."

Young Sam had scrambled cheerfully each day to bring something in
for the family. Unwarranted optimism was not without psychological cost
in his case. Deep depression haunted Sam. He may have had mood swings,
or manic depression. He certainly drank more than he should have, and
finally collapsed and was treated for nervous exhaustion for months in
around 1917. This was the breakdown that Norman vaguely but incorrectly
associated with the collapse of his father's business. The business collapse
occurred years before Norman was born.

Norman recalled visiting the Adams Nervine asylum, "apparently an
old estate." Only six or seven years old at the time, Norman found his bedridden father a scary sight. He said, "He had wasted away almost to nothing." For several long months, the family worried that Pa might die or, if he
lived, might never recover his health. Without question, McKenzie paid the
family's bills and kept the household alive during this period.[24]

Pa survived, although he was never the same. To the end of his long
life (he lived to be 110), Pa was also a histrionic food faddist. He required
that the family's drinking water be boiled and banished forever from the
Corwin table several common foods, including pickles, sauerkraut, and hot
dogs. In characterizing his diet as a centenarian, Pa, ignoring his smoking
and drinking, described good, vegetarian-rich fare. He prescribed "nothing
pickled, nothing fried, nothing greasy." He was also an evangelist of mental activities. "Are you doing something to keep your mind and time occupied?" he would ask his children frequently.[25]

Ma, not unaffected by Pa's illness, needed a different regimen. In its
wake and caring for her husband and children, Ma fell ill herself. Norman
knew comparatively more about Ma's illness than his father's. He told Bannerman, "My mother's illness was a hereditary illness, a thyroid goiter. You
know that people of Hungary and Switzerland, they're prone to this disease
because of a lack of iodine in the soil. And a great many Hungarians came
to this country, many of them settled in Cleveland, in addition to having
this hereditary weakness, the soil of the great lakes was lacking in iodine
too. This created a big problem. So that, we had on our mother's side of the
family an extraordinary example of disease running through our family. Of
eleven members of the family, almost all of them had this condition. Thyroid. When my mother had it, she had to undergo two or three operations.
It grows back. And these were rather costly."

Pressed by responsibilities that seemed only to grow by the day, Pa went back to work at the McKenzie company—he sometimes called it "the factory." Pa's doctors did not want him to do heavy lifting or exert himself (orders that he ignored). His workdays were long. Em, as the oldest son, recalled trips toting lunch bags many nights. Presumably, he took the Boston Elevated and got off at old Scollay Square. Then, when Em arrived at McKenzie's shop on Congress Street in downtown Boston, Pa would interrupt his tasks briefly and eat whatever Rose had prepared, probably most often a hot meal but, one trusts, nothing fried, pickled or greasy.

Pa was working harder because McKenzie had more work than he had workers. Business was actually booming. Pa told Bannerman that McKenzie had trouble finding printers. To fill out the rest of the production line Pa seemed to have recruited all possible adult or near-adult relatives. The 1920 census lists, within the Ober family living in Eastie at 238 Bremen Street, two plate printers, Samuel, 24, and Edward, 21, employed by an unnamed "Engraving est(ablishment)," and their sisters ("press feeders"), June, 19, and Helen, 17.[26]

His Mother's Boy

At home, Ma, more than Pa, encouraged Norman. After all, by convention it was "the mother's job" to raise the kids in those days. And, before she married Sam, Rose had experience in raising children. As the oldest daughter, she was born into the job of helping her mother raise her siblings. Moreover, Norman was not her first child but her third. By his birth, if not years before, Ma was an able, attentive, and adaptable parent of a gifted child. Ma said of her maternal experience, "I can't think of a better way to learn child psychology." Her wording is insightful: the child's *mind* was what interested her.

In a brief memoir, Ma said that she detected Norman as different from Alfred (known as "Al"), Norman's quiet middle brother, born in 1906, and Emil (known as "Em"), his more vocal and pragmatic oldest brother, born in 1903. They were, she said, "both normal, lovable youngsters with healthy tempers." Then she was stumped. Norman was not so easy to characterize. Grappling to distinguish her third son from his brothers, Ma said carefully that he was "healthy, inquisitive, lovable, and tempestuous."[27]

Not so, not really, not quite.

First, Rose imputed to Norman a health he possessed only in adulthood and then only intermittently. Not vigorous like his athletic brothers, he was fragile at first. Em remembered the baby as "very, very frail" with "a yellowish tinge to his cheeks ... so delicate that you could blow into his

cheeks and see the inden-
tation." Ma admitted that
Norman gave her concern,
writing: "I found it very difficult to find a formula that
Norman could thrive on."
Em, who recalled long walks
in all weathers to "the milk
station" was backed up on
point by Ma. She said, "This
was before the day of the
pediatrician but fortunately
the Straus baby clinics and
milk stations were just starting to operate."[28]

Norman survived to
shape up (he could have
played Tarzan in the mov-
ies by the 1920s) but that was
in adulthood. In his twenties
he bicycled and exercised
but, even up through high
school, Norman declined
to take part in sports on
the basis of an undefined
"injury." Em said flatly that
his youngest brother "was
not very much to look at as

Rose "Ma" Ober, the oldest child of twelve siblings of Eastern European immigrants. "The
Belle of East Boston" broke her engagement to
a richer beau to marry handsome, garrulous
and persuasive Sam (courtesy Diane Corwin
Okarski).

a young man." In his unfinished and unpublished memoir, without dates,
Norman described struggling with chronic colds, bouts of flu, and frequent
digestive problems. His above-average concern (or possible hypochondria)
is probably rooted in sickly years which his mother chose not to recall.[29]

In calling Norman "inquisitive" Ma accentuated the positive. To others, inquisitive Norman was a nuisance. Ma wrote of a paperhanger who
discovered "Norman and his paste spilled all over the floor" and recalled
a similar incident with a cream separator in the country. Her little boy's
rapid-fire series of questions could overwhelm people. Ma said that no
family member was exempt from being "put on the rack." His fond mother
was sure that "almost everyone whom he questioned eventually became
interested in him." The key words here are "almost" and "eventually."[30]

It was Ma's last word for her son, distinguishing him from Em and Al,
"tempestuous," that was spot on. Norman could (and did) storm about with

a temper, but he not seldom threw himself into a tight-fisted, disciplined effort. He was moody and sensitive. His mother tolerated this better than his father did, and Norman seemed to favor her in turn.

Norman's kid sister, "Booie," (Beulah) recalled Norman not only running ordinary errands but insisting that his mother relax as he scrubbed the floors and did the ironing. So unusual was it for Norman to be at odds with his mother that a single occasion—when Ma threatened to send him away to reform school—shocked his little Booie, who began to sob and beg that Ma not do it. For a long time, Booie thought that it had been her plea for mercy that saved Norman from reform school.

Ma had grown up more protected than her husband. She had blossomed within a close-knit family with two able and active parents. Hers was a happier household than her husband enjoyed. Em said, "My mother was born in Hungary in a place called 'Kleineardein' and came to this country when she was about 5 and settled in Boston with her family." Rose seems to have read aloud often to the younger Obers. It is not clear how long (or if) she attended public schools. However, she was literate, had a good vocabulary, and loved books. Off duty as an adolescent, Rose was indulged and allowed to retreat into books. Books remained a primary entertainment for her. Speaking for all four Corwin children later, Em credited their mother with "our love of the written word because she was interested in writing and literature. She read, my father never, or rarely did."[31]

Curiously, Norman recalled less reading, "Books were not conspicuous in our house, and small attention was paid to the nuances of language. Yet both my parents spoke well, with vocabularies and usage beyond their education."[32]

Besides reading to her children, at least to the ones who would sit still, Ma introduced them to visual arts. Ma was a self-taught artist. The story is that teen-aged Rose had worked before her marriage in a photo retouching lab. One day, she was moved to ask for some worn, old brushes to take home. It was the start of a lifelong hobby.

"She was interested in finding out how to use them and bought paints," Em said. The family was too poor to afford canvases or frames. Em described his mother "painting subjects on a board or anything she could get," even on clam shells. "She was very good at painting satin subjects which would be used on pillow covers," Em said.

While Ma brought some color into drab Bremen Street, her activity opened her children's eyes to the possibility of bringing imagined scenes to life. Em marveled at how Ma "was doing these creative things, while she was living under very difficult circumstances." Could Norman have marveled less? Em's praise of homemade art nonetheless stands alone.[33]

Pa impressed the family as an inventive mechanic. When the family

moved from the first to the third floor at 218 Bremen Street, they suddenly had a view—although carrying coal up from the cellar got harder as a
result. Pa pondered this problem and solved it. Em recalled, "My father had
a very ingenious device to spare us from carrying coal up from the cellar to
the third floor. My father developed a pulley device to haul coal up from the
backyard up to the third floor."[34]

Pa worked more magic that warmed their hearts, literally. At first,
a single coal-fed Franklin stove was the only source of heat for their
five-room apartment, consisting of a living room and a kitchen besides two
bedrooms, one for the parents with little Booie and one for the three boys.
Eventually, however, in the living room, there was "a small round stove that
had a little isinglass window" installed that Pa used to light on the coldest
nights or occasions that they had company.[35]

Neither Pa nor Ma prevented boys from being boys. Consequently,
ways to be injured abounded. Heat waves drew tenement boys out of their
sweltering rooms day and night. Drivers of jerky autos without power
steering, good brakes, or lights, were everywhere. Near misses were common. Automobiles were not the only dangers. Playing "kick-the-can" once,
in reaching the can by going up and over the railroad yard fence, usually
agile Em fell awkwardly. Hitting the iron track, he broke his wrist and was
in a cast and sling for weeks. When he was up and moving, he competed
again, running around the block. Em described their urban track: "We used
to run around the block. One would run one way and the other would run
the other way to see if we could end up at the point of origin, one ahead of
another."[36]

The world of Eastie did not feel very safe. Norman's radio shows later
were rarely set on sunny days rich with good humor. His radio world
most often featured people in danger, some making sacrifices and fighting
while others stoically suffered. No wonder. In Eastie, horrors came at them
around the corner. A couple of blocks away from their tenement stood "an
old barn where horses where sometimes taken out and shot in the street."
A man would "run home" a pistol to the unfortunate old or injured horse's
head, and "crash, the horse would tumble over."[37]

Norman's world then was far from isolated or homogeneous. Walking
to their neighborhood school each morning were kids, new immigrants or
children born here to immigrants, who ate bagels and lox, heaps of pota-
toes and corned beef, or plates of steaming lasagna with fresh garlic bread.
School, at least for Norman's first several grades, was a melting pot. It held
no terrors for Norman, who already spoke better English than many classmates. Starting school for Norman meant a new audience. For a show-off
who recited poems, public speaking never made him shake. In classrooms
that were often overcrowded, poorly lit, ill-ventilated, poorly insulated,

either overheated or underheated, Norman stood out. Addressing a classroom of his contemporaries was a breeze.

After graduation from the James Otis Primary School, Norman's visibility rose higher yet in elementary school. His former mainstay, reciting, took a backseat. He discovered something new: writing. Norman parleyed it to prominence, "writing sentences" in his phrase. It was by writing sentences that he caught his teachers' attention.

"As a schoolboy, his precocious talent for writing was encouraged by his teachers at the U.S. Grant Elementary School in East Boston," Norman fondly concluded in the third person. Soon, he was writing sentences at home as well, every day.[38]

Norman's First War Story

Not long after his sidewalk success as a teller of tales, Norman moved from speaking stories to writing them. Ma recounted with slight exaggeration but transparent pride, "When Norman was eight, he decided to write his first novel."[39]

Norman in adulthood always emphasized the element of luck in his life, and at eight years old he did have some good luck. In exploring the attic of their Bremen Street tenement, he had found something that some luckless prior tenant left behind: a large-sized, heavy volume of lined pages of the type commonly sold to businessmen. Such ledgers were intended for entries of income and expenditures in black and red ink. The absence of any entries in this one revealed an American dream deferred, if ever fulfilled. In its unpromisingly blank pages, Norman made his own dream come true. He produced his first bound book. As his mother said, it was a novel.

He began his "novel" at the right time. The world war had gone on for three years. When it started, the people of Eastie had been pulled in all directions. In the Corwin family to take sides implied cheering on Hungary, the Old Country of the maternal side of the family, whose Emperor found common cause with Germany's Kaiser Wilhelm II. On the other hand, Pa had grown up in London and was a devoted anglophile. Norman at four, five or even six would have struggled to sort out good guys and bad guys.

But Norman was an author at eight. The fog had cleared. America was in the war and on the Allied side. Norman's inspiration came from across the street. Troop trains parked on his doorstep. Due to the influenza of 1918, khaki-clad doughboys were barred from leaving the cars, but Norman could glimpse them in passing in the switching yard. Through sooty windows he could take in blurry visions of leather-strapped, uniformed doughboys wearing wide-brim campaign hats.[40]

Left to right: Em, Beulah ("Booie," born 1914), Ma, Norman, Pa, and Al, c. 1925 (courtesy Diane Corwin Okarski).

The ledger book's genre he later characterized as a tale of "blood and thunder" but it was a war story, and his first. To write it, he applied his imagination to current events—his trademark in radio during the 1940s. Not yet capable of poetry himself, Norman made do with prose. Self-taught but precocious, he sagely took up the story of a single soldier, one of the Tommies in the trenches. He also drew pictures to illustrate his text. He called his episodic illustrated stories *The Adventures of John Ransford.*

His mother remembered only its eponymous hero and the hilarious fact that John Ransford had a sister six months younger than he was. Timing was everything. Norman dutifully made daily entries as the war ground down. Soon, on Armistice Day, November 11, 1918, Norman had a proper ending. The first poem that four-year-old Norman had memorized described a wartime messenger's dramatic demise. The same theme he enlarged while he let John Ransford survive. His story was a celebration of the triumph of singular heroism. Ma said in summary that John Ransford was the hero who "won the war single-handed."[41]

In the end, Norman documented his father's side winning. Norman looked at the war through British eyes. These might be said to evoke his future wartime radio shows. On the other hand, emphatically to the contrary, Norman wrote no "Lone Ranger" serial of a bold and daring soldier overseas and on the front lines. His characters were thoughtful and reluctant warriors, anti-war in their hearts, playing honorable parts in a necessary group struggle to defend civilization for all of humanity, even for the enemy after peace.

Besides his "novel," another event may have been more significant, for it was the type of terror that haunted Norman in his adulthood. And it was the closest Norman personally came to this war. He wrote of it, in part. Some part was omitted. For example, if David Hoffman was given a back slapping, kissing and hugging send-off, if not a party, cheered by the neighbors all along Bremen Street, Norman said nothing of it. The classic scene of a next-door, long-term neighbor, 21-year-old David, proudly leaving for war in his Navy-blue sailor uniform is absent in Norman's memoirs. His bravery is not on display or alluded to in Norman's abbreviated discussion.

Norman instead and exclusively reported the mother's grief. A Navy officer brought a telegram to her. David went down with all hands when his ship, the cutter *Tampa*, was sunk off the coast of England by a lurking German U-boat. Word spread up and down Bremen Street. Then the Armistice was announced. The sounds of bells and cheering crowds prevailed on the day peace came versus unsettling quiet in this one home. David's mother, Minnie, left the black-creped front door open to receive visitors. Visitors were not constant; most everybody was celebrating. Through that open door, eight-year-old Norman helplessly saw Mrs. Hoffman alone, weeping, and he dared not intrude.

When Norman wrote the script for the day of victory in Europe in 1945, that eerie Bremen Street mix of celebration and mourning was reprised. "On a Note of Triumph" reflected Norman's bittersweet observation of victory and its dreadful costs. So much was in place as early as November 11, 1918. Norman shook off the romantic fallen boy hero of Robert Browning. He left off writing his own war story of John Ransford. He took up realism, Walt Whitman, Carl Sandburg, and others.

Looking around him then in Eastie, any half-awake boy would glean that the world was not a safe place. It was a sobering time and place. The pandemic of 1918 struck down especially young men and women in their prime, healthy, and active one day, dead the next. Likewise, war dead were as close as next door. Even after the war ended and the influenza epidemic burned out, death could suddenly strike. Across the Charles River on an exceptionally warm day in January 1919 a huge molasses tank on high steel stilts exploded, flooding the North End, killing 21 people and several horses.

That year, one could rely on nothing. In September 1919, the Corwins woke up one morning to find that the Boston police were on strike. National Guardsman and volunteers were directing traffic and patrolling downtown with rifles to prevent looting. Opposing the strike, Massachusetts Governor Coolidge won national fame and became the Republican Party's unanimous choice as its candidate for Vice President in 1920. By then reading the stories below the headlines, he may have begun to consider becoming a newspaper reporter.

Annual commemorations of "The War to End All Wars" hammered home how dearly bought the peace was. Each year after 1918, Norman would have stood with other pupils at the U.S. Grant School, all of them silently facing east on the eleventh hour of the eleventh day of the eleventh month, remembering the fallen. Any note of triumph was countered by a degree of dole.

Norman Types and Discovers Radio

Norman was but ten when he lost his idol and best friend. In 1920, Em became the first Corwin to attend college. Beginning in September, Em lived more than a hundred miles west of Eastie at Massachusetts Agricultural College, "MAC," the state university in Amherst. He and Norman no longer saw one another at breakfast, or swapped stories each evening, telling about their day. Em was no longer Norman's sounding board or confidant.

The unprecedented move did not seem ordinary. Norman must have been surprised, perhaps shocked. Higher education was nothing that Pa had ever planned for his sons or drilled into them as needed. Em said that neither of his parents ever told him to go to college. What could either of them tell him about it? Neither one was a high school graduate. Rather, Em consulted his peers. He told Bannerman that "because most of the boys in my senior class at East Boston High School were going to college, that I decided to do that, too."[42]

"I had to borrow money to get in. We were that broke," Em said. Apparently, Pa supported Em's plan and went to Mr. McKenzie for help. Pa's boss contributed nothing personally but did put a word in for Em to get a loan of $350 from the Boston Rotary Club to "tide him over at Amherst the first year."[43]

Em's resulting absence marooned his moody, pre-teen and prolific writer brother, Norman. Em did not return often. It cost money to travel and Em was on campus working his way through college. Further, Em was living on a co-ed campus crowned by a beautiful chiming chapel next to a small pond.

Norman tried to make do with Al but they fought. They fought over everything, even the Sunday paper. They fought over the comics supplement because Norman thought that Al was "stalling to provoke me, knowing how impatiently I awaited." Their argument was raucous enough to draw Ma's attention. She confiscated and destroyed the *causus belli*.[44]

Sooner or later, Norman took steps. He could not save his stories and poems and wait patiently. He splurged on postage and mailed his stories to Em for comments as soon as he finished any. Em's replies were a great joy to him. Whether vocally or not, Norman's parents certainly noticed their youngest son's devotion to writing.

Deciding to intervene actively in that, in the spring of 1922 Pa found the perfect birthday gift for Norman's twelfth birthday. It was a typewriter. Not widely remembered today (the company went bust in 1928), the Oliver Typewriter Company of Woodstock, Illinois, made the first million typewriters produced specifically for use at home. The olive-green, heavy, balky machines were bought by ordinary folks, mostly on credit. The Company repossessed its machines for resale, used, when purchasers fell behind. With the short, sharp recession of 1921–22 came a flood of repossessed Olivers. Pa exactly then doubtless caught a break either by bargaining for a repossessed Oliver or by making the last few payments for some prior owner in default and taking the discounted machine ($ 50 new) home.

The machine itself was good. Pa doubtless tried it, and found it responsive to his touch. Sturdy Olivers packed such a powerful punch that business firms used them chiefly to cut stencils for mimeographing. A typist at home on an Oliver hammered away, facing paper visible between two wings of standing keys, seeing about two inches of text at a time. Doubtless, Norman looked down that tunnel and composed many of his stories and poems in sprints of a few words at a time.

Thus it was, thanks to Pa, the Oliver Typewriter Company, and a recession, at twelve, Norman was off and running. Persistence paid. Self-taught with a lot of practice, using only two fingers, Norman developed a fast typist's concentration and coordination.[45]

Meanwhile, on his own, the two-finger typist discovered radio. As Norman revealed in a videotaped interview in his nineties, he was hanging around doing nothing much with his Eastie peers in 1922 or 1923 when, out of the blue, somebody told him four fateful words:

"Harold has a radio."

It turned out that Harold Merchant had made, or had been given, a crystal radio.

"What's radio?" Norman asked.

"Sounds from the air," was the answer, which only mystified Norman further. Contacting Harold was, naturally, next.

Harold, a year younger than Norman, was one of five kids of an Irish family on Bremen Street. Norman knocked on the Merchants' door. When he entered the apartment, Norman promptly observed Harold in earphones. Harold handed them over to Norman. After following Harold's instructions on using the cat's whisker over a coil of copper wire, Norman put them on and understood the phrase *sounds from the air*.

The sounds were the dah-dah-dit Morse code traffic between ships in the harbor, but Norman was both amazed and thrilled.

It was no longer possible for him to live without this marvel. Norman wanted a radio set of his own—and Pa had no objection. Traditionally, Pa's motto was, "Keep your time and your mind occupied." He may even have contributed the few coins needed to buy parts. Ma surely soon provided the cylindrical Quaker oats box. Though Norman had seen a radio set, put on earphones, and cradled the cat's whisker in his own fingers, it was up to Al next to read plans, perhaps from *Popular Mechanics*, though there were many other sources at the time. Al had the patience and discipline needed. It was not Norman but Al, the family's Harvard man and second Corwin to go to college, who assembled the family's first radio. Al wound a length of thin copper wire to make the classic radio of the early 1920s.[46]

Soon, family members took their turns hearing the marvel.

"Not even a battery was needed. Nothing. God did it all," Norman wrote joyfully in his memoir.[47]

Two commercial radio signals were available on the air, one from Boston and the other from nearby Medford. Of the two, Shepard's store in Boston was strongest. The downtown department store owned its own radio station, WNAC, beginning 1922. WNAC broadcasts reached people's earphones from a 100-foot antenna on top of the department store. Not fading in and out, WNAC was an easy find. Its still-strong signal reached across the harbor. At one point, it carried news to the youngest Corwin, who heard that a miracle was coming—"on Thursday night a show would be aired, coming from New York."[48]

Norman made certain to be ready, earphones on, to hear this show. When it happened, he marveled at hearing sounds coming live from New York, "hundreds of miles away."

He described himself as forever after "sentimental about radio's annihilation of earthly distances." The distance separating him from his beloved but absent Em might someday be waved away. Norman's world grew larger with radio. He felt a part of distant events and people. The sentiment he expressed was a variant of Norman's trademark theme, the oneness of the globe's people.[49]

After their homemade crystal set, when did the Corwins get a "real" radio? The answer is speculative but soon afterward, probably. Every family felt under increasing pressure to keep up with current events as their neighbors did. In the summer of 1924, radio owners heard a political convention in progress. A microphone up on the speaker's platform during the Democratic National Convention held at Madison Square Garden provided results in real time.

These first live "breaking news" broadcasts simultaneously comprised the start of radio's competition with newspapers. Norman, in his years as a reporter, would confront this very challenge himself. To some editors, radio was poison. Those in charge of other papers embraced the new medium. They set up special "Radio Rooms" to receive, transcribe and issue radio bulletins. Among these, the *Boston Daily Globe* stood boldly—some would say recklessly—as a radio news pioneer.[50]

If Norman by then had access to a radio, he heard good, strong, clear signals from state-of-the-art facilities in New York. The numbers of people listening further soared when the convention turned into a snake pit. For several days in early July 1924, anyone interested in politics—or entertainment—tuned in to hear the bombastic speeches, bands, crowd noises and, finally, over a hundred alphabetical roll calls. It took 103 ballots for the Democrats to nominate a Presidential candidate, ballots that always began, "Mister Chairman, Alabama casts twenty-four votes for Oscar W. Underwood."[51]

The new medium took wings. Sheer repetition turned Alabama's favorite son into a household name. His instant fame no newspaper could have accomplished. One wonders if Norman heard and understood the unprecedented and loud demonstrations and prolonged disruptions over an anti–Ku Klux Klan plank in the party's platform, a resolution that failed by the tiniest margin.

Finally, late one July night shocking news was piped into the country's living rooms. It was the first non-political "breaking news" story and it was accidental. From Maine to California, people were tuned in to their stations at 10:30 p.m. Eastern Time on July 7, 1924, awaiting the reconvening of an interrupted session. This audience across the country heard instead the chairman announce that there would be no session because the President's son, John Calvin Coolidge, Jr., had suddenly died.

As the *New York Times* reported, speaking of the country's capital, "[T]he people of Washington—like those of most of the nation—received the news first by radio from Madison Square Garden, when it was announced that the National Convention would adjourn immediately through respect to the President."[52]

This news about the Coolidges, so long linked to Massachusetts, had to hit Bostonians hard. Sadder still, it turned out that for several tense days the President and Mrs. Coolidge had been keeping a secret bedside vigil. Their 16-year-old son, a vibrant athlete, feverishly fought before he fell prey to blood poisoning.[53]

Norman himself never said when the family's first "real" radio arrived. We do not know whether the Corwins had a radio in February 1925 when an amateur cave explorer in Tennessee named Floyd Collins became trapped. His story played out publicly over the air for over a week. At first, hopes ran high. Then a secondary cave-in blocked an originally promising rescue route, although Collins survived. Without food or water, he continued communicating with his would-be rescuers in hoarse and increasingly weak shouted words. Then, one day, the rest was silence, a silence felt more intimately by radio listeners than by readers of newspapers. As Norman said, listeners were not separated from events by hundreds of miles but were *there*.

If the Corwins had no radio as 1925 began, the pressure increased. Neighbors shared radio news and brought friends over to listen to baseball games and music in real time. This radio boom generated the manufacture of cheaper sets in a wider variety of styles and sizes. Competing companies putting out several models so good and, importantly, so *cheap* that Pa, although now paying for their new house in Winthrop, would have considered joining the crowd and buying one, too.

No Bar Mitzvah *for Norman*

The last big personal event in Norman's life that occurred in Eastie illustrated Norman's difference from others. A *bar mitzvah* was an easy decision and no dilemma for many twelve-year-olds around him. But Norman, as his mother had noticed and said since his childhood, usually with pride, was that he was "inquisitive" and "tempestuous." In his case, between his inquiring mind and his tempestuous spirit, Norman was impressed by the ethics of Judaism but not its rituals. He spoke and he acted from that position. He was not open to a *bar mitzvah*.

He decided not to attend Hebrew lessons, not to prepare himself and not to take part. His decision was not casual. It was not an aversion to a fussy cer-

Norman in gritty East Boston in early 1920s (courtesy Diane Corwin Okarski).

emony. It was not a rebellion against authority. And, God knows, it was not stage fright or nervousness about being the center of attention. Instead, detailed edicts and seemingly arbitrary prohibitions regulating life were revolting to rational thinkers, one of which Norman counted himself. His decision seems almost predictable. What may be surprising are his parents, especially his father, who must have allowed him to make his own decision. It is a clue both to his strong-mindedness *and* to his parents' forbearance to impose upon him that Norman had no *bar mitzvah*.

No part of any argument survives. The hint of a family argument over this is vague and ambiguous. It appears in one early letter. Norman thanked his father for discipline that was "never rigorous or entirely lacking." What stood behind those words? Did Pa assert to guide but ultimately support his son's freedom to make up his own mind?[54]

Of course, Norman's stance toward Orthodox Judaism in 1922 or 1923 was not unprecedented in immigrant families across the country. Sometimes it was a conflict between faiths of intermarriage. Cross-cultural conflict between Jew and Gentile, between pious and secular Jews, was hot stuff, literally box office. A play on this theme, like *Abie's Irish Rose*, opened in 1922 and did not close until 1927, a Broadway record. Notwithstanding this stellar example, Norman never made religious conflict the subject of a radio play. Religion led him to ruminate rather than to romp or to rage. This is obvious from a letter he penned in 1933.

In that letter, fully ten years after his own determination not to follow the orthodox path, Norman criticized what he called "clannishness" and superstition. Norman wrote Em after the passing of their Hungarian grandmother. He noted that the family excluded him from the house of mourning. He reported (complained may be the better verb) that he was barred from approaching the body of his grandmother for not being "of the proper tribe."[55]

His eyes were open to this snub, as to everything else. Alertness may have led him to his decision not to have a *bar mitzvah*, Alertness was the source of both pleasure and pain to the perceptive youth. He was made for conscious and acute perception. In his childhood, sights and sounds and books possessed him. Poems? He literally turned himself into a poem on legs. Although it is not ever clear, and his attitude could have varied and shifted, Norman seems in his teens and twenties not to have thought that he could be both an observant Orthodox Jew and a full citizen of the thinking world in which he wanted to live.

Further evidence of this is late by almost seven decades following his decision in Eastie. When he was 80, Norman advised a dear nephew against orthodoxy—"mindlessness" was his term—in any form.

"Most of the atrocities of history have been either initiated or fueled by orthodoxies," Norman said in his 1990 letter to Robert Kaiser.[56]

Without stating that the question was one that he had put to himself in his youth, he asked his nephew, a budding physicist, "How do you feel when you read Galileo's recantation to the priests—this genius who advanced astronomy by the power of his mind?"

Norman said that he could never forgive the tyrants of orthodoxy. Inculcated and imposed uniformity Norman distinguished sharply from Judaism, which he followed. He believed in God and in "ancient Judaic ethics," he said. To Norman it was "inconceivable that a majestic, omnipotent, omniscient God could be fooled by flattery or ritual, or hold against anyone transgressions of minor codes relating to diet, or punish anyone for going into a place of worship with an uncovered head."

Again, these are Norman's much later words. His pronouncements doubtless constitute a far more articulate and authoritative argument than teen-aged Norman would have been capable of mounting or thinking. But might not its core reflect Norman's youthful thinking?

"I urge you not to be beguiled by any system of thought which *demands* conformity," Norman told his nephew.

No argument over his *bar mitzvah* appears of record, but he must have hurt the feelings of pious family members, including his father. A great tree may have fallen in the forest of Eastie, though nobody ever said they heard anything. On its face, Norman stood alone and unopposed against orthodoxy. On its face, as his much later letter demonstrates, his decision against a *bar mitzvah* shaped him for later battles.

Freedom to think was a cause he expressly espoused as an adult. It was a great theme in many of his radio scripts. He attacked Fascists and, later, McCarthyites for their stultification of free thought and free speech. But Judaism is not Fascism. And the faith of one's fathers is no small legacy to decline. Adolescent Norman's decision not to take part in a *bar mitzvah* was perhaps as easy and joyful as many boys' contrary decisive and enthusiastic participation. Norman may have experienced unwelcome yearning and involuntary waves of melancholy or sadness of which he never spoke or wrote.

Winthrop

No ambiguity over emotions accompanied the move. No melancholy or regret was aroused by the Corwins' departure from Bremen Street.

Norman in Winthrop, c. 1926. No longer in a tenement, and close to the sea, Norman, as a moody teenager, had many reasons to love Winthrop (courtesy Diane Corwin Okarski).

Instead, joy over the family's move to Winthrop seems to have been unalloyed and enduring. Norman promptly made and sent a snapshot to Em, who was at that time working in Cleveland. Norman's well-framed photo captured paradise: a big, roomy house perched on a tree-lined side street near sunny Shore Drive. The picture reflected the charm of small town, contented life even though the salt air and surging waves of the nearby sea had to be imagined.

Em's fellow workers in Cleveland swooned. Em wrote back how the "super nertz pix" was seen in urban Ohio. "When I showed it around the office, they said I must be nuts to come out here to work."[57]

The photo did justice. The Corwin family's new place on Perkins Street was a well-situated three-story building "one lot removed from Shore Drive." After using the big house for rental income in 1924 and part of 1925, while they remained in Eastie, Pa finally moved them all to Winthrop in mid-spring, 1925. The house with a large, open porch and a real cellar on a tree-lined street near the sea amazed them. This was living. Small wonder that Norman took a photo to show Em.[58]

For Norman, who lived to listen, their move away from Maverick Square traffic and the railroad yard on Bremen Street was a removal from chaotic noises to smack in the lap of beguiling nature. This thrill was not on Perkins Street itself but on the other side of the sea wall at Shore Drive. Waves and sea breezes made forays into his very being.

In his autobiography, he proclaimed the chief grandeur of their new place with respectful solemnity, saying, "The sound now was that of the sea." Norman found solace in fair weather sea sounds, the "susurrant stirring" he called it, selecting onomatopoeia. Susurrant stirring, however, was punctuated by occasional hard slaps of huge waves against the sea wall "as though to remind the brooding shore who was boss."[59]

Of their new home, a large old place that could house four families, Norman spoke fondly. The sweltering third story apartment of an Eastie tenement must be imagined behind his appreciation of the Winthrop homestead, a "four-tenement duplex" where (in his memory) it was always summer:

> The house in Winthrop was once a very fine home and was when we'd moved in. The rooms were cozy. The living room looked out on the ocean. My mother had a garden and grew flowers, was very proud of the flowers. It had a porch for the summertime. We made use of the porch a great deal, and of course, anyone who lives on the beach is very popular with the relatives in the summertime. Everybody comes out to swim. And they used our house to change out of their clothes and my mother was always busy all summer weekends serving refreshments to friends and relatives from other parts of the city.

Summer or winter, the move to Winthrop was freighted with social significance. Em spoke of it as "getting away from that underprivileged side of the city and really the beginning of the North Shore." Although the family only moved a bit over a mile, a mile went a long way when it reached up toward the North Shore, along lines of a move from Brooklyn to the Bronx.

The North Shore was well-known for its hotels, summer cottages and the large houses and mansions. President Wilson's closest adviser, Colonel House, lived on the North Shore. President Calvin Coolidge, who assumed office upon President Harding's death in 1923, took a house in Swampscott for his family vacation in July 1925. When the Corwins moved into Winthrop, they settled in ten miles south of "White Court" in Swampscott, the "summer White House."

The Corwins were only on the lower edge of the North Shore, a toehold actually closer to the Deer Island House of Correction than to the summer White House, but they were also no longer *tenants*. They were *homeowners*. And—with no trains in sight—they were literally a stone's throw from the sloshing sea.

Em experienced the contrast upon returning from Cleveland for some recreation before starting a new job in the summer of 1925. He said, "These were very happy days because we had a lot of elbow room, we were out, overlooking the ocean, the streets were cleaner, the air was pure, the school was better."[60]

Because Em was done with public school, as was Al, by "better school" he could only have meant Norman's high school, which implies that a "better school" for Norman was a motive and had been discussed as such around the family table.

Norman found outlets for his energies and stresses. He began to keep a diary. He awoke early and walked the beach alone in the morning. Without new friends yet, he made a lighthouse a sort of companion. He declined Ma's offer of curtains. Nightly, the beam of a lighthouse swept through his attic room. The rising sun was his alarm clock but by night it was Graves's Light's "short flashes, resting, short flashes."[61]

One day early that summer, Norman apparently stayed up too late counting flashes. His "tough kid" resurrected that morning. Em and Norman got into such a hot argument—not likely started by Em—that they agreed to don boxing gloves and duke it out in the basement.

"We really had a terrible slugging match," Em recalled. "We came up exhausted, we were living in Winthrop at that time and we both went to the same room. He stretched out on one bed and I on the other, and that was the end of it. But a half hour before we were beating the stuffing out of each other."[62]

The brothers hung up the gloves after that memorable and exhausting fight in Winthrop in 1925. Wishfully moving the last brothers' fight back

Norman (c. 1926) made use of the Winthrop seashore to walk, to swim, and to contemplate. A lighthouse beam swept his uncurtained room throughout the night (courtesy Diane Corwin Okarski).

further, Norman told Bannerman, "There came a big turning point and after about when I was 12 or 13, or 14, there came a very close bond."[63]

The world turned outside, too. A courtroom battle divided the country. One wishes that any member of the family told Bannerman whether they listened to news from Tennessee in July 1925. The "Scopes Monkey Trial" was on the air, the case that put religious belief on trial. Clarence Darrow for science sparred with William Jennings Bryan for the Biblical view of Creation.

How could Norman not listen to the radio and root for those who opposed superstition in favor of science? It is a great speculative leap, but Norman's sense of a link between personal decision-making and the world's future could date back to this trial so vigorously covered in newspapers and over the radio.

With or without a radio connection to the outside world, the brothers came up with the affectionate Yiddish nickname of "Perkinstrasse" for Perkins Street. Their Perkinstresse was a short byway between the Atlantic Ocean on the northeast and Crystal Cove, a shallow part of Boston Harbor, on the southeast. A half-grown kid could run from sea to shining sea in under three minutes. They need not foot it to get around, either. They were only two streets down from the Winthrop Beach station, where a railroad shuttled people between Lynn and Revere Beach, some of that journey up on stilts over Crystal Cove. Under shady trees in summer, in a pretty spot as if designed for boys and girls, Perkinstrasse was to them exotic and different, if not idyllic.[64]

So situated, the Corwins had a near front row seat on the ongoing drama of humankind's precarious hold on earth. Houses on Perkins Street literally trembled each full moon and spring tide. Waves hit and shot up like geysers against the sea wall. "Susurrant stirring," indeed. The high winds of one Nor'easter tossed two-ton slabs of granite squarely onto the Corwin's oceanfront neighbor's lawn. The entire thin peninsula was declared at risk of being swept over and claimed by waves during the next hurricane. A startled team of engineers promptly planned first two, then doubled to four, protective breakwaters that were all built in the first few years after the Corwins moved into Winthrop.

Deer Island, in colonial times an unconnected spit of rocks and pasture that ultimately reached out a skeletal but increasingly fleshed arm of sand to touch the rest of Winthrop, had been a prison since the French and Indian War. Still taking advantage of its remoteness and, by 1925, its three-sided ocean moat to keep prisoners from escaping, the House of Correction for Suffolk County stood at the tip of Deer Island. For a long time, Norman had no curiosity about Deer Island. Although he loved the beach and the ocean, Norman was actually ten years in Winthrop before finally taking a free tour of the prison. He noted that, in cells with no-seat toilets, the inmates were given earphones to listen to the radio.[65]

On Shore Drive, possibly while strolling of a morning or swimming to beat the heat, Norman found a new friend, Barney Zieff, Winthrop High School Class of 1926. Barney lived at 56 Shore Drive. Their friendship seems to have been one more example of Norman's extended connections with reclusive or fringe people. Two years older, Barney was born in nearby working-class "sin city" Lynn on March 7, 1908, to an immigrant couple, Isidore and Ida Zieff. Barney had an older brother, Henry, who was a pharmacist in town. Barney's father died before Barney knew him.

Norman's family (his two brothers, a sister and two living parents) would have seemed large to Barney, a serious student who took no part in sports or, indeed, any extra-curricular activities. He worked after school as a clerk at a drug store and hoped to become a pharmacist, like his brother. In school, Barney took no part in sports and it was only in senior year—possibly egged on by Norman—that he squeezed together any time for any after-school activity, a role in the annual operetta. (One suspects that Barney never actually sang. His name was not listed in a role or as part of the "Chorus of Village Maids and Young Men." He was not in the photo of 36 costumed cast members. *Ergo*, did Barney work behind the scenes, handling lighting or stage cues?[66])

Norman never chronicled his high school adventures with his best friend, Barney, but bespectacled, introverted Barney must have served as a helpful guide early on. Soda jerk Barney knew everybody, and everybody knew him. Who dislikes the soda jerk? If not while strolling or swimming, Norman might have met Barney during his first weeks in Winthrop where teens gathered, at the centrally located town pharmacy.

Barney had a serious side, too. Barney, if not by nature a born workaholic, was the dutiful wage-earner in his widowed mother's household. Barney indulged his sense of fun only in a few, rare spare moments. Norman, who appreciated a struggling underdog when he saw one, and a good audience, took to Barney immediately.[67]

In Winthrop, Norman separated from his family in four ways. First, he kept to his room a lot, the attic room through which the beams of a nearby lighthouse swept. Second, he walked the empty beach at five each morning. Third, he found time for a best friend, Barney. Fourth, Norman threw himself into his senior year in high school. These are documented.[68]

Whether the house had a fifth attraction, radio, seems likely: nationally, between 1920 and 1945, radio grew to reach over ninety per cent of the country's homes. On the 1930 census, the Corwin family reported that it owned a radio. Of course, their radio ownership probably went back into the mid–1920s. Pa read the papers, liked to keep up on current events and no print media could beat the immediacy and emotional impact of radio broadcasts. Likewise, radio's diverse entertainment, day, and night, as free as the air, were attractions to everybody. Rose herself may have asked for a radio. When Pa was at work and the children were in school, radio banished loneliness and temporarily excused housework. To keep up with soap operas—so-called from their sponsoring detergent manufacturers—required fifteen-minute breaks several times a day. Without more, we are left with the simple probability that the Corwins moved to Winthrop with a radio.

Restart in High School

Norman (third row, second from right), hair parted in the middle, "dusted off" his violin to pose with the orchestra of Winthrop High School. His senior year (1925–26) was spectacular. He was co-editor of the yearbook, and wrote the class play, a fantasy of radio reports about the future doings of class members (courtesy Diane Corwin Okarski).

The story of Norman Corwin, the giant talent of wartime American radio, must always be reported as having begun in Eastie, in Eastie's public library where Norman had discovered classical music, in Eastie's public schools where he first won his teacher's praise for reciting and for writing, on Eastie's sidewalks where he staked out his own storytelling stage, even in Eastie's streets, where he was known as a tough kid, nobody to cross.

Then, in an instant, as if picked up by a tornado, he was not in Eastie anymore. He was in Winthrop—where reinvention was possible. Although Norman spoke fondly of Winthrop, he never wrote up anything like the full story of his transformation. Evidence is skimpy but consistent. His mother made a list. Also, when interviewed, speaking of that first year in Winthrop, both Pa and Em spoke of Norman as a changed son and brother. Clearly, Norman's unlikely story definitely took a sharp turn in Winthrop and, most of all, restarted at Winthrop High School.[69]

In the first page before her list, his mother remembered the exact date. They moved, she said, on May 1, 1925. After renting the place for income for a couple of years, the Corwins bid farewell to their tenement across from the railroad switching yard and entered the green world. A big house on a tree-shaded road near the ocean was suddenly home. A double celebration was in order immediately as Norman turned 15 on Sunday, May 3. Barely unpacked, the brand new 15 year old began classes and initiated his reinvention the next day, Monday, May 4 at Winthrop High School.

At Winthrop High School, the delinquent disappeared and Norman, a brilliant, even precocious boy, shined. Transparently, he auditioned well, pleasing the school official in charge of transfers to seat him with juniors. In the last six weeks of the school year, beginning May 4, Norman was part of the Winthrop High School Class of 1926.[70]

Norman jumped into the pool. He could not have acted shy. During the final six weeks of junior year, he managed to introduce himself as a writer. His mother was so happy. In language arts, her Norman stood head-and-shoulders above others. We can visualize Norman running up the steps of their new home with the good news. Ma exulted, "In the six weeks before school ended, he made such an impression that he was elected associate editor of both the school publication and the yearbook for the following year."[71]

In the bittersweet way that is life, Norman soon shared less with Ma. Ma was aware of fewer of his triumphs as he gained traction in Winthrop. She recalled that he was editor of the school paper, associate editor of the yearbook, also master of ceremonies at the class banquet. He obviously shared with her his essay "WORDS" and his "Class Prophecy" play, as well as several stories and poems she did not name. But he no longer rushed to tell his mother *everything*. During 1925–26, her son took wings and flew far beyond his mother's reckoning and her short list remained forever incomplete.[72]

For Norman, this year was a year like no other. At Winthrop High, the fifteen year old in the swarm of seventeen year olds unpredictably surpassed everybody else. His 1925–26 year was like something out of Horatio Alger. Start with chemistry. The school's chemistry teacher was charismatic and apparently legendary. For his senior elective, Norman unerringly picked chemistry. He promptly fell head over heels for the new subject. Norman spoke of being "in love with a chemistry course at the time," employing a word he did not use even for his old favorite, English, which was likewise taught by a gifted pro.

The budding scientist, buoyed up by the fun of school demonstrations, dazzled by lab experiments and field trips, set out to become a demonstrator himself. Pa's mantra, "Keep your time and your mind occupied," insured his easy approval for Norman to set up a chem lab in the basement on Perkins Street. Besides, chemistry enjoyed a history in the Corwin family. Pa had "spoken of agricultural chemistry as a coming thing" before Em left in 1920 to begin his studies at Mass Aggie. Em's first major was chemistry because he "went along with Pa on that."[73]

Norman invited kids in the neighborhood to see his shows. (In an essay published as part of his 1945 radio play anthology, Norman admitted that his home lab was built for "sheer exhibitionism" rather than research.) Goggle-eyed youngsters crowded in to see magic performed in the Corwin's cellar. They watched him dissolve gold leaf in fluoric acid. He pranked around with the ever-popular compound, hydrogen sulfide, otherwise known as "rotten eggs." Ma smelled trouble and complained. She declared that her son had become "a specialist in noxious odors." Despite stink, Norman reveled in his role until the explosion. He heated nitroglycerine in a double boiler. Then Pa shut down the mad scientist.

How close Norman came to blowing up the house, starting a fire or seriously injuring himself (luckily, he had no audience at the time) is unclear. In jeopardy of losing an eye or being eviscerated by flying shards, Norman later compared the event to the atomic bomb. Norman wrote, "I'd had doubts about the stability of matter ever since I almost blew up a house at 36 Perkins Street, Winthrop, Massachusetts, when I was a high-school student."[74]

Unlike Norman's passionate but passing link to chemistry, his connection to English became one of steel. In his English course, Norman appeared for a year before a woman who displayed an enthusiasm for words, written and spoken. The latter elicited consonance in Norman. Being herself something of a showman, she loved reading poetry aloud and encouraged her students to read aloud. She also led them to memorize and to recite poetry. Norman, who had been memorizing and reciting poems dramatically since age four, an erstwhile moody adolescent who walked the beach near his Perkins Street house and sat in bed, his eyes open as the lighthouse beam swept over him, rediscovered his poetic voice. In English class, he made words thrill others as he reached an audience not only of his peers but also an appreciative, intelligent woman.

His Ma excepted, no woman in Norman's youth had a bigger impact than Lucy Drew, "Miss Lu." Before her and classmates all older than he, Norman recited as never before. Moreover, for her, face-to-face, give-and-take, living interaction was education. Her students adored her for animated discussions and lively debates. Young minds passionately engaged characterized time spent with Miss Lu. As this exceptionally gifted teacher told Bannerman, she "didn't take packs of paper that high home with me and make crosses here, and cross out words there and [so forth.]"[75]

She foresaw a future for Norman in arranging words on paper. She thought of him chiefly as a reporter, though, probably accurately replicating Norman's own modest newspaper aims at the time. She said some fifty years later, "I thought he was an unusual boy. And when he was going into newspaper work, I thought he'd do very, very well." Then she added, openly and honestly, "I had no idea that he'd actually do the things he has done."[76]

Miss Lu heard Norman recite poetry with flair but neither she nor Norman saw him at the acme of American radio followed by millions. It may have been his choice of clothes. As Em described, "[Norman] was very sloppy … his pants were always hanging down and his stockings were always hanging down and he used to wear these decrepit looking clothes, he used to wear a cap and everyone wore the cap with the peak in the front, but he wore the peak in the back. You know, this kind of thing. He was an individualist even in those days."

However he dressed, Miss Lu paid attention to Norman and attention had always been the key to Norman's responsiveness. In courses without a lively teacher to encourage him, such as Latin, Norman struggled. The *schloomper* who made wisecracks and obstinately held unconventional opinions was not inclined to double down when he was ignored.

He loved attention but he also paid attention as well, sometimes to unlikely people. Norman, the youngest by far of the Class of 1926, who lived as a poet, a storyteller, and a music lover, was that extraordinary rarity: a *kind* teenager. In this, an abbreviated account by Norman in his incomplete memoirs stands corroborated on point by his mother's earlier eight-page memoir of the 1940s, more detailed than Norman's, and by Em during an interview with Bannerman recorded in the early 1970s. They all spoke about Eddy Torgussen. That Eddy was in some way crippled is clear—according to Ma, an accident cost Eddy two years' absence from school, left him lame, his arm "semi-paralyzed" and his speech "halting."[77]

Eddy was the kid who eats alone. Early on at Winthrop High, when Norman still confided in Ma, he told her about one boy who "didn't mingle." Ma gathered (we do not know how, unless told this by Norman) that Eddy was afraid he might be pushed and jostled by "the hungry boys" at the lunch counter.[78]

One might pause to analyze that explanation. The longer considered, the more awful it sounds. Had the boy been pushed because he was slow and boys were *hungry*—or did someone euphemize the differences and verbal disability that made Eddy a constant bullies' target?

Norman asked his mother if he could bring Eddy over their house to visit. He warned his mother that Eddy was sensitive and shy about the contortions required in the course of eating. Eddy came and he ate with the family at table. (Eddy's mother later called to ask if she could visit Rose and they became friends. Eddy's mother told her that her son's friendship with Norman was the nicest thing that ever happened to him.)[79]

Because Eddy missed two years of school, that probably made him the oldest student in high school. Norman was the youngest member of the senior class. Because Eddy's speech was "halting" while Norman was endlessly verbal, the set up for a speaker with an intelligent, older audience obtains. An adolescent injured and recuperating alone for two years, finally attending school but now an outcast—his friends already graduates and gone—would have had something in common with a cerebral and sensitive new kid for whom listening was a fine art, and thinking was life's biggest blessing. As the year progressed, why would Eddy not achieve vicarious satisfaction from his active friend's rise in life, and adventures?

Em likewise said that Norman brought Eddy over. Neither Em during his interview nor Norman in his page adverted to an extended friendship. They instead both described a positive but passing friendship, shared for a year or so, before each of them looked away and went on to other topics.

We are left with Ma's report on Eddy's life after high school: that "he is able to keep himself occupied by raising flowers and vegetables on the grounds of his home. He visits me once in a great while, and we talk about Norm."[80]

That year, as he befriended Eddy Torgussen and Barney Zieff, Norman also beat high odds in high school as a vote getter. He must have spoken with anybody and everybody. Without previous connections in Winthrop and totally without the means to shine materially among teens, who so often judge by fashionable appearance and conformity, he was the only student to win three of the 26 class superlatives. (And—this was despite a hindrance that, for some categories, such as "Biggest Feet," "Tallest," and all of those allotted to girls, Norman was not in the running.)

Norman was voted the Class Poet, the Class Orator—tied with Frank Bauer (in the words of the yearbook, "'Norm' Corwin appears to be quite glib, while his accomplice, Frank Bauer, shares the distinction")—and the Class Bolshevik, this latter an ironic superlative for one who was fated to fight blacklisting.

Remarkable, resilient Norman was the proverbial and popular Big

Man at Winthrop High. It was no momentary success. It continued to the end of the year. He broke through later to become the chairman of and emcee at the annual Class Day Committee.

Outside of school, Norman's name first appeared in print. He won the *Boston Traveller*'s top prize in its "Best Short Story" contest. The single boast he made in his memoirs of that year was that his name appeared in this newspaper as winner of its annual story competition but the record is clear that in Winthrop, in smaller classes and given closer attention than in Eastie, Norman not only fit in, he outdid others.[81]

For the yearbook photographer, Norman assumed a sober mien, really a neat and earnest mask. Unsmiling and serious, he could have passed as a Coolidge Republican. You could not see the shirt not tucked in, and nothing revealed the maverick that he had been, was and always would be. His inner revolution was obvious only in missed assignments and failed tests. Driven by his own priorities, Norman fell behind in some of his classes at the same time that he owned the high school after hours.

For the first time outside of the front stoop on Bremen Street, Norman acted. The part did not require a great voice, however, nor any memorization—neither did Hollywood, at that time still producing flickering silent movies. Norman appeared in "The Charm School." He played one of four benumbed war veterans, mute props of a comedy that actually starred ten (count them) 10 girls. Satisfied with being seen and not heard presumably, he did his part.

Norman seemed not to have told Ma about the play, nor that he was active in the French Club (mostly girls, too) or that he played with the school orchestra. It was comprised neatly half and half of boys and girls, to enter which he had to dust off and take up his abandoned violin after a five-year lull.

Norman was likewise seriously active in the co-ed Science Club, which required no small investment of time. Through this club, Winthrop students attended demonstrations and lectures by professors in the metropolitan area, including (very memorably to Norman) Harvard Observatory's famous director, Harold Shapley. However, girls were not required to lure him into action. In the Debating Club, all boys that year, Norman excelled. He did not sit long on the bench but won a coveted place on the school's competitive inter-scholastic Debating Team.[82]

In writing, as Ma well knew, Norman served as assistant to the editor-in-chief of the *Echo*, the yearbook. The editor, she may not have known, was the bespectacled, long headed and prematurely solemn Frank F. Bauer, Jr. Slow but steady Bauer was a favorite of the English teacher who fascinated them both, Miss Lu. In this triangle, to his advantage Bauer had had Miss Lu as his teacher longer. When Miss Lu judged Norman's year-end essay second best to Bauer's, she was sensitive of their rivalry and met privately with Norman to console him and to explain where his theme could be improved.

For the yearbook, Norman outdid Bauer by bursts of writing and more writing. Nothing if not prolific, Norman filled pages with his long script of the Class Prophecy and a short "thriller" suspense story, "Smooth," which became the sole short story published in the yearbook's Literary Section.[83]

In the end, while ominously setting aside and neglecting the Latin textbook, Norman outplayed, outwrote, and basically outdid anybody, including Bauer, the reigning English wizard. The energetic new kid became so ubiquitous and popular that his classmates wanted him to emcee their Class Day banquet. Unruffled Norman accepted and made it look easy.

The most difficult, time consuming and (most essentially) name-studded part of the Class Day ceremony was the Class Prophecy. Norman put himself in charge. For it, Norman worked up a skit which displayed front and center the power of radio. Crafting a simple, economical setting, he let voices and sounds do the work. The work in miniature embodied the fast pace and urbane wit that he would later dish up to a national audience. Norman wrote, directed, and starred in it, opposite the lovely Laura Atkinson. The vehicle he entitled the "Midsummer Night's Scream." Norman simply had "James" in his living room tune in from station to station to hear about various named classmates' doings in the future.

While Norman would refine his techniques, zooming in or out of scenes, going inside minds, even animating and giving voice to the dead, and would never saddle himself again with such a preposterous title, the script itself was eerily prophetic of Norman's future. His first "radio show" was a well-paced crowd-pleaser. The audience of his classmates and parents who heard his "Midsummer Night's Scream" at the Winthrop High School auditorium would one day grow into tens of millions. Nothing he did for the next ten years would come as close to his career on radio as this play, presented in June 1926 by 16-year-old Norman Corwin, which began: "The rising of the curtain finds James, a bachelor whose only joy is his radio."[84]

Was it Barney who invited attention to Laura Atkinson? Norman made moves quickly in the direction of the lovely local princess, curly-haired, dark-eyed Laura. Or did Norman only follow his own eyes? By year's end, Norman had twinned up with her very publicly. She served literally as "The Woman" in the cast of two voices of his "Class Prophecy" production. One imagines perfectionist Norman, if not romantically smitten as well, requiring lengthy and frequent rehearsals.

Meanwhile, at home, Pa sneaked a few of his son's poems out of the house on Perkins Street. For decades, Pa's highest authority had been his boss, the greeting card magnate, McKenzie. Pa passed the poems to

McKenzie. McKenzie, no poetry critic, took it to someone else. Norman's poetry was judged favorably. One wonders about Norman's reaction. He received attention. That was good. But who had he pleased? Certainly not McKenzie, a Rotarian and golfer whom Norman thought boorish. Moreover, his father had betrayed his privacy. The moody adolescent genius boiled over and refused to talk with his father.[85]

Ma ferried messages between them. Norman wanted $65 for a suit. He needed it to dazzle audiences at his play and as an emcee. For Ma to tell the elected chairman of annual Class Day, Pa said, "I wouldn't give him 65 cents." Pa also pledged not to attend, saying, "He wouldn't appreciate my presence." As may be expected from a man whose surface was harsh but whose heart was soft, Pa nonetheless made arrangements. A certain Hymie Schwartz provided the suit for Norman, in return for which Pa paid a dollar a week.

True to his word, however, Pa did not attend the ceremony. True to his cryptic values, he did buy ice cream and cake for a party at home afterward. Following the ice cream and cake, Norman (again, only just turned 16 years old) came around the table to where Pa was sitting, hugged his old man and said, "Pa, I know I've not been a good boy, and have upset you many times. But I will never forget what you did for me. From now on I won't be the same boy."

Pa said of the end of high school that Norman "changed from that time on," but one wonders how. Didn't Norman really change a year *before*, upon the family's relocation in Winthrop? And what did Pa notice? Did Norman become more serious? more passionate? Norman's fifteenth year may have comprised a manic series of documented successes. By contrast, the record of his sixteenth year is a blank, a virtual lost year. If he changed, was it for the better? Or did Norman fall from a manic year into a depressed one? Nothing Norman wrote makes this clear, and Pa's comments are too vague to add very much.

Why did Norman never write about this marvelous year? Possibly because he did not graduate. The principal withheld his diploma for failing Latin. He could not graduate.

Shocked people go into denial or amnesia, and, in this instance, Norman's denial or amnesia was astonishingly deep. His failure to earn a diploma was one thing he kept to himself for over half his life. Norman seems to have told nobody before he disclosed it to Bannerman. When he shared the secret with Bannerman, Bannerman was jolted to discover that it was not known by his older brother, Em, with whom Norman had always confided everything.[86]

Luckily for him, parental pressure was minimal. Pa was garrulous about education but only suggestive. "I was crazy about education and I never had any," Pa said when he was interviewed in 1987 at age 110. "An education can make you somebody." He told the same reporter that when people ask him what matters, "I always give them one answer: education." However, one notes that Pa conditioned speaking out with being asked. Doubtless, Norman did not ask and neither Pa nor Ma made an edict. On college, Em stated categorically, "[Our] folks at no point dictated what their children should do."[87]

The only pressure Norman faced was sibling pressure, indirect and subtle but real enough. Both of his older brothers were "college men." At the start of the summer, 1926, Em had already graduated from the Massachusetts Agricultural School in Amherst, while Al was nearing the end of his studies at Harvard. Notwithstanding their examples, Norman, seemingly a high school graduate, was not going to college.[88]

Norman did feel obliged to offer an explanation, no matter how glib, in his memoir. He said that it was on account of "grades" that college was out for him. He said that he was "not college material." Perhaps this reflects an adolescent's bad judgment, pessimism, or self-loathing. As an explanation, the explanation rings false. Norman had demonstrated—literally—for a time that he was good in chemistry, and he excelled in English. He barely passed math, true, but he passed, and if he flunked Latin, his teacher may simply have rubbed the excitable and sensitive youngest student in the class the wrong way. Moreover, most education is self-education and Norman was an awesomely disciplined autodidact. Given most subjects and most professors, Norman was "college material."[89]

In the end, his decision against college remains an insoluble mystery. Norman's earlier decision against a *bar mitzvah* signals how stubbornly strongly he felt about choosing reason over religion. His decision against further education seems inconsistent. When his class graduated without him in June, the brightest light of the Class of 1926 dimmed and was left academically stranded.[90]

Ultimately, a wondrous year like 1925–26 could be lived but it could never be relived. His spectacular senior year is absent from his memoirs. Transparently, Norman (who kept his yearbook, now at the Norman Corwin archives in Thousand Oaks) elected not to recover the year but to revere it—in private reveries. It was as if Winthrop High School never happened. He chose not to describe his feelings, his motives, to narrate his high school year, or otherwise explain in any detail his decision not to pursue college. Norman was simultaneously done with school as a student. He shelved his most amazing year under O for Obscure. Norman would enter classrooms in the future only as a professor.

Be it noted, though, that something clearly did not sit right with Norman back then. His decision against college, and the secret that he had not graduated from high school, may have torn him apart. He admitted to emotional storms. He recalled them in a letter in 1937. He wrote about being bitterly consumed by what he called "secret gnawings" of his mind. The year and a half after June 1926 is perfectly befogged in his preserved writings, which pick up the trail of his life only as he departed Winthrop and began to reinvent himself again, this time in Greenfield.[91]

The "Lost Year" and Greenfield

Before Norman left Winthrop, Ruth Gersin, Norman's firecracker distant cousin, a pretty woman with a crackling wit, came into his life. Ruth illuminated; her cousin's dark moods during the late spring and summer of his lost year between the summer after he left high school, 1926, and fall, 1927, when he arrived in Greenfield. His 1937 letter to Ruth is one of the first he selected for the collection of his letters published in 1972, and the only surviving letter that sheds any light at all on the lost year.

They met at the hospital. Ruth brought Norman a book, *Cyrano de Bergerac*. He had had his appendix removed. In April 1927 he was 16, and so was she. They clicked. In her he found convivial company. Norman praised her in his letter as "the sensitive, vital, brave girl who came into my life when my appendix went out of it and who brought *Cyrano* with her."

Stalwart Ruth became thereafter his steady date to dances and his guest on midnight promenades. She was a good listener while he seethed. Norman wrote her of "the dark night on the roof when I confided in you the secret gnawings of my mind and you soothed me with cool and sane words." They shared and whispered wicked thoughts as well. In his letter, with obvious ruefulness, Norman reminded Ruth of her "sister's wedding and the cynicism with which we profaned it."[92]

That letter and a little story in his memoir (without dates) about how he found a job in Greenfield sums up the record of Norman's missing year. Except for his appendix removal and sporadic promenading with Ruth, Norman's lost year is a mystery. The same autobiographical hand that would not write a word about his incredible 1925–26 school year also left this next year almost completely blank. Sleuthing out what Norman did from June 1926 to October 1927 begins here.

Norman may have boiled over in part doing without creative writing on a deadline, classes and the everyday novelties and excitements of a school, the sudden absence of friends, attentive teachers like Miss Lu, the end of awards. A succession of empty days may have sunk Norman into a depression. His mother, who listed his accomplishments in 1925–26, had no list to offer for the following year. With his unshakable resolve not to consider college, he had to find a job.

That is, in 1926 it seems implausible that for months or a year teen-aged Norman was housed, clothed, and fed by his parents while he simply loafed. Instead, Norman was likely pressured into a job—a job at an enterprise that he hated or for someone whom he came to hate. If his father ever used connections to get his son a job, Pa had no stronger connection than with McKenzie of the McKenzie Engraving Company.[93]

Norman's abundant surviving letters to Em only begin with Green-field. Why? It cannot be that he did not write. He was a great letter writer. Almost certainly, Winthrop High's poet laureate, yearbook editor and playwright typed or wrote up many letters, many of them to Em, during this year. What did Norman shroud? A biographer's dilemma arises because Norman cloaked this period. A biographer must confront the potential significance of silence. After June 1926, when Norman's senior year photograph and list of accomplishments become obsolete, and the yearbook can help us no more, what was going on?

Again, one speculates along the course of least resistance. Following doggedly in his father's footsteps, apprenticed at his father's company, under his father's boss, a hated, egotistical buffoon, leaving home each morning in work clothes and getting home with his father, smelling of the same chemicals of plate making, would have predictably revolted this sensitive teenager, especially so soon after his reign as the big man of Winthrop High, his name in the newspaper as a successful author, his head full of dreams.

As lucky other classmates headed to college, something positively Dickensian, the fate that befell sensitive Charles Dickens, who was set to work pasting labels on bottles, perhaps befell Norman. Perhaps. Norman ignored this period when he wrote his autobiography, but that would not be because a Dickensian sketch did not make a great story. It was more likely because the fiasco remained painful.

He did not seem to have left home. He did not seem to have traveled even briefly. (When he spoke of a later trip to New York, he said that it was his first and, moreover, that he had only been as far north as Lake Winnipesaukee, New Hampshire, and south as Coventry, Rhode Island, on family trips.) It seems certain that Norman stayed in Winthrop, within a trolley car or a long walk of downtown Boston, with Lynn and its booming shoe factories reachable by train from Winthrop Beach.[94]

We need to circle back to it again: did Norman really not work for over a year? Possibly. Norman made clear that he arrived with only nominal money in Greenfield in October 1927. Of course, this did not mean that Norman had not earned and *spent* money. But living under his parents' roof and given the fact that in his later life Norman was frugal and a saver, something seems to have served as an obstacle to his steady employment for over a year and that obstacle was *not* ill health.

Although Norman complained of colds and was a prodigious, self-styled hypochondriac, only a bout with appendicitis was serious enough for him to report in his memoirs. After the operation, his belly sewn up and the doctors gone when he awoke, words came to him. Flat on his back, young Norman said, "Well, if this isn't the damndest allegory."[95]

The recovery room nurse's reaction is lost, but we are free to react ourselves now. A young man had just faced and survived a medical emergency. His appendix was removed, lest he die. The oldest allegory in the world is death and rebirth, one of the universal myths embodied in many parables. Immersed in literature and in storytelling as he was, Norman awoke to a strong impression: his experience presented "the damndest allegory" imaginable. In fact, in radio, he would present the speaking dead as voices on the air many times.[96]

His successful surgery took place, he recalled, in April 1927. In Norman's memoir, he implicitly left after high school for Greenfield, as if immediately. He said similarly in an interview in 1966 that he "went right into newspaper work at the age of seventeen." In fact, he was at work on a newspaper at age *seventeen*—but he was *sixteen* when high school ended for him in June 1926. He did not turn seventeen until May 1927. Whatever Norman did (whenever he was not in surgery) spans the year from June 1926 to about June or July 1927, when he arrived in Greenfield, the same year of which Pa said in two words, with admiration, "Norman changed."[97]

What lies behind the transformation that Pa noticed without otherwise describing or explaining its history?

One thing Norman surely did—and wrote about in fine detail in his memoir, without dates—was to seek a writing job. Norman described drawing a 150-mile radius on a map. This was farther from Winthrop than Norman had ever traveled. He plotted his escape within this circle by identifying all of the area's newspapers.

Next, upon finding over eighty, he listed their editors' names and addresses. Thereupon, his clunky old Oliver typewriter, his parents' gift to him at twelve, became key. To find a job in journalism and, thereby, leave home, on his old, clattering Oliver, he repeatedly typed until he had the perfect template of a one-page business letter. Whatever Norman typed (no copy survived) his youthful age, absence of a high school diploma, and inexperience were likely omitted or somehow obfuscated.

Pa (or Norman himself?) took Norman's template to Mr. McKenzie's "factory" to print out identical copies on a multigraph. Each copy looked original. These Norman then signed, placed into addressed envelopes which he licked and sealed, to which he affixed three-cent stamps, and off they went. (Probably each one also contained a stamped, self-addressed envelope, considering that he eventually got so many replies.)

Awake nights listening to the surf hit the seawall, walking the beach mornings, seeking consolation with Ruth, Norman waited. He also grew a moustache "to look older." Photographs demonstrate that Norman adopted the expression of a world-weary man.

Norman received a staggering number of replies; however, one imagines Norman's disappointment and increasing frustration as he excitedly opened, one after another, for days and weeks, only rejections. Not one of the first 55 replies Norman received were job offers.

Norman did not say that he looked locally in person, though he did. As his letters were being rejected everywhere, Norman was being rejected in person as well. At the *Traveller*, Norman, who had won that daily's short story competition during his fabulous senior year, was rejected. This led him to try his luck at *The Boston Post*, the *Traveller*'s next-door neighbor on Newspaper Row. He found himself seated in a chair as an earnest young interviewee before Charles E. Young of *The Boston Post*.[98]

Clearly a gracious gentleman, Young, the Assistant Managing Editor of *The Boston Post*, took time. He discussed Norman's future options. Norman told him where he had applied by mail. One of the papers seemed to Young to be Norman's best chance. Presumably after Norman's grateful nod at his offer of help, Young then typed up and signed a letter of recommendation. Dated September 4, 1926, Young addressed it to John W. Haigis, the publisher-editor of *The Greenfield Recorder*, Greenfield, Massachusetts.

Young's note to Haigis said:

> This will introduce Mr. Norman H. Corwin [*sic*], the young man with whom you have had some correspondence and who is very anxious to get started in the newspaper business.
>
> It is on my recommendation that he is trying to ally himself with a paper in some smaller city or town. I believe that the very best training is to be obtained there, much better than in a big city where the staff is larger, and the reporter is likely to get into a terrible rut.
>
> Norman is an ambitious young fellow, who writes very well and who is anxious and willing to work hard. I think he will make a good reporter.[99]

Actually, Haigis had no compelling reason in 1926 to hire a sixteen-year-old, even one favorably recommended by Young. Nor was Norman himself inclined to ship out so far from home. He simply held the nice letter until circumstances changed.

Near the end of this lost period an unprecedented drama unfolded in the skies in May 1927, with ripples throughout that summer. Like Norman's *The Adventures of John Ransford*, it was the drama of a lone, intrepid hero: Charles A. Lindbergh. "Lucky" Lindy made a solo flight across the Atlantic, won an international prize and instantly enjoyed of world of acclaim.

Encouragement for Norman to enter media was literally in the air, on every radio and in the shouts of all of the newspaper boys. Newspapers were bursting with headlines, maps, and photographs of Lindy and his "Spirit of St. Louis" single-propeller lane.

In tandem with radio bulletins, newspapers tracked Lindy (and his plane) headed by battleship back home, where he was greeted by President Coolidge as cameramen cranked and gaggles of newspapermen scribbled notes. Norman saw himself in his dreams not as the pilot but as one of the reporters. His mother said that Norman, from childhood, had always told her that he wanted to be "a newspaper man."

In Winthrop, his ear to the radio, Norman heard news happening, stories begging to be written, unprecedented incentives to become a reporter *now*. His older brother and idol, Em, a reporter in Springfield, was already doing what Norman wanted to do.[100]

Norman released the letter from Young to Haigis. Haigis invited Norman for an interview. As a legislator, Haigis had an office in the State House. That is likely to have been where Norman and State Senator John W. Haigis first met. Norman would have traveled by streetcar and subway to hear Senator Haigis say that he anticipated a vacancy soon. In fact, Haigis had plans beyond hiring another reporter. A step-by-step, rung-by-rung politician, the cigar-chomping publisher-editor of the *Greenfield Recorder*, already a legislator, was going to make his first bid for state-wide office in 1928.

Knowing that the state's incumbent Treasurer was aiming to be the next Lieutenant Governor, Haigis was going to aim to be the next Treasurer. He had massive western Massachusetts contacts, of course, but Norman was an energetic young hustler with obvious connections in Boston whose brother worked for an influential newspaper in Springfield. So, what was not to like?

Haigis offered Norman fifteen dollars a week, or half of the going rate for experienced reporters, but then Norman was not experienced. Norman accepted. The deal actually ought to have required his father's approval because he was not yet twenty-one, but Pa's approval would have been given. Pa, then doing hard manual labor for $18 a week himself would surely never have argued with anybody's offer of $15 a week for his son to write articles.

It had been a good ten or twelve months, going back to his last year in high school, since Norman had last known the high of success. Norman, 17 years old, failed Latin scholar, explosively failed chemist, accomplished reader and writer of poetry, great and sensitive classical music lover, was going to be what he always told his mother he would be, what Miss Lu foresaw for him: a newspaper reporter. And his boss was going to be Senator Haigis.

Too young not to have been seen off by his parents, Norman likely went by train to Springfield in about June or July, where either Em, most likely, or their glazier cousin, a man disguised under the name "Fred" in Norman's memoirs, met him to drive him the last leg of the journey up to Greenfield. Norman likely got no grand tour of Greenfield before moving in without ceremony or hoopla with Fred in one room of the no-frills Mohawk Chambers rooming-house on Main Street.

Greenfield and Its Paper

Norman in 1927, apparently with the family car. A couple of years later, he bought an old jalopy in Greenfield. He then drove it as a reporter in Springfield without a license for six years (courtesy Diane Corwin Okarski).

Greenfield was not totally foreign to Norman, although he had never been there. To Norman's nose, eyes and ears, printing was not exotic. The Corwins were intimately familiar with printing through Pa. As a consequence of his work, distinct and sharp smells imbued his father's sweat, including resins, which were the aromatic, piney, incense-like ingredients he needed to apply to plates in progress. Fainter smells of metal, typically (but not exclusively) copper, also clung to Pa's clothes. Finally, when plates were made near the printing room, pungent printer's ink asserted its veritably intoxicating presence. Before the boys could speak, they knew the printshop smell when Pa came home to reap their hugs on Bremen Street.

As soon as Norman walked into the *Recorder* office, he smelled print-er's ink blended with a tang of hot metal. Machines were bolted to the floor over where half of the office space was devoted to the newspaper's physical production. An idle staffer could observe the typographer toss slugs of lead to melt in the "hellbox," the red-hot part of the machine—hands off!—from which malleable metal then flowed. This recycled metal the typographer dexterously pounded away at via his keyboard on a souped-up, noisy sort of typewriter requiring more strength and concentration than any type-writer. Next, an automated plate maker (his father's trade back in Boston, but here greatly accelerated and no longer manual) created pages that were finally set into long, mechanized, whirling printing machines that ran off copies of the daily newspaper. Surrounded by smells of printer's ink and hot metal, clicking and clacking, the noisy office was much like cacophonous Eastie. No wonder Norman felt at home at work.

The whole newspaper operation thrilled Norman. Enveloped in a heavenly ambience, a frantic effort to fill columns on time compelled every-one's attention. In 1958, Norman happily reminisced with a *Greenfield Recorder* reporter, recalling in detail "the chattering telegraph bar which brought the news of the world, and the big, placid telegraph operator with the gentle face of a scholarly beagle. He was a preacher on his days off. On the job, he sat before a bumpy Underwood typewriter with an air of benign expressionlessness, decoding dots and dashes, and setting down words with no apparent feeling one way or the other about the sinning continents, the ceaselessly revolving squirrel cage of mayhem, disaster, rape and rev-olution or the regular respiratory movements of law and commerce and sports."

The office was more interesting than his dwelling. After all, the win-dow of the Mohawk Chambers did not overlook the sea or catch the beam of a lighthouse and display all colors of the rainbow. Nothing like the sound of waves or an isolated beach at dawn was nearby. Norman *was* awakened by the doleful whistle of a freight train coming through at three in the morning, a sound which probably made him feel no better. The sun was no longer his alarm clock. Most likely, Fred was.

Norman wrote in his memoirs of leaves changing colors when he arrived. More probably, he arrived in mid-summer. For a period, he was probably more the office "gopher" and message-taker than a reporter. Phone duty could nonetheless be a dramatic spot, and he wrote on this point in his memoirs.

On the night of August 23, 1927, alone, working late, Norman fielded questions people asked about an old criminal case that was in the news again. Pioneer Valley radio stations were not licensed to broadcast after sunset, but its newspaper offices were open late. To get the news in

Greenfield after dark, people phoned the *Recorder*. When they phoned in the summer of 1927, they got Norman.

Norman found himself telling about two Italians whose names he knew very well. In Eastie, especially among the Italians, "Sacco and Vanzetti" were rallying cries. For years, Norman witnessed protests and marches as Sacco and Vanzetti were tried, convicted, and sentenced to die. Persecuted as anarchists during the Red Scare of 1920, the men's fate reflected a great injustice. Many thousands favored their reprieve or a pardon. August 23 was the night of the men's executions.

In Greenfield, Norman, a rooter for Sacco and Vanzetti, was thus ironically the one who had to tell others to abandon all hope. Years later, he recalled the night that he relayed news from telegrams that arrived in the office:

> Yes, Sacco has been executed. Yes. Four minutes ago. Vanzetti is now on his way to the chair."—*Ring*—"Yes, they have been executed."—*Ring*—"Yes, both men are dead."—*Ring*—"Yes—yes—yes—yes—yes—"[101]

Norman finessed the usual rough patch that all rookies face. His editor cautiously assigned Norman the office boy to cover local sports. He was instructed that the most important thing was to get the players' names right. The sports pages (while the 1928 Yankees burned up the charts) were a well-read, turn-to-first and important part of any paper.

At first, Norman primarily enjoyed a tyro author's most intoxicating pleasure: seeing his name in print. Thousands of people read his accounts of ball games under the byline "By Norman Corwin." The baseball league tagged him to be league secretary, as his scorekeeping and notes for the newspaper was something they needed, too. A modern reporter might quibble about serving, essentially, both as official spokesman and news source as well as the reporter, but there was no such bar in those days.

Cheeky stories in sportese slanguage were acceptable as well. Norman soon took advantage of that extra freedom. He loved to use poetry, rhyming or free verse. He turned in a report of a football game in the form of a rhyming poem. His doggerel was published as is, making some splash as a novelty item.

Working late, arriving early, getting stories, innovating with poetry and wit, Norman was recognized and rewarded. He felt good about it. In an interview years later, he called the office *home*, though Norman actually lived with "Fred" in a small room three stories above several small businesses. That was the trouble. Young Norman's first time away from home, despite good, familiar smells at work, would have been bleak. Coming in later and rising on a different schedule, Fred was probably a disturbance to the young man who, when his eyes were closed, was especially sensitive to sounds. No letters survive from Greenfield except one to his parents in which he does not mention his cousin at all.

Tensions rose between Norman and his older, sophistication-aspiring cousin. The dynamics were set for friction and heat. Norman needed a brother and Fred was not Norman's brother. Unmet expectations are a potent and common source of misery and Norman, not only seventeen but a young seventeen, ached for family. Having little in common—by Norman's own admission, he "had nothing in common with him but half the rent"—the cousins had precious little to say to one another. Norman never quotes Fred. Without conversation, they shared nothing but the air.

Norman spared Fred few words. In his memoirs he described Fred only (and somewhat mockingly) as the "lady-killer Ravenal type." Active bachelors make poor hand holders for homesick teen-agers. Fred had a car, but he was not generous with rides. Mentioning a ride through spectacular foliage once with Fred, Norman dubbed it "rare." Fred and Norman may not have had fist fights, but Norman hastily found another place. Greenfield directories show that Norman moved quickly, the 1927 edition already listing him at 31 Garfield Street, and the 1928 edition, at 133 School Street. Before he married, Norman never thereafter attempted to live with a roommate besides his brothers.

(Pity Fred. From Fred's viewpoint, he was doing the kid a favor. He was saving him some rent money. Was it his fault that he had a full dance card while Norman had "no life" but his new job? Minor irritations grew into serious aggravations, transparently. Whether Norman decided to depart, or Fred forced the issue, Norman separated from Fred before the new year.)

Norman lived in Greenfield but remained tightly connected to Winthrop. Although Norman wrote a lot of letters to his folks, somehow only one survived. (This was a note on his birthday in May 1928.) But besides exchanging letters frequently for three cents a pop, Norman spent the extra dough required for staticky toll calls to hear and to be heard. As always, sounds were life to Norman. The Los Angeles Times ran a story about Norman and his father in 1987. Their regular weekly phone calls going back sixty years (to 1927) were the hook. Like clockwork, Norman called home every Sunday.

If Norman thought of the office as his "new home," in part, this was due to Haigis. In Boston, Haigis was interesting but in Greenfield, he passed as exotic. Norman stated in his memoirs, without explanation, that he was at this time a Republican. The reason he was a Republican was probably Haigis, his boss, a living example of self-made success, the American dream realized. A family man whose highly visible vice (as for Norman's father) was his omnipresent cigar, Haigis was an extrovert extraordinaire, as in loud, and Norman thrived on sounds.

Haigis had good reason to toot his horn. He had gone from being a local stringer peddling copies of the *Greenfield Recorder* in Turner's Falls (population 6,150 in 1900) up several rungs through all of the elected fiscal offices of the town of Montague (population 6,866 in 1910) to becoming president of a small bank and, in 1915, the owner and publisher of this regional newspaper in Greenfield (population 15,462 in 1920). He took a big risk, turning a weekly into a daily.[102]

Haigis, a cigar-chomper "who never opened his mouth when he spoke," wanted to be Governor. The example of Calvin Coolidge, who had gone from a seat on the Northampton school board on up to Governor (and was now President) inspired his fellow frugal western Massachusetts Republican. During Norman's first year at the *Recorder*, Haigis won the Republican primary, became the party's nominee for Treasurer by acclamation, and handily won the job of State Treasurer on election day.[103]

Norman was an enthusiastic Haigis campaigner before he was old enough to vote. It is obvious that when Norman affixed a Haigis bumper sticker to the family's Plymouth in Winthrop, he did so with inner pride. He probably hoped that somebody would ask him about the sticker so that he could brag about his boss. Haigis liked Norman, whom he paid $ 15 to start but gave regular raises to later (first to $17, then $18, then $20 a week) before he sold the paper in late 1928.

(It may be that while working for almost two years in his late teens for a man who truly seemed to know how to do it all, who could make money, manage money, run a business, win elections, do good in office and be kind to family and friends, Norman had his first mentor and a model besides Em. However, Norman does not describe Haigis as being so significant in his life, or an example, and perhaps it misreads his relationship with Haigis to suggest this. On the other hand, Norman did not often wrestle in writing with the process of his maturation. The coming of age theme that had fueled Mark Twain's books on Tom Sawyer and Huck Finn, and such perennial classics as *Seventeen* by Booth Tarkington, never grabbed Norman. Coming of age did not interest him as a topic or figure as a structure in his memoirs. The period between high school and Greenfield is a stark vacuity. Any argument over a *bar mitzvah*, any adolescent *angst* acted out is omitted. Norman preferred episodic or unconnected stories or scenes over exploring his personal evolution in depth. Haigis may be an omitted, but real, erstwhile model.[104])

In the end, a biographer must remain at least partly baffled by the *lacuna* or heavy curtain draped over the years after Norman was given a typewriter and used a radio but before Norman turned eighteen, even over a lot of his time with the Greenfield paper. Happily, one extended story survives to save us from a sense of utter gloom, dark clouds, and storm throughout late 1927 and to early 1929.

Curiously not set in Winthrop or Greenfield but in New York, the story reveals commendable spunk on Norman's part. It candidly exposes the naiveté of an inexperienced youth who took as literal the open invitation of a celebrated author. At its core, the story displays Norman at seventeen talking shop one Sunday morning and in all innocence (and, likely, *gravitas*) handing some of his writings for comment to Heywood Broun while that Broadway *bon vivant* was still in pajamas, bathrobe and slippers. Because it was told in full detail, by taking it as representative, we may believe that Norman in his old age finally looked back on his younger self during his Greenfield period not just with tolerance but with positive affection.

Meeting Heywood Broun

Before Norman left Winthrop, Em had introduced his brother to Heywood Broun's column. Broun was a writer who looked like a writer, a paunchy fellow who slept in his clothes. However, unusual among writers, he led a rich social life. A phenomenon who burned his candle at both ends, close shaven, round Broun was a familiar figure at opening nights on Broadway, bouncing through Manhattan's speakeasies, and dancing in nightclubs. At the drop of a hat, he spoke at dinners and fund-raisers. The first nationally syndicated columnist and the best paid, Broun was one of the country's few writer celebrities.

Today, one tries and fails to recall anything that Broun wrote. As literature, even when examined, his appeal is difficult to explain. The elements of his verbal stew, wit, sophistication, gossip, and political opinions, were available elsewhere even in his own time. Broun's mix and match, however, with surprises and contrasts in every essay, somehow hit the spot before the Depression. Broun daily offered a reliably entertaining variety column of tasty tidbits. His column captured the attention of millions.

Broun was a natural hero for a young writer and, if Broun was not already Norman's hero in Winthrop, he certainly rose to become his hero as he sat homesick in Greenfield. He could keep up with proletarian, earthy Broun for free. The copy room at the *Recorder* had New York newspapers on a table for reporters.

Norman typed out a letter to Broun. Perhaps egged on by colleagues— they eventually all knew about Norman's letter, including his boss—whatever Norman said of himself, his new job, his hopes—and it is unlikely that he did not disclose to Broun some autobiographical facts—Broun was moved to dash off a comradely welcoming telegram. Norman recalled a phrase forever, as if words of fire branded into his memory. Broun's telegram said that Norman might "see him when in New York."

See Him When in New York?

Greatly taken by the cosmopolitan phrasing "as though I had got a cable reading 'when next on safari in Kenya,'" the boy proudly showed it around. The gang at the office were quickly on him to go to New York. Broun was a writer who not merely survived but thrived. Broun lived a reporter's dream, writing his opinions, original short poems, descriptions of oddball characters, human interest stories, anecdotes, and a sprinkling of choice news items of his own selection.

Someone told him how to get from Grand Central station to Times Square while others came out with other tips and encouragement. When Haigis got the word, even frugal Haigis—perhaps smelling a great local human-interest story involving one of his reporters and a real celebrity—authorized Norman to use company credit at the Hotel St. James. He then could not get to New York fast enough.

On Saturday, January 28, 1928, getting to Greenfield and catching the train proved easy enough. Weather became the issue. The closer the train came to the city, the whiter the landscape grew. More obviously by the mile, New York City was in the grip of a big blizzard. With cabs impossible to find, after trudging through knee-deep drifts, Norman dried his clothes in his small hotel room while he made calls to Broun. He got no answer.

Norman decided to pass the time Heywood Broun–style with an evening out. He bought a heavily discounted ticket directly at the box office of the half-empty Roxy Theater. Still, Norman did not watch much of the show. He kept leaving his seat to make more calls, always getting no answer.

After a night's light sleep, Norman began a new round of calls Sunday morning. Only at noon did Norman reach the man. To his eternal credit, Broun, in a groggy voice, told Norman, "Come right up."

Norman trotted—doubtless, luggage in hand—through high snow to 333 West 85th Street. Broun, in pajamas and swathed in a large bathrobe, brought his young visitor into his library, where Norman promptly thrust an article at Broun. No matter how he felt, easy-going Broun, champion of the underdog, was polite. Smiling over Norman's writing, possibly scanning, possibly not, he passed it back without criticism. Norman recalled Broun telling him, "Keep on writing. Don't be impatient with yourself or the world."

After a little more conversation, Broun stood and plucked from his bookshelves a copy of *Gandle Follows His Nose*, which he inscribed. That copy, now preserved at the American Radio Archives in Thousand Oaks, California, was simply inscribed "To Norman Corwin from Heywood Broun." Norman kept it, even adding to it. Inside it is a yellowed clipping from an unidentified newspaper dated in pencil April 8, 1931, in which Broun was quoted as follows:

Once I wrote a book which pleased me to the hilt. It was short. But it contained all that I believed and had ever dreamed. Few read it, and I seemed to be almost the only one who found in it wisdom and a tragic significance. In fact, once a year I read over "*Gandle Follows His Nose*" and say to myself, "You were good when you wrote that."

Indeed, I try to reach my right hand above my shoulder and pat myself enthusiastically upon the back. But I'm not as limber as I was once.

Norman emphasized in his memoirs that he returned to his humble role "at the Greenfield *Recorder*, circulation 11,806 (paid)." His hero was addressing more people in print daily than all of the people Norman had ever seen in his life. He went back to serving 11,806 paid subscribers, and (soon, if not already) living alone.[105]

The boss liked Norman and picked him up to join the family for Sunday meals at a nice restaurant. In the boss's big Packard, Norman joined Haigis, his wife, a son and two daughters, one named Rose, just like Norman's mother. Norman banked half of his pay weekly in Haigis's bank. Norman was riding and dining with a successful, self-made man who spent more time in Boston than in Greenfield and who was a friend of President Coolidge. Haigis was also a Republican. And so, Norman said in his autobiography, was Norman then.

1928, After Broun

On his first birthday away from home, Norman indulged himself with fantasized success, such a success that others would come around to interview *him*.

"If ever I am famous, and they come to interview me, I shall be prepared," Norman wrote his parents. On May 5, 1928, having just turned eighteen, he fingered the small rose molded out of Bakelite from his mother, and his father's encouraging note covering photos of his brothers. Norman speculated airily, "When they ask me, what accounts for my success, I shall show them your letter, Ma's bakelite rose and the pictures of my fraters."[106]

An interviewer should have asked him then how it felt to be in Greenfield. A virtual addict in withdrawal as a classical music fan here, Norman was no longer up to his ears in music. Symphony Hall was a hundred miles away. Northampton's well-appointed concert hall was about 15 bumpy miles by road and, besides, he had no car. But he might be upbeat in answering the question. His ears pulled Norman out of his funk. The Greenfield soundscape came to please him. In his memoir, he spoke nostalgically of the clatter of machinery in the *Recorder*'s office. Other novelties made up for other losses. The accents of the rural baseball players, the local football coach, the tobacco farmers, and the Polish immigrants, so different from Jewish, Italian and Boston Irish voices, struck his sensitive ears as unfamiliar and stimulating. Gone were the sounds of sea against the seawall and cries of gulls over a beach, but here Norman heard birds, the grinding gears of tractors, and backfiring model T's rather than city traffic. These sounds overwhelmed his homesickness. Although Norman said nothing expressly about missing Boston's sounds, he was well aware of the Boston & Maine freight train's "long whistle" as it rumbled through town at 3 a.m.[107]

At the paper, eventually, some non-sports stories—rejected or heavily revised at first—found print more as originally written. No home ever fascinated him as much as this office did. Studying characters like the "scholarly beagle" typographer, roving Main Street, reporting ball games, he lived through a year at work.

Half of the people in Greenfield were female but Norman, later among the most impactful communicators of his time, seems to have had classic difficulty as a young man communicating with them. Norman was self-conscious about barbarity, lacking "certain common decencies" embodied by hospitable Em, an impeccable gentleman who knew how to please his companions. Telling this to Al, Norman reverted to Yiddish, worrying that he'd always be "a *schloomper*" (a slob).[108]

Notwithstanding Norman's self-conscious *schloomperism*, at least one romance flared. A local girl whom Fred cast off became Norman's passionate love. Norman spent few words on its narrative arc, but his words compressed a sad story. He wrote of falling "desperately in and out of love."

Norman seems to have ended as he began in Greenfield, a lonely stranger in a quiet town. He wrote Em about his down days, if not their cause. Em was less than impressed with his doleful moodiness.

"Your last letter brings me to the verge of kicking your arse," Em snapped back.

Then, the teenager was named the paper's poetry and movie critic.

Sam Corwin, when a few years younger than 17-year-old Norman, had spent two weeks in the hold of a ship in steerage class. Most of the time while crossing the Atlantic, Sam and his family had but one source of air and light. He became familiar with it and he recalled it as the best of his voyage: being in the dark staring at a single, small porthole. By contrast, Norman sat in the cool dark looking at the latest movies. Ecstatic Norman dubbed his bylined movie column "Seeing Things in the Dark."

Unlike Pa's ship, the theater offered music. In movie theaters of the time, tinkling tunes, popular and classical, were pumped out by pianists to accompany silent films. Readers who turned to his reviews saw flashes of Heywood Broun's wit. Norman's column became popular enough to be feared for bad reviews. Norman experienced the inevitable first clash with a reader.

One review was so snarky that the movie-house manager threatened to bar him. Despite the threat, he panned a few movies and was never barred. Given perspective, he saw that the manager was right. Norman criticized his own criticism. "Never so jejune," he said. In the end, Norman more often found bright bits than blots on the silver screen.

His perks at the paper ameliorated much of his misery. Norman saw as many movies as he wanted on his press pass. Not only was the public library a particularly nice one, a 1797 mansion with bannister stairs, Norman enjoyed first dibs on the latest books. He was the *Recorder's* reviewer. Social events, many with refreshments, were open to him as a reporter whenever he wanted something to do—and something to eat.

When Norman was 18, working full-time but too young to vote, a ballot issue about child labor led to a media frenzy. The Massachusetts child labor referendum—a national "test case"—stoked a state-wide political firestorm. Nowhere was it fought more intensely than in the Connecticut River Valley, so dependent on tobacco growing farms and other farming operations that employed even pre-teens for some tasks. Professional speakers, big rallies, bands, and billboards overwhelmed sedate Greenfield. The vote tallied in November 1928 shocked the country: not a single city or town in Massachusetts voted against child labor. The majority of every municipality favored the proposition that children could work, and the government ought not to interfere.

That same summer, Coolidge had famously not chosen to run for another term. One envisions the telegrapher at the *Recorder* behind his big, balky typewriter, stunned by that item. Coolidge did not choose to run? A great struggle between the two major parties ensued, during which a Catholic ran for President. Over the radio, Al Smith's raspy voice was grating, loud—and clearly from New Yawk. Bigotry revived the Ku Klux Klan. Crosses burned in the hills of western Massachusetts.

These issues came at him as news. Norman himself was a working "child" of 18, and the son of a working child, when the issue of child labor was being fought over. Norman left no writing on this issue, or when Smith lost.

Of personal importance, Haigis won. His boss's win meant change, and change quickly. Within two weeks of winning election to State Treasurer in November 1928, Haigis sold the *Greenfield Recorder*, effective December 1, 1928. (Haigis had good luck in his timing; a year later, after the Crash, his newspaper would have been a distressed property.)

Norman inhaled only the fumes of vicarious satisfaction. No state job in Boston was his. The young man Haigis had hired, cultivated and who had excitedly volunteered and campaigned for him was left behind. Norman, who still knew Boston far better than he knew Greenfield, who loved the symphony and much else about the state capital, who earned little and saved small sums each week, would surely have moved back to Winthrop and commuted to the State House for a better-paying job had he been invited.

Clearly, however, no job was offered. The role of conquering hero was not yet his to play. Instead of becoming a government clerk in Boston with Haigis, he moved to Springfield for a bigger, better-paying reporter's job. Probably in addition, even then, he was thinking about radio.

Station WBZ broadcast from both Boston and Springfield. Newspapers in the *Recorder* office carried news stories in 1928 about WBZ announcers going to New York for better jobs at NBC network headquarters. In January, it was Alwyn Bach, best known for broadcasts of the Boston Symphony Orchestra, and in October, John Shaw Young, who did shows in both Boston and Springfield. The same story repeated, only the names differed, as other announcers went to NBC from WBZ. How to break into network radio lay between the lines: get to Springfield and get on WBZ.

With Haigis gone and new people in charge, Norman had reached the acme of his possibilities on a small daily in a small town, but the 18 year old with such limited experience was stranded. Thus, when Em called with his news, Norman welcomed it and congratulated him. Em was going to New York to work for the country's major wire service, the United Press.

But there was more, and it involved Norman. When Em served early notice of his departure from the *Springfield Republican*, he had, ahem, audaciously proposed to his editor, crusty, grumbly Bill Walsh, his kid brother as his own replacement. Walsh had not been interested. He knew how to fill vacancies. Without tipping Norman off, Em thereafter lobbied Walsh. The two men had worked together for years, but Em and Walsh had little in common off the job. And they were different personalities. Undaunted, Em plowed on, cajoling, and teasing until he got Walsh to agree on one point— to interview his brother.

Springfield

Em surely advised his brother on how to make a good impression. Dress his best, shake hands firmly, sit up, speak slowly and clearly. If so, Em did not speak in vain. For his interview in Springfield, Norman recalled dressing better than ever in his life, fashionably parting his hair in the middle and sporting his lucky mustache. He had to have brought a portfolio of his writing. He spoke seriously and answered directly whatever Walsh asked.

The *Springfield Republican*'s newsroom on Fort Street, about 1930, was a crowded and busy eyrie overlooking downtown and near eateries and saloons (courtesy Diane Corwin Okarski).

As they talked, Norman studied Walsh, whom he called "another splendid advertisement for the Irish-American," otherwise describing him as "a thin man, bald as a melon, with an honest, big nose, a prominent Adam's apple, and thick lenses in his eyeglasses."[109]

Doubtless, Walsh took Norman's measure as well. There was no glossing over the fact: Norman had only had a year of reporting experience. Walsh saw before him a sorry specimen who had barely cut his teeth on sports and movie articles, soft features, in Greenfield. The *Springfield Republican*'s reputation was national. The *Republican* ran few intentionally funny stories, no comics or humor column (Norman would later suggest that he write one), or rhyming accounts of baseball games.

Norman was right to make his strongest pitch. By a point little appreciated by Norman at their first meeting, Walsh was the very boss he needed. Haigis, for whom political interests were primary, wrote the editorials. Indifferent to nuts-and-bolts journalism, he delegated those tasks. By contrast, Walsh was a skilled reporter. A consummate professional, he cared passionately about prose and picked up on good or bad writing. Luckily, Walsh, a good questioner, detected a caring capacity in Norman, only he was far too wily to say a word about it.

Instead, glumly, as if put upon, Walsh made his move. He made no attempt to conceal how "grudgingly" he was hiring the teenager. However, he simultaneously offered Norman $ 32.50 a week. The *Republican's* reporters were unionized and had negotiated higher rates than the scale at Haigis's newspaper. $ 32.50 was double his pay in Greenfield. It was a great offer when a loaf of bread was twenty-five cents. Suddenly, life was beautiful. Norman did not hesitate. He jumped up to shake on the deal.[110]

Not so fast. Walsh now made clear that the opening was not immediate. For one thing, Em had to vacate his seat first, and, for another, Walsh had to give the high sign as well exactly when to fill the vacancy. Well, that would be all right, too.

Em worked on Walsh to bring his kid brother aboard as soon as possible. One day, exasperated or persuaded, Walsh gave the high sign. Interestingly, he did not call Norman but mailed him a letter. Em wrote, "Mr. Walsh crushed the Coolidge coolness tonight and said you can come any time you wish."[111]

Next, Norman was the mopey one. Conditionally hired sometime about mid–December 1928, Norman still only left Greenfield to begin his new job in late February or early March. He may have soon realized that delay had been a mistake. Springfield later seemed so much like a birthday gift or a rebirth that in his memoirs he stretched the calendar back and spoke of beginning at the *Springfield Republican* "eight weeks before (his) birthday" in 1929.[112]

Instantly keeping a close eye on young Norman, Walsh had to be his 18-year-old rookie's harshest critic at first. Ultimately his friend, mentor and biggest booster, Walsh worked his magic. A master in the art of managing a colorful and diverse crew of reporters, Walsh found ways to make each shine. Norman was but the latest of a rough-edged series of men whom Walsh had molded to do their best work.

First, Walsh assigned Norman to character or "local color" stories. This proved fortunate because Norman wrote such articles well. Norman, like his garrulous brother, could engage people, get them talking and get their stories. Secondly, when any article of Norman's caught public interest, he kept Norman on the story, mining that person or topic into a series. To Norman's and his editor's pleasure, Norman developed a following.

Norman was simultaneously expanding his knowledge, analytical and verbal skills. His job improved his mind. "It was my liberal arts course working for *The Republican*," Norman said in an interview years later. He did not name Walsh, but Walsh lives between those lines. During his college years, in his early twenties, Norman was in a seminar led by one professor, Bill Walsh.[113]

Unlike the Eastie of his youth, here Norman lived near a community of thousands of Blacks, most of them living in a few segregated blocks with their own churches and schools. Springfield was otherwise Italian (almost all of whom came from the less developed and poor farm belt of southern Italy), French (often French-Canadians) and Irish, each of these blocs largely living within a respective geographic section. A smattering of Polish, German, Jewish and other ethnicities filled out the city's diverse population.

Besides fires and accidents, Walsh saw to it that Norman learned about local institutions. He sent Norman to the courts, to public hearings and occasionally on a run to the State House, by train. Perhaps Norman ran into Haigis in passing and saw his folks in Winthrop. But all the while Walsh and Norman knew that his true beat (and *forte*) was "the offbeat." Look at people, he was told, and find stories.[114]

Besides Walsh, Em kept an eye on Norman. Writing from New York, he praised his kid brother's report of an accident. He loved especially that Norman eschewed "gaga and saccharine sentiment." Norman obviously complained about getting too much critical attention from Walsh. Aghast

In Springfield, Norman enjoyed camaraderie in a large news staff under editor Bill Walsh, who named Norman to be the newspaper's "Voice of the News" on local radio each night, beginning 1930 (courtesy Diane Corwin Okarski).

at his brother's self-pity and gloom, Em instructed Norman, "If you are bluesy over your work just write me a letter of explanation—your attitude is beyond me."[115]

Norman had gotten along most of his time in Greenfield by walking and cadging rides. To pursue stories here, Norman drove—illegally. During his months in Greenfield, Norman withdrew a few bucks he had salted away and bought a vintage used car. It did not bother him that he had no license to operate a motor vehicle. Perhaps swerving a bit, maybe a little erratic in his signals and turns, but cautious—Norman was never a fast driver—he made his way slowly about that small town. It was the same in the city. Even through rain and raging snowstorms, the self-confident young man made it through Springfield's increasingly familiar streets without an accident.[116]

Norman always knew that he ought to take a test and pay a fee, but he kept putting it off. Norman, by then 24, finally confessed in a letter to Em on June 8, 1934, "I plan for a license-test Monday. I've been driving illegally for five or six years now, and it's high time I got a license." Either his by-now-ancient car had seen its day, or he felt entitled, as a licensed driver, to better wheels. Norman said that he had his eye on another reporter's 1928 Pontiac, which he knew to be available for $ 85.

Besides the "ordinary extraordinary" people about whom Norman wrote, and with whom he lived when in the Spicers' international rooming house, there was waterfront. In his old age, Norman nostalgically associated his affection for Springfield with its river. This was characteristic of his taste. Flowing waters anywhere, including tidal harbors or coves, in Eastie and Winthrop, or the Hudson River in New York, always bucked up Norman's spirits. The many Depression stories that Norman had covered, and some sad, if not tragic, memories were merged in his mind into a general impression of personal contentment. In an interview forty years later, Norman said, "My heart is still along the riverfront in Springfield. It was a happy time in my life."

Norman had forgotten all about, or (more likely) chose not to regale the interviewer with his recollections of the book that failed and how his co-author had turned down his marriage proposal flat.

Norman Proposes to His Coauthor

Norman's memoirs, otherwise so full of Springfield, do not explain how they met but Norman asserted that when they met, Hazel was being pursued by "social lions," men who "in competitive courtship, could rend me limb from limb." Shrewdly, he cut off competitors by organizing some private time together. When alone with Hazel, he avoided comparison with other suitors. He announced his upcoming book project and his problem. Norman said that he needed a collaborator. Had he found one? Oh, yes, she loved epigrams, too.[117]

Hazel Cooley, several years older than Norman, lived with her mother on the far side of the city, near Forest Park, at 408 Sumner Avenue. Her mother, Sarah, was a widow whose husband, Max, a local merchant, had died in 1908. Hazel, "the belle of the city" by Norman's smitten sighs, possessed "great dark levantine eyes, a regal cast of mouth and chin, an effortless grace, a warm and generous spirit, and a carriage of natural dignity."[118]

Even Em knew Hazel, though not very well. When Norman asked him, Em cheered Norman on. He wrote his younger brother, "Cannot say how much or by whom she is rushed," before he insisted, "Seeing as you are a figure of some prominence, your chance is as good as anybody else's."[119]

Aiming at two birds with one book, Norman thereafter kept her company, at the same time confirming what Miss Lu said, that Norman stood out for "his use of words. He loved words. He *loved* words. Really did. And he had a very, very good vocabulary."[120]

That earlier strong bond between Norman and his English teacher became the basis of his relationship with Hazel. "I sighed every time the streetcar passed your house," he confessed to her forty years later. Working together daily for an hour or two, they found hundreds of quotations for a book of wisdom. They were both reading (admittedly, mostly Norman), copying and putting together strings of unrelated great sentences. Norman's often ecstatic and lifelong love affair with language proceeded.[121]

Too shy to kiss the girl, Norman one afternoon finally squired her out from under the watchful eyes of her mother to Forest Park. There he proposed. He recalled delivering the proposal ponderously, "like asking President Hoover if I could replace his Secretary of State." Shocked though Hazel may have been, she had her wits about her, promptly refused, kissed him, and suggested that they work on their book together until it was complete.[122]

Still not rushing the job, largely flailing Heywood Broun's columns for verbal gems—apparently certain that his old friend, Broun, would not mind their borrowing—Norman and Hazel finally had a scrapbook long enough to publish. Just as he had the prior year to meet Heywood Broun, Norman set himself in motion by train to New York. He had the high degree of confidence granted only the naive. Astonishingly, his simple and direct approach worked. In a hotel room with his manuscript, flipping the Yellow Pages listing of publishers, Norman picked one, phoned, made an appointment, brought his draft, and left the building that same afternoon with a signed contract.

Their book, entitled *So Say the Wise; A Community of Modern Mind*, was in his hand when, on September 29, 1929, he advised Em, "I went to see Hazel (at her invitation) at her sumptuous quarters some 15 blocks from my encampment last Friday night."[123]

She was dazzled but the Roaring Twenties did not roar long after that. The stock market crashed in late October 1929. Neither Norman's relationship with Hazel nor with the publisher prospered. As the Depression deepened, the couple's big book of credited plagiarisms failed.[124]

Norman did not stay alone. He dated a lot. He neither proposed more book projects nor marriage. When he left Springfield, Norman referred to leaving "three girl-friends" behind. Earlier letters from Norman to Em suggest the possibility that the three may have been Anna Segal, with whom he wanted to attend the controversial movie *Maedchen in Uniform* in 1932, Beatrice S. "Bess" Waldo, a "tall, knockout brunette," the oldest daughter in a large family, for whom Norman obtained a voice audition at WBZ, and one Betty McCausland who, though older, was, like Hazel, literate but, unlike Hazel, quite a gadabout and was a co-worker on the newspaper.

McCausland, the newspaper's art critic (born in Kansas in 1899), had come East for its arts and artists. Her apartment was a virtual salon at which new and often impoverished artists could enjoy sympathy, a bite to eat or something to drink and a degree of peer visibility. The photographers Lewis Hine and Alfred Stieglitz won her devotion.

Some future gifted sleuth of the Springfield cultural scene of the 1930s might be able to provide details of the extent to which its writers and painters engaged during the Depression. Often, times of social distress upends previous forms and experiments are the rule. Writers and artists feel a kindred rebellious *Zeitgeist*. Absent more evidence, Norman's attendance at McCausland's salons is a question mark.

McCausland seems to have made an effort to bring to the public obscure but progressive painters. Among others she gave attention to—and about whom she wrote monographs—were "cutting edge," abstract or fringe modernists like Marsden Hartley, A.H. Maurer, and Edward August Landon. Landon, who probably was introduced to Norman by McCausland, painted a portrait of Norman in 1933. It was a boldly colored surrealistic image he kept, unframed, for the rest of his life.

On a tantalizing note, McCausland certainly introduced Norman to her mother when she was in Springfield on a visit from Wichita. She reminded Norman of it in a 1947 letter, writing him, "I stopped off in Wichita and saw my mother. Though she is not much interested in the arts, she inquired for you from an old visit to Springfield, and I was glad to report only the best news."[125]

At the least, Norman's association with McCausland may have been the beginning of a relationship through her with a thriving and fast-changing

world of visual arts. Because stories about Norman's art appreciation in
Eastie, Winthrop and Greenfield (even by his watercolor hobbyist mother)
do not exist, the art bug does not appear to have bitten him any earlier than
his years in Springfield. Through McCausland, he would have met struggling artists. In this respect, Springfield reflected Norman's most celebrated
movie script, "Lust for Life," nominated for an Oscar, about the life of Vincent Van Gogh, the neglected but great artist.

Apart from these three close women friends whom he mentioned, Norman engaged in many platonic relationships. Acutely shy or high-minded,
he frequently acted outwardly as if books, lectures, concerts, and paintings
attracted him more than caresses, hugs and kisses. (Even after he moved to
New York and his dates became more physical, it was fifteen years before he
would talk about marriage and focus on just one woman.)[126]

Salons or no salons, Norman was himself a part of the Springfield cultural scene. What he had done in Lucy Drew's classroom he did on local
stages. Norman lectured on poetry, and found an interested audience.
His name sold tickets. He made some money, but these public exchanges
favored him in a more dynamic way. Norman accumulated face-to-face
feedback priceless to him as a future producer and performer of live radio
shows. He discovered the poems, the very words that worked and simultaneously the ways of delivery that appealed to the general public.

Scores of hours at a podium before diverse audiences sharpened his
already keen senses. It was in Springfield in the early Thirties that Norman made the leap up into diverse audiences of fifty or a hundred people. From entertaining them, and occasionally failing to do so, he came to
be able to gauge the poems best suited for broadcast to an unseen audience. From eye contact, laughter and applause of this earlier time, when
he later lacked immediate reactions in a studio in New York, he possessed
a built-in, well-honed detector of tasteful content, pace, tone and sounds
overall that charmed most people most of the time.

Enter "Jumbo"

Norman's "off-beat" beat on the *Republican*, human interest stories,
led him to an especially colorful character in 1929 who would change his
life. Norman was still cutting and pasting with Hazel in the family parlor
when he first ran into big, vocal Carlo Felice "Jumbo" Tranghese. Having
grown up in Eastie, Norman was cozily familiar with Italians. In Jumbo he
discovered a character of enduring appeal to him, and one thing more: with
Jumbo, Norman backed into radio broadcasting.

In mid–1929, Bunyanesque Tranghese, the athletic son of an athlete,

Jumbo, son of Jumbo, was coming back into the limelight after having been in Springfield's shadows for many years. Jumbo had gone through a long, dark period following the death of his first wife. The high-school sweetheart he married had died in 1922, soon after giving birth to a boy. The young widower could barely function. His father and mother took on the raising of their infant grandchild, despite the busy boarding-house they ran for Italian immigrants and workers on short-term visas. Burly but broken, Jumbo, Junior, hung around the house, frequently overcome by crying jags, and worked only intermittently.[127]

Then something good happened. From Italy, a merry group of five brothers came to Springfield on six-month work visas. Fortuitously, they stayed at the Tranghese rooming house. Just about the time Norman arrived in Springfield, the musical, upbeat brothers, got Jumbo, Jr., back on his feet. By their sheer proximity and contagious high spirits, these gleeful strangers in a strange land, intent upon saving money, hardly leaving the rooming house, made fast friends with their mopey contemporary. Jumbo came out of his shell, talking and walking. A key moment in his transition arrived when somebody asked Jumbo to referee a sporting event. In a good mood, or strongly encouraged by the brothers, Jumbo agreed. Thus, Norman met Jumbo.

Norman's editor, Bill Walsh, saw a story. It was not Jumbo, of whom Walsh knew nothing. To cover the two-man "barrel bouncing" contest one Friday night in the schoolyard of the Howard Street elementary school, he sent Norman, the new guy. Technically, Norman's assignment was the contest, but Jumbo ended up prominently in the story Norman filed.[128]

In truth, the match itself between Arthur Lisee, 119 pounds stripped, and Samuel Santaniello, Jumbo's cousin, 160 pounds, was predictable, boring, and amateurish. It proceeded in fits and starts. Delayed an hour until two ashcans could be found and filled, the event became farcical. It was a race to which nobody brought a stopwatch. Norman had to keep time on his own wristwatch and still take notes. Norman managed to pump out a twelve-inch story, nonetheless. It was published with Santiniello's photograph as winner and printed under a double headline on June 29, 1929. It was Norman's kind of story and exactly what Walsh wanted.[129]

Jumbo was seared into Norman's memory. That night beside the giant, boisterous referee whom the crowd of 150 clearly loved (and whose backstory they probably all knew) was enough. Norman sneaked a few words about the big judge, urging him to turn competitive. Unused to seeing his name in the paper, Jumbo was moved to remember Norman. He would contact him again more than a year later.

Meanwhile, tragedy struck. Half the globe away, a young farmer was struck by lightning and died in his fields. Shortly after the competition, the brothers received the news: their sister's fiancé was dead. Before their visas expired, the brothers came up with a plan. Jumbo would join them on the boat back to southern Italy. The family may have coaxed him there but, in any case, Jumbo courted and married their sister, Paolina. When Jumbo returned to Springfield three months later, he brought a bride with him.

The couple soon had a baby, a son. Having reclaimed his health and strength, Jumbo found a job with the city. It was the toughest and most physically demanding job in the city: rolling and dumping trash and ash barrels into the backs of trash trucks. Far from depressing Jumbo, heavy lifting gave him a new lease on life. He was on top of the world at the top of his game. It was at this point that Jumbo remembered Norman.

A side street off Main Street hosted the *Republican* reporters' eyrie in the 1930s. The paper's upper story editorial offices stood strategically at 20 Fort Street. Through tall windows on the third floor, the staff had an unsurpassed and broad view—before present-day buildings blocked it—of City Hall, the Superior Court, Steiger's department store, Main Street and downtown. They sometimes spotted fires, and could always monitor traffic and estimate the numbers of shoppers out on Main Street any day without leaving their brightly lit, warm quarters.

When Jumbo came bounding up the steps asking for him, Norman remembered him. He could not have been more delighted. He introduced Jumbo to any nearby reporters, photographers, copy boys, editors and the cartoonist on a high stool before his easel. They all looked on as the giant spoke. Loudly.

They heard (and could not help hearing) Jumbo's record of successes. Undefeated, he had beaten Samuel Santiniello on home turf, and he had easily beaten one Benjamin Conway in faraway Lawrence. He, Jumbo Tranghese, dared anybody to roll full ash barrels faster than he did. Would Norman write and print his challenge?

Jumbo's timing was perfect. Light stories about ordinary folks doing extraordinary things were in vogue. Tongue-in-cheek sports heroes spun off as the most diverting stories of all. In 1930, a leggy, lurching, loping horse like Triple Crown winner "Gallant Fox" graced magazine covers, not just the sports pages. The public could not get enough of boxing champs like "Battling" Battalino and Tony Canzoneri. Foreseeing readers among sports enthusiasts and Italians alike, Walsh gave Norman the go-ahead.

On Sunday, January 11, 1931, the *Springfield Sunday Union and Republican* (a jointly produced Sunday edition) ran the first of Norman's several stories about Jumbo Tranghese. For a couple of months thereafter, Jumbo, the man, his challenge, and any challengers and upcoming matches were revealed and headlined. By Saturday, January 24, 1931, Jumbo had a manager, George Precanico. The *Springfield Daily Republican* photographed the two with Jumbo's ashcan, "Pegasus." Jumbo had "accepted the challenge of Luigi Cavardossi of Rochester, N.Y., to battle for a world's championship." (Jumbo exhibited confidence by boasting, "If I had $ 5,000, I would post it, but I don't need no money.")[130]

As soon as Cavardossi turned out to be a hoaxer, however (which only led to more stories both in Massachusetts, i.e., *The Boston Globe*, and New York newspapers, i.e., the *Herald-Tribune*), little Arthur Lisee (whom Santiniello had infamously defeated in 1929 in the schoolyard match refereed by Jumbo and timed by Norman) asserted that *he* would compete.[131]

"Who's he beat?" Jumbo rightly wailed, as Norman quoted him. "I ain't rolling against any toothache like Lisee unless he's beat somebody."[132]

In another 10-inch story on January 29, 1931, Norman repeated Jumbo's boast that he was "the Enrico Caruso of ashcaneering," and (apparently thinking again of New York) said that he would meet "anybody, anywhere, and for any distance."

On February 3, 1931, the New York State Athletic Commission discussed Jumbo's petition for an ashcan match to be held in Times Square. The Commission, stumped, dumped the petition upon the street cleaning department, asserting that it lacked jurisdiction over ashcan rolling.

No barrel bouncing match actually came off in 1931 but Jumbo's and Norman's publicity stunt enjoyed a long and highly visible run. Just before it winked out of the news totally, Bill Walsh wanted Norman to bring Jumbo to the attention of the station manager of WBZA. It promptly got Jumbo—and Norman—on the air. Despite employing several radio announcers, the manager asked Norman, with his expertise in barrel bouncing, to interview Jumbo. Jumbo's fifteen minutes of fame thus fell into Norman's ever-creative hands.

On the night of February 5, 1931, Jumbo answered (or, alternatively, avoided answering) Norman's questions during a fifteen-minute interview that was reported as news in the next day's papers. Awaiting the cue to be audible to thousands of people in a wide radius, Norman stood beside the champ inside a sound-proofed studio. The strongest signal in town, WBZA broadcast from the elegant hilltop Hotel Kimball at 140 Chestnut Street. WBZA's richly appointed, thickly carpeted digs were only three blocks from the *Republican*'s editorial offices.

Norman was thrilled that people in Greenfield would hear him. His parents in Winthrop might hear him. He would have told Em, in New York, to try and tune in. Locally, Hazel would surely listen to hear her old friend and co-author. He could imagine lodgers at his old rooming-house on Union Street gathering and asking, surprised, "Is that our Norman?" Co-workers of the *Republican* would be listening to his every word. Upon getting the high sign, introducing himself and Jumbo (more formally as *Carlo* Tranghese), Norman began:

> You know, Carlo, there must be something wrong with our educational system. Why, even at this late date there are hundreds of innocent people who've never heard at all about ashcan-rolling. Suppose you tell us something about it.

The proud champ was then good for over two minutes. Laying it on thick, first, that barrel bouncing was no easy competition, Jumbo then shifted gears and spoke of overcoming the only man who ever had enough courage to challenge him. That had been in a match held away, in Lawrence, Massachusetts, the previous June. "This man felt sorry for it afterward, beaten as easy as pie" Jumbo said.

Underlining Jumbo's status, Norman asked, "Just where do you stand in the ashcan registry."

"I don't mind telling you I'm champion of the world," Jumbo said with candor and finality.

Norman delighted many listeners by bringing up a recent sore point: the New York State Athletic Commission, which had referred a request for a barrel bouncing match to the Street Cleaning Department.

"Listen, boy, where do they get that wise stuff?" Jumbo said with histrionic indignation. "I don't need nobody to clean up after me when I roll. I never spill ashes, see? I ain't no amateur."

After more back-and-forth, Norman's last question again brought the bear out of his lair.

"Do you ever hope to meet a foeman worthy of your steel barrel?" Norman asked.

"Not if they hear about me first," Jumbo said.

Broadcast statewide through Boston, the short show of the odd couple was a memorable hit. Norman quipped later about Jumbo that "for about ten minutes he actually became a national celebrity." Moreover, the interview had gone without a hitch. Although radio was done with Jumbo, it was not done with Norman.[133]

His interview put Norman in the spotlight just as the *Republican* shook hands with WBZ on an unusual deal. In the Twenties, when the management of newspapers and local radio stations were not distrustful enemies, they were self-conscious competitors. In Springfield in 1931, Bill Walsh had the foresight to gauge that a nightly broadcast of the news could be a win-win. With the right man, he could enhance the paper's prestige without hurting circulation, and maybe helping it—by night, after all, the day's newspapers had already been sold.

The next question was: who was going to be the Voice of the *Springfield Republican*?

Norman was still a very junior man in an industry that valued and traditionally rewarded seniority. On the other hand, Norman's interview with Jumbo was an undeniable hit. Walsh was not going to ignore what people liked. Norman later characterized the interview, which had been heard by "all the staff," as the key to Walsh's selection. Who did the interview? Norman. Walsh accordingly picked Norman.[134]

The radio assignment pleased Norman greatly although it paid no extra. Its non-monetary dividends were several. It turned half of Norman's evening shift into a sort of sinecure. Half of his editor's expectation that he research, interview and write articles for print vanished because he was allowed time to prepare his script, travel time to and from the station, as well as time on air with time to spare.

Norman also fed his hunger for recognition. Nightly, his voice was heard over thousands of radios in New England, literally bringing home the news of the day. In terms of sibling rivalry, Norman was doing something that Em had never done. In addition, Norman was the nightly newsman not only in the Pioneer Valley but also in Boston, as the *Republican* broadcast was routed to the affiliated Boston station. That meant a clear signal for Ma and Pa, who could invite the neighbors to tune in and hear their son give the news.[135]

In retrospect, Norman was unprepared for the radio assignment. He was the first to notice that reading aloud items from newspaper did not work. It surprised him that satisfactory print copy often made for a wretched delivery. "What was written for the eye would not necessarily go smoothly in the ear," he learned. He delivered his nightly broadcasts in streaks and sputters, thinking that Walsh would get the hook, until the idea of revising his text struck him.[136]

All of this, however, was easier said than written or revised. No manuals existed for radio copy nor were models to follow (like newscaster Lowell Thomas) yet established in their daily news shows. By default, Norman taught himself to write for radio. His poet's ear helped him and familiarity with the rhythms of classical music informed his choices as he reorganized pieces for a cadence "to make them more listenable." With practice, he could hear the sound of what he wrote. This skill was of indispensable importance to Norman in Springfield but even more later when he had to write a script a week for radio.[137]

Managing to overcome all obstacles, with a bit of time on his hands, buoyed up by rising recognition, and overall feeling his creative oats, Norman wanted to extend the fun that had begun with the jolly Jumbo interview. Norman was certain that he could write stuff that was funny. Because the *Republican* ran no comics or jokes, he supposed that it lacked humor. Submitting an idea above Walsh's head, Norman proposed a humor column to Sherman Bowles, the *Republican*'s owner, and publisher.

Bowles scrawled a reply to him in pencil on scrap paper first praising Norman's *predecessors* as humorists who had "kept the humor to themselves" and adding next with an exclamation point that Norman ought to
consider "the shock to our readers!" Finally, exercising a stiff joke of his
own, Bowles told Norman that a humor column to the *Republican* would
be like putting a pole-sitter on top of the First Church. Thus, Norman never
did become the paper's resident humorist. But that was all right. For his
vehicle of creativity, Norman remained the *Republican*'s radio man.[138]

PART TWO

Norman in His Twenties
(1930–1939)

Taking a Reading in 1930

The year before Jumbo ran up the stairs at 20 Fort Street and ignited Norman's radio career, nobody should understate the odds against Norman becoming much more successful. Of the Winthrop High School Class of '26—without actually graduating with his class—Norman remained extremely likely to stay a career newspaperman in 1930. After the stock market crash, it was downhill economically for the country for years. Anybody who had a job held onto it. Why would Norman, who was elected the head of his reporters' guild, who had recognition in the area in print and on the air, leave to pursue allegedly greener pastures? To prophesy change was irrational, even to imagine an ash-barrel bouncer changing Norman's life would be quite a stretch.

Rather, Norman had found employment and settled comfortably into the middle of the state. Others he knew got no farther than Winthrop, and some still resided with their parents. The lovely, dark-haired Laura C. Atkinson, the daughter of a French Canadian and an Irish immigrant, Norman's co-star in the senior class play after winning "Best Debater" in her junior year (which was remarkable because her team of four lost the team competition), clearly possessed talent. Laura nonetheless did not leave home soon. The 1930 census taker found her at 22 in Winthrop with her parents. She stated her occupation as "commercial artist self-employed." Thereafter, records of marriage, children and addresses appear. Certainly, gender discrimination and the economics of the 1930s blighted women's opportunities. However explained, this bright star of Norman's class vanished into child-rearing and housework.

Similarly, the Class President married the Class Secretary and they settled in Winthrop. None of the Winthrop High School jocks turned professional. Norman's best friend, Barney Zieff, who had beaten Norman into

Norman courted several eligible young ladies and even proposed to one (who said no) but here he poses by the sea with an unidentified young woman, possibly his sister, Booie, c. 1930 (courtesy Diane Corwin Okarski).

the workforce as a soda jerk at the local drugstore in Winthrop, went to pharmacy school. By 1930, he had become a licensed pharmacist, but any other distinctions eluded him.

Meanwhile, in Greenfield, Norman had saved money, viewed, and reviewed films on a pass, and read everything that he could. In Springfield, he took out classical music from the well-stocked city library and played them on a borrowed Victrola. He attended concerts, kept up with *avant-garde* movies and explored Springfield's culture while contributing to it. He lived ascetically while, especially through poetry and radio, he grew intellectually and socially.

Norman developed a following as well as growing circles of friends. Locally known, Norman was sometimes resented and even feared. His liberal views led one judge (ironically, Webster Thayer, the same one who had tried Sacco and Vanzetti) to accuse him loudly of being "a spy." But "spying" on judges was his last interest. He moved forward cautiously but steadily, increasingly prepared, ever self-contained. Learning by doing how to script and speak on radio, he girded himself to shoot rapids that his classmates never undertook to face. By his mid-twenties, Norman had accrued the linguistic resources to succeed, at least at an entry level, in New York or in Hollywood.[1]

In sum, none of Norman's old classmates turned into a notorious criminal or a spectacular loser but neither did they shine brightly in the world. Norman did shine, in spite of being born in woebegone Eastie, a late comer into elite Winthrop. He might be judged objectively a bit ahead of his classmates, much as he seemed to be during that extravagant year of 1925–26.

The Tragedy and Norman's Resolution

Charles and Ida Spicer's home away from home sat squarely in the center of a row of several other lodging houses. From 1929 through at least 1931, the big, bustling building at 264 Union Street, Norman's first and longest stop, near his newspaper's 20 Fort Street office, ought to have reminded Norman more of Bremen Street than of his Winthrop or Greenfield diggings.[2]

Norman probably chose it on Em's say-so. In letters, Em asked about the landlord's cats and the landlady's latest capers, and he probably lived there first himself. His references to the couple show that he certainly knew them well.[3]

The Yiddish-fluent Spicers were immigrants who had previously run a deli on Main Street. Childless and long-married, Charles and Ida were in their fifties. Ida seems to have been depressed. Certainly, she was outwardly cranky. Although nobody seems to have judged her state to be critical, it would turn out tragically so.

In his memoirs, Norman immortalized the Spicers and this residence in several detailed and mostly affectionate pages. It was natural that he would. In part, Norman associated them with when he fell in love, his first marriage proposal, his first book, his first important job, working with a colorful newspaper staff, and his start on radio between age 19 and 21.

Besides Norman, the other roomers' average age was in the mid-forties. His fellow boarders included four men and four women. Working nights, Norman did not likely interact with all of them equally. How much was Michael Morrissey, the Irish locomotive fireman, actually around for Norman to talk with? The candy factory foreman, Samuel Pember, too, likely worked days. On the other hand, Jacob Brown, the manager of the local bowling alley, who presumably worked late afternoon and evening hours like Norman and Donald Burt, who seems to have been disabled, a good conversationalist and, Norman said, "a good listener," functioned as his *ersatz* brothers and confidants.

Women boarders included a 29-year-old single Swede who typed at the electric factory and a 40-year-old married-woman-living-alone who was a local lawyer's secretary. Older women boarders were a 50-year-old widow and a 64-year-old teacher. According to Norman, one of these women came out on summer nights naked, her door open, ostensibly for air.[4]

Norman lived up in a room on the second floor, where he shared a bathroom. Above him was the apartment of the Spicers. Charlie liked and trusted Norman enough to loan him his old hand-cranked Victrola with a "morning glory" horn to amplify sound. (Why did the Spicers no longer use their Victrola? The Victrola's availability was symptomatic of something: that the music had gone out of their lives.[5])

Norman, whose shift at the newspaper began at 2 and ended at 11, could always sleep in. In mid-morning, he got up and, first thing, cranked the old Victrola. Beethoven, Brahms, Mozart and other classic 78 rpm phonographs from the public library he played "full blast, or as blasty as the machine could manage" while he showered, shaved, dressed and made a little breakfast with a toaster and a hot plate. At night, under a sheet, turning Charlie's machine down to its lowest setting, Norman listened to orchestras playing the world's greatest music very, very softly.

One spring night, Norman and other boarders were startled awake by a crash. Norman wrote in his memoirs that Ida committed suicide. She may have. Norman erroneously remembered that she landed and died on the sidewalk. However, the *Springfield Republican*'s report suggests a different, longer saga. After reporting that Mrs. Spicer died at Springfield Hospital at

3:15 p.m. on May 30, 1931, the *Republican* concluded, "Mrs. Spicer, who had been ill since last August, was rushed to the hospital from a private nursing home Thursday morning following a fall from the second floor."[6]

In 1931, social safety nets were not in place. Social Security did not exist. Some couples lost everything they had ever invested or saved (in banks that closed), and money was tight. To hire help in her place or a caretaker for her would have been a great burden.

Any illness of ten months' duration, running from August through the entire winter and into spring, could have been depressing. The stresses devouring her may have driven her to a desperation. Most falls from either the second floor or even third floor are not fatal. As typically, this fall was not. She was instead brought to a private care facility.

From the newspaper's omission to name or to characterize the facility, it is likely that it was a privately-run facility for the mentally ill. In any case, within two days, whether from effects of a long fall to the sidewalk or from her original long-term illness or even from some new desperate act, on Saturday Mrs. Spicer was rushed to the hospital only to be pronounced dead. Norman conflated the series of shocking events into one immediate death and, within months of his shock, reacted in a "do it now" resolution to make his dreams come true. He plunged headlong into life.

Innocents Abroad, 1931

Norman had plans to write in Europe. Having acquired a Smith Corona, he was going to bring it with him. In addition to his trusty typewriter, Norman recruited both Em and his old buddy, Barney Zieff, to join him on his jaunt overseas. The idea for the trip went back to his first trip to New York and meeting with his cosmopolitan idol, Heywood Broun. The 17 year old who had never been farther from home upon returning to Greenfield promptly asked Em with a fetching casualness, "How about Europe next spring?"[7]

In fact, three springs came and went before Norman finally organized his dream of a European tour. A limited budget would not stop him. Norman suggested that "steerage will give us proper hardening for the adventures to follow. Columbus, I am told, had no ballrooms on the Santa Magaziner."[8]

Accordingly, Norman's stocky brother, Em, short, bespectacled friend, Barney, and increasingly athletic Norman, now 20, left New York for Hamburg on an ocean liner, and probably *not* in steerage.[9]

The trio included no experienced world travelers. They were, in Mark Twain's famous term, "Innocents Abroad." One adventure they experienced in Europe wins the prize for unplanned hilarity: their visit to a much-hyped brothel show in Paris. Its sights proved disappointing even to their unjaded eyes.[10]

In RE ME, Norman painted his recollection in broad strokes. With Em and Barney beside him, Norman realized himself suddenly as one of three fully clothed and highly self-conscious Yankees, mute, stiffly seated on straight-backed chairs, impassively watching what Norman dubbed a "gynecologic display." He became uncomfortably aware that they all witnessed the girls' performances with "little more expression than that of visitors viewing the Laocoön."[11]

It was too much of a good thing. Norman recalled being "more aroused by advertisements for brassieres." As a nugget of wisdom that he earned from the episode, he offered the observation that "modesty is more of an aphrodisiac than flaunted prurience."[12]

Meanwhile, back in America, Walsh submitted samples for peer review in competition for "the best broadcast of news bulletins by any newspaper in New England." Feeling that he had a decent chance to make a mark in radio history, Walsh put the *Republican* into competition for a newly minted journalistic award. His judgment was good. Upon words written and delivered by Norman, the *Republican* won.

Walsh was right about broadcasting. It was a good and profitable idea. So much so, it was outlawed. Laws soon passed and legal fences were erected to prevent newspaper-radio media monopolies. But before being shut down, the *Republican* had been an on-air pioneer. As the Depression deepened, Walsh understood that people who could not afford a daily paper would still listen to news on the radio. Ahead of his time, Walsh realized just how powerful a newspaper-radio combination would be.

(Thus, Norman's timing was incredible. He had come to work for a newspaper whose editor was far-sighted enough to welcome radio. The same editor actively promoted the nightly news which now brought Norman his first radio award. Moreover, Walsh kept the nightly news going even in Norman's absence. And all of this could only have happened before Federal regulations, which kept newspapers separate from radio stations beginning in 1934.)

While Norman was taking in the sights of Paris, other reporters vied for the exposure on the air. Walsh had no difficulty finding a replacement announcer for Norman. The difficulty was finding anybody any good. By default, a senior reporter named Pelletier, without any on-air experience, and not really ready for prime time, became Springfield's voice of the news.

Walsh allowed monotone-mike Pelletier to fill the gap but also clawed back some slots for himself to play broadcaster. In the end, by trial and error, Walsh found Norman irreplaceable. When Norman returned, apart from courtesy gigs to Pelletier, delivering the nightly news was once more Norman's job.

Walsh wished to encourage Norman. Norman had been back for months when, in May 1932, Walsh gave Norman six months' notice that an upcoming huge radio audience was going to be his. Norman would handle the *Republican's* election night program. He would prepare. He would present. Gathering research, background color, little-known facts, the incoming returns, analysis on the spot, everything, whatever he wanted to do. Off the air, behind the scenes, at the microphone, on the air, it was his show.

"A big assignment, buddy, a big assignment," Norman crowed as soon as he could tell Em. Norman showed himself to be pleased and confident. On that one November night, everything would be up in the air and at risk. He would be noticed for a highly public success or a highly public failure.

His future on radio was suddenly worth thinking about. The possibility of becoming known wherever the WBZ signal reached was in play. People would be at their sets switching stations, searching for the most comprehensive and interesting coverage. Scouts for the networks in New York would be on duty.

Norman had at least one good reason to feel confident. He heard something that he immediately told Em. One of the county commissioners confided to him that Sherman Bowles, Norman's phantom-like publisher, who never complimented Norman, had told the commissioner, "Corwin has a nice voice on the radio."[13]

Elated that the *Republican's* owner was listening, Norman hungered for mail. He sought vindication from somebody outside his family. A letter appeared a month later, his first listener pucker. Writing Em immediately, Norman lamented that "a dizzy dame" in Putnam, Connecticut, found fault with his delivery. He "spoke too close to the microphone," she wrote—then she said that it was probably her set. As summer ended, Norman stood actively appreciated by his editor, secretly praised by his publisher, loved by his family, and probably excused from a perceived fault in his first fan mail.

Looking ahead to election night prominence, Norman had every reason to think that 1932 would unfurl as his banner year. Soon to reach the five-year mark as a print reporter, he was setting sail for radio's deepest waters. Heard statewide each night, it was only a question of time. Someone would listen and be impressed. He could hope, on a solid basis, that he might soon receive a call, and be recruited by NBC or CBS.[14]

Em was listening, too. Instead of praising his brother's baritone voice, he told him to slow down and to enunciate more clearly. Indeed, Em, the now-experienced European traveler, offered a correction in pronunciation. Doubtful, Norman checked out what Em suggested.

"It is neither ZURITCH, as I pronounced it, nor SURICK, as you suggest, but ZOORICK," Norman said, settling their argument, underlining the conflicting verbal incarnations of the largest city in Switzerland. He was then gracious enough to say to his critical brother, "You were nearer, though."[15]

The "Interruption"

As summer began, Norman, 22, was itching. He had studied authors. Scott Fitzgerald put out *This Side of Paradise* at 23, Ernest Hemingway published *The Sun Also Rises* at 27. One's twenties was time. He must create time for words. Norman resolved to take on no more lectures and side gigs after those to which he was already committed. Next, he told Em, would come serious writing, probably poetry but possibly a novel. Norman was doubtless up in the air himself. Either way, he foresaw an "intensive program" that fall and winter.

Then, suddenly, "[T]here was an interruption in the Springfield period," in the formal understatement that Norman used to introduce the subject in his memoirs. His "intensive program" of writing would have to wait. Alas, the election extravaganza, the first real Norman Corwin show, would have to be reassigned. One day after a little bicycling in Springfield, he started coughing up blood.[16]

Although Norman had not known consistent great health and was frequently laid low by colds, this "interruption" was possibly deadly. It easily trumped a mysterious period of difficulty breathing in his boyhood and emergency appendectomy as a teen. Yet Norman wrote little, even to his brother.

"(Y)ou don't want to be kidded along," Norman told Em before he said almost nothing. He was steely careful not to invite panic. He managed to state diagnosis, "I am low with a touch of tuberculosis," before he went mute on prognosis. Inwardly, Norman had to be calculating his risk of dying. Years later, when talking about a young man who died of cancer, Norman hoped that he had not known of his imminent doom as "I daresay it is not a comfortable knowledge."[17]

At the end of his letter to Em, Norman listed authors who had suffered from tuberculosis (Keats, D.H. Lawrence, and Eugene O'Neill). Expressing no worries over medical mauling, any feared possible surgery, prescribed isolation, or likely medication, he told Em, "I have accepted the disappointing revelation with what I like to regard as philosophic calm."

Philosophic calm may have accompanied him up to the very doors of the sanatorium but when Norman arrived at the sanatorium, he was for a shuddering moment appalled and apprehensive, if not in full panic.

"Though it was mid-afternoon, the window shades were drawn and there was absolute silence. Was *this* the way one recovered from TB—by lying still, as though dead, in a darkened room, vegetating?" he asked.

Mercifully, the answer came quickly: definitely *no*.

"Suddenly there was a burst of laughter, explosive and loud, from all of the beds at once. It began so uniformly and peaked so high that I knew it could not be laughter at me; besides, none of the patients was paying the slightest attention to my entrance. And then in the dimness I made out the cause: each man in the room was wearing a set of earphones, and listening to a comedy radio program. I had chanced to enter during the daily Quiet Hour, a two-hour period in which patients were supposed to sleep— or to try to. No reading, no conversation, just rest. Once in a while they got dispensation to listen to a special broadcast during Quiet Hour, and I had chanced upon such an occasion."[18]

Norman's illness did not lead to a stretch of great pain or misery, but a period of intermittent stress and fluctuating anxiety. Despite external flamboyant aplomb and good spirits overall, he was constantly plagued by the worry that he hosted a life-threatening germ in his body. Norman diffidently, fastidiously teetered between hope and horror. He characterized his months in the sanatorium as hospitalization for "a lesion suspected to be tuberculin."

Few lives are as dramatically interrupted as Norman's life was, and few interruptions are as fortuitously timed. He *needed* a break. He was a mess. Beginning back in high school, he had declined even tennis due to unspecified past "injuries." Through seasonal walking, swimming, biking, and skiing he avoided total deterioration, but he recognized that, despite this intermittent "sporting," he was not in great shape. The congenital gift of a muscular build was not enough. He smoked, drank, and paid no heed to his diet. He faulted his time management, too. He "had worked too hard on the newspaper and radio, at unnatural hours, and done additional writing at times I should have been relaxing, or sporting with my girl of the season."

In addition, the "sentence maker" whose little forays were prized in grammar school in Eastie, whose essays were acclaimed by teachers, whose short story as a teenager won first prize, whose works publishers of two newspapers received with pleasure, was bored with routine. In part, that was why he was searching for something to write about, and had his hopes pinned on success in November during his election broadcast. He wanted change. He felt that he was in a rut.

During the interruption, Norman was gratefully not chasing down the same stories over and over. ("A fire is a fire and a flood is a flood," Norman said in his memoirs later, echoing letters to his brothers in the early Thirties.) As he recovered, Norman recalled that he was *cheerful*. "I surprised myself by almost unbroken good cheer," he wrote of his months at Rutland State Hospital. The food was good, the air was clean, and he loved playing chess with a doctor named Philbrick, as neither of them were, he said, "good enough at the game to spoil it."

Another undoubted source of his cheer was Bill Walsh's hearty promise that whether Norman was gone "four months or four years," a job with the *Republican* was his upon his return. Liberated unexpectedly from the mundane world, from August 1932 through May 1933 he burrowed into literature.

In the sanatorium, the voracious but usually time-strapped reader digested more books than ever. He wrote more imaginatively. Once discharged to rest at the old homestead in Winthrop, he additionally sought the consolations of music. Em suggested that he dust off and repair his old violin or sit at the piano. He may have done so. Certainly, for the first of only two times in his life, he composed some music.

In his autobiography, Norman omitted (and perhaps had forgotten) tracking how his hopes both rose and fell. First, that he might not have TB was one hope—the spot on his x-ray could be an old scar, something common enough. However, when his x-rays were sent to Massachusetts General Hospital, doctors there discerned that the spot was fading. This indicated healing after a *recent* tuberculin infection. Good news superficially, this determination carried with it an ambivalent prognosis—and an order to stay home that winter.[19]

His hopes flattened, he told Em and Al not to expect him in New York by Christmas, but make it Memorial Day. As he shuttled between Winthrop of a Boston specialist named Dr. Floyd, he was all ears for a second opinion. Dr. Floyd, on a chest exam before an x-ray, said that Norman was fit and could go back to work any time. That was what Norman wrote Em, his hopes soaring, adding that he did not think the x-ray Dr. Floyd took would change his opinion. Apparently, it did: Norman did not return to work until the following summer, 1933.[20]

As the doctors kept checking, he kept worrying. During batteries of tests, x-rays, diet, rest and a strict regimen in a series of sanatoria consulting with a long parade of doctors—as Massachusetts General wanted to follow his case from a distance—Norman aged from 22 to 23 facing the possible end of his active life, if not of life itself. Even in his autobiography, the interruption is Kafkaesque, narrated in a dream-like account. Throughout this nightmare, he moved often from hospital to hospital, switching doctors as he went. Names, dates, and places are missing. The spot on his lungs was ambiguous, experts disagreed—an old lesion or recent tuberculin infection?—active or inactive?—and prognosis?[21]

Sidelined and sometimes silenced, outside of stories for a period that seemed that it would never end, Norman burned to be at work. His *consistent* philosophical calm and uninterrupted good cheer may be questioned, despite many letters written in that tone and his repeated explicit insistence on his serenity.

First, his life savings were being drained. Remarkably, for a reporter in the depths of the Depression, Norman had some money. He began making small but regular weekly deposits in Greenfield, and did so for four years as a better-paid reporter, while accruing small sums for recitals and lectures. At the start of his illness, Norman had a few dollars shy of $ 1,000 in the bank. Through his illness, Norman survived without debt. However, diagnosed with "a touch of tuberculosis," after several months in a sanatorium, he had to worry. As it was, he lost almost half of his savings.[22]

Second, Norman always obsessed over his body, especially any respiratory problem. He found illness distressing but, most especially, difficulty breathing unsettled him most.

Taken at his word to Em, did Norman nonetheless do no "soul searching." He wrote his oldest brother and best buddy, "Soul-searching always costs some sleep, but it's temporary and it has no more merit than the Quest for Truth." He then shared his lusty conclusion: "I have come to believe that man was not destined, let alone created to track down Truth. He was created, like gnats, rabbits, and weeds, to perpetuate his kind, and his development has been incidental and well as accidental."[23]

After over a year of rigorous medical regimens, tests and worries over health, money, and death, he was 23 and alive and he sounded ready to perpetuate his kind. He was certainly ready to replicate one thing in writing: the paradox of isolation from the rest of the world and simultaneous merger within a small group. This was an experience that he would transform again and again into radio drama. Sharing one person or one crew or one small group as representative of millions, synecdoche, his trademark structure, might be the most lasting and the most positive legacy of his long and unexpected "interruption."

Hits and Misses

One day, Norman could stand no more. After cooperating with an extended "wait and see" so-called plan, and starting a novel, he forsook philosophical calm and unilaterally declared that his life had been interrupted long enough. It was time. Norman pressed for his release. He yielded to compromise in late May 1933, agreeing to a condition: he would rest. The same doctors who released him—possibly because Norman was becoming too restless to hold—would absolutely not yet clear him to work. Thus, he exchanged a bed in the hospital for one in Winthrop. He was released without being cleared as TB-free.

"I moved back into the attic room of my boyhood," he said in his memoir, "took up my old conversation with Graves Light, and resumed dawn-watching through the uncurtained window."

Contemporary evidence confirms this. Back on his back in the attic, he felt at home instantly. He promptly wrote from Winthrop to one of his Springfield girls. He wanted her to know that the transition he made was not only complete but immediate:

> When I left Rutland, there was an apple tree in full bloom right outside my ward. I looked back on that tree just as we were leaving, and I thought I might miss the place. But three hours later I strolled up to the sea wall and gazed once again at my old friend the Atlantic, and I had completely forgotten my three months at Rutland, and the apple tree...[24]

The doctors' condition, that Norman rest, left Norman to define "rest." He defined "rest" liberally. He listened to music and the radio and, in addition, Norman not only read and wrote, as he had at the sanatorium, but also practiced speaking. Concerned about his voice, he performed elocution exercises on a dictaphone. Clearly, he was rehearsing for his return to radio. Ordinarily a business device, in the mid–Thirties a dictaphone was the most practical way to record and to replay spoken words.[25]

Norman's goal was clear. As he lived and breathed, the nightly news assignment still existed. Although Walsh had divided it among staff including Walsh himself, this part of his job—and he thought of the nightly news as part of his job—motivated Norman. Walsh made no promises, but Norman would later wax indignant and even insult him over what he assumed to be tacitly implied, namely, that he could return to exactly the job he left, intact, his nightly news broadcasts included. He took more woodenly than Walsh's original promise that "a job with the *Republican*" was his upon his return.

But that bad news lay ahead. Before that, and underscoring mortality, Norman was hit by sad news. His maternal grandmother died. Although not fully well himself, he attended her funeral. It was the first funeral he ever attended, or actually partly attended. Initially, as a non-practicing Jew, Norman was barred from the house in which Grandma's body lay in repose. Later, he had to remain outside the cemetery during her burial service.[26]

Obviously, Norman's temper was less easily triggered than it had been in his younger days. In tranquility, Norman brought both his grandmother and grandfather to mind. He made little lists of what had made each one happy. Norman the lists to Em and Al. They were: "Grandpa: pinochle, humming old Ungarische tunes, playing jokes, dirty stories, mending stoves," and, "Grandma: going to the movies, receiving visits from her children, making strudel."[27]

If Norman ever made a similar list of the things that made him happy, the list has not survived. But one may project such a list. After family, sounds—even before girls. He loved classical music and almost every popular song. Although he rarely composed anything complete, he loved to jot down short pieces as snatches of music ran through his head. With sounds, music, real or imagined, poetry, symphonies (with his eyes closed), writing or storytelling and *radio* his list would have been at least half finished.

By the end of the first summer after his scare, however, even Norman had had enough music, solitary reading, and writing. He was well enough and more than ready emotionally to socialize. He reached out to Bill Walsh and his wife, along with one of his Rutland doctors, Dr. Kahalas (was his invitation a lobbyist's gift?), and "Miss Rubin." When could they all come to Winthrop for deep sea fishing?[28]

Given the ongoing Depression, which beached many Boston boats, Norman could hire a 48-foot cruiser "with a cabin and a toilet," and seats and room enough for the large party to fish without entangling lines. To his brothers, he confided with a sound of pride at his bargain that "bait, gasoline and a pilot were provided" for $ 20. With that bargain easy on his budget, Norman, who had spent little all summer, felt flush enough to fund a series of fishing prizes in total sum of another $ 20.[29]

Greeting the Walshes, Dr. Kahalas, Esther, he and his parents were joined by another 18 friends and acquaintances Norman had invited. Norman exulted upon being among so many familiar people in unfamiliar surroundings. Norman joyfully penned an account of the grand fishing trip for 25. His report's light tone reflects Norman's exuberant feelings about liberation, even temporarily. With a reporter's eye, he depicted his editor finally meeting Pa and Ma. Lastly, his voice when talking with his brothers, Em and Al, comes out when he affectionately saluted them at his three-page letter's end, "mein tzwei menschen (sotch nize tzildwen)."[30]

Each guest appeared wearing, as directed, comfortable "old clothes." The spacious but packed boat then departed from Crystal Cove. On the Boston Harbor side of Perkins Street, Norman noticed the quiet. No wind, no waves, only the purr of their engine, over "water as calm as Corwin during a news broadcast." He quickly found his sea legs and attended to his party.

Transparently, Norman played the role of convivial host with verve and personal joy. In language came unity. He led the ocean-going party in "gaiety, quips and puns." Following "corned beef sangwiches and beer and ginger ale," the boat was far enough out. They could lower their lines. One imagines the hullabaloo when it was the host who quickly snagged a couple of small cod. Someone asked him how he held his line and Norman shared with his doubtless amused brothers how "pontifically and with great belching of technical terms, I explained my method." After that, Norman confessed, he went fishless.[31]

During the five-hour cruise, Ma—who had never fished before—caught seven "(b)ig blue haddock weighing about five or six pounds each." Norman noted her method. "Ma would drop her line, wait a few seconds, and then proclaim that she had a bite," Norman saw to his awe. "She'd start to haul in, and then stop halfway up to see if the fish was still fighting. For any of the rest of us to have used such unorthodox tactics as to stop and give the fish a chance to get away, would have meant no catch at all. But Ma would satisfy herself that the fish was still on the hook, continue hauling and land her fish."[32]

Far away now from his attic room and resting alone, his eyes devoured the sight of almost everybody caught something—"the Walshes catching three small fish between them"—while others reaped another dozen fish. Only Pa, "with a floppy felt hat down over his ears and a cigar in his mouth," was skunked, having dangled his line all day "without result." More than bragging rights were at stake. The fishing party had a pool for most fish caught, biggest catch by weight, etc. In the end, "(a)ll prizes went to Ma."[33]

So Ma not only hooked seven eminently edible haddock but also brought home $ 20 in cash, a rich haul in 1933, indeed. Norman, to whom adventures had been scarce of late and who longed for tales to tell, was the son of the big winner. Hopefully, he was also able to put an arm around Miss Rubin at some moment, perhaps when the boat was "mildly roller-coasterish" as they plowed through the wakes of great liners passing near them. Either way, he probably felt the richest of anyone aboard.[34]

Norman personally hooked something bigger than two cod. Before the boat reached port, Walsh, obviously impressed by Norman's vivacity, asked him to clarify his plans. Norman ebulliently promised his faithful editor that he would return to the paper the second week of September. On a ship at sea before the storm broke—a thunderstorm approached and they saw lightning in the distance—Norman, in full sail, had set his future course. With lightning and a strong wind behind him, he was headed for Springfield soon.

He's Back

He followed through. On schedule, beginning in mid–September exactly, Norman stormed back to work as if he never had left. The staff treated Norman's long absence just like the simple "interruption" Norman himself declared it to have been. If everybody else's good behavior did not mystify him, it should have. No banter, no wisecracks. It was unnatural.

Walsh had spoken to them all: no teasing, no references to Norman's long absence.

This time, no crowded rooming house for him. Norman found new quarters. Intending to write, he looked for a quiet place in a natural area. His next two addresses were 63 Mulberry Street and 15 Avon Place, both within sight of his old Union Street abode but different. Both were located in the same quiet, tree-rich residential neighborhood that surrounded the Milton Bradley Elementary School. At the address of 63 Mulberry was a three-story private house with a large wraparound porch and a gabled roof. It had a lawn. Norman rented a room. After he vacated 63 Mulberry and sold his car in haste when he expected to

Upon returning to work in Springfield after hospitalization and isolation for almost a year, skinny Norman sat for this portrait in 1933. Signed by Edward August Landon and possibly arranged by the newspaper's art critic, Betty McCausland (courtesy Diane Corwin Okarski).

move to New York in early 1935, he returned to his last address, apparently one that he used least, 15 Avon Place. Probably for a year but possibly much less, his refuge off duty then was a blocky four-story brick building without any lawn.[35]

Freed from parental oversight, he picked up the pace of his social life. Norman was a bachelor but, then as now, unmarried did not necessarily mean sexually inactive. A letter to Em shows as much. Norman's brother struggled with whether to propose to his teacher sweetheart. His struggle led Norman to a revealing comment. In a list of criteria for deciding whether to marry, Norman advised Em to monitor some ten things, including whether "she is sexually stimulating three nights in a row or twice in one night." Was Norman quoting someone else or speaking from experience?[36]

In the rest of his letter, Norman revealed a spectrum of romantic experiences. After Hazel he remained wary of what he termed "the logical conclusion," marriage. At the same time, he wrote of "being fiercely in love … and then outgrowing (that) ardent affection" as well as "starting out with a Platonic agreement not to love a girl, and then finding (himself) in love."

If Norman had to guess about his own feelings, the girls may have had to guess about Norman, too. He said that he never wrote a love poem. Nor was his face very often expressive. Even candid photographs mainly captured a reserved demeanor, a guardedness. To his girl friends of the time, Norman was probably a mystery no matter how long any of them went out with him, or how many times they pleased him.

Norman only implicitly documented a robust sex life. The only Springfield girl he named, Hazel, was the chaste co-author to whom he had proposed. Hazel was followed by a hazy reference to a parade of unnamed women. He kept looking, not unhappily. Insulated from proposing by his long list of criteria and pure logic, Norman did not struggle as Em did over marrying anybody.

Norman was almost as busy as he wanted to be, but not quite. The one element lacking from the time before was a *radio show*. Cool, quiet dignity, and immovable calm are great traits for radio work, where deadlines and performance frenzies up to the minute hand on the clock require a firm hand. To be outwardly unflappable is the mark of a great director.

These character traits made him ideal behind the microphone as well. The trouble was that Norman could not reclaim the nightly news exclusively. Walsh did not want to reassign reporters like Pelletier, who had been faithfully filling in. Other reporters experienced the cachet and name recognition that came with reading bulletins on the air. They had overcome their "mike fright" and tasted the plum. The winter ahead made the duty of selecting, writing, and broadcasting news in a warm studio sound a lot more pleasant.

Thus, for the first time, the nightly news was a battleground. Walsh gave Norman some slots—to exclude him would have been insulting—but not all. Norman consequently brooded. Having to share the nightly news in rotation with Pelletier, of whose microphone talents Norman was bitterly critical, grated him the sum. The newspaper's original newscaster, who had by far the best diction and voice of anybody on staff, could not avoid fretting.

He had recovered. Norman felt entitled. He was passionate, painstaking, a perfectionist while, Norman felt, Pelletier cut corners. When he brought his concerns to Walsh, Walsh committed the greatest offense in Norman's universe by standing between Norman and radio.

With a truly unjust pen, Norman wrote to Em, "Radio goes along the same, with Pelletier still chiseling and Walsh too yellow to bring it to a showdown." Em, of course, knew his brother, Walsh, and Pelletier, too, from his own days of working on the *Republican*. Em never had such rapport with Walsh to invite him fishing, nor to be invited by Walsh in turn to Christmas dinner, an invitation Norman would accept. He would have had reason to chuckle if not to chastise Norman. But before Norman resumed good terms with Walsh, passions actually ran higher.

On the evening of October 27, as Norman was newscasting, a WBZ staffer he did not name passed him a letter from a listener in faraway Taunton, who criticized Pelletier's delivery and demanded Norman. Norman showed it around. Norman wrote Em the next day that everybody told him there was no comparison.[37]

Winds of change blew in from outside to cool off this tiny but heated controversy. It turned out that the battle over the nightly news might not be worth fighting. National press associations were tugging all of the country's newspapers into line and that line was to stick to print journalism. As 1933 ended, Norman, quite savvy about radio and print relations, wrote Em that the *Republican*'s nightly news broadcast would "probably go down the toilet bowl soon if and when an agreement between press and radio goes through." In the same letter, Norman, obviously fatigued, wrote, "Reporting is not hard work for me mentally, but rather exacting physically."[38]

After the new year, abandoning one fight for another, he directed his rancor to the size of his paycheck. The man who never did anything solely for money wrote up an angry memo. His request for a raise, a sarcastic, bitter, and rambling communiqué to his avuncular publisher, Sherman Bowles, was in terrible form. Norman concluded with a pumped-up list of his past accomplishments, leading up to the improbable and unintentionally funny climax of "publication of a book in 1929." Having ventilated, Norman then set his blistering blarney aside, let it cool and never sent it. The draft remained filed among Norman's papers without a specific date, with no comment in pencil nor any reply among his 1934 materials at the ARA.

He got cracking constructively. He could control his own time and he did. Revising his immediate priorities, Norman became a much more active public speaker. He got a gig addressing the "Book Club of Filene's" in Boston, and tried to line up more such paid events. It was not only the money (often nominal, sometimes free), it was the feedback. More clearly than elsewhere, he wrote Al about his simultaneous observations of reactions and delivery of a poetry lecture.

"For a half hour I talked to them informally, and read them poetry calculated to make them laugh," he told his brother of a lecture to a thousand high school students. "They interrupted my speech several times with applause, and I could see the look of pleasure and anticipation in their faces which is a sign you have your audience in hand."[39]

His greatest fan, Em, grumbled and nagged him to *write* something.

When Norman did, he wrote speculative radio scripts, including one called "Heil Hitler," a satire. Of this prescient play—Hitler had been in charge of Germany for less than a year—Norman updated Em with glib optimism, "It needs only revision, tightening up and copying" to be ready. (His remark sounds much like Hemingway's remark that what was hard about writing was "getting the words right.") His early "Heil Hitler" idea came to nothing, as did all of Norman's Hitler scripts, including one later based on Hitler being trapped in a dentist's chair. Some subjects would just not yield to his efforts.[40]

Off the air except for stray news broadcasts between Pelletier's shows, as he wrote his useless radio scripts, Norman was stymied. He had dutifully written WBZ. Months in advance of his actual return to Springfield, he sent a letter offering to renew his weekly poetry show. Sitting in the Corwins' Perkins Street home, Norman had projected WBZ managers being glad to air his show. He had a following. His ready audience in the Pioneer Valley would still cost them nothing. Once back in town, his byline would be out there every day to accrete more recognition and more radio listeners. After dawdling without a reply for months, WBZ suddenly said no.

"Nothing new on my radio program of poetry and music," Norman quickly informed Em in September 1933, "except that today I wrote WBZ a scorching letter demanding to know why they took so long in answering."[41]

He waited six months. Then, well settled and working in Springfield, he took another stab, with a new twist. A piano accompanist propelled Norman back on the air. The slightly older Benjamin Kalman's precise connection with Norman before and apart from this program is unknown but Norman, who attended classical concerts, was surely one of Kalman's best-informed fans. "I conspired with one of my friends, a pianist named Benjamin Kalman, to create a program," Norman summarized in his memoir. Promptly responding this time, WBZA asked Norman to fill a fifteen-minute slot every Tuesday afternoon (later changed to Thursday afternoon).[42]

Probably stemming from his original "scorching" grudge over delay, Norman disdained to name the one responsible for his return to the air. Although he named his WQXR station manager and his later CBS bosses, Norman sentenced his WBZA contact to perpetual anonymity. Somebody unnamed approved the broadcast of a 15-minute weekly hybrid poetry-and-music show hosted by Norman, this time called *Rhymes and Cadences*.

Norman enjoyed name recognition, but it was Kalman who reeled in the audience. A long-time member of Springfield's Jewish community, Kalman had been a celebrated local musical prodigy. Born in 1900 in Riga, brought to the United States in 1904, he lived without a fixed home as his family rotated frequently between Springfield and nearby Providence, Rhode Island.

When Bolsheviks came into power in Russia in 1917, the Kalmans decisively became American citizens. Naturalized in 1918, Kalman traveled for the sake of his music. His studies in war-torn Europe involved hardships of which no documents survive. Following years of musical studies abroad, Kalman returned to earn his living in Springfield. His 1922 passport photo shows a robust man in a suit-and-tie, a face evenly featured, with alert eyes. A thinner, more serious, long-faced man with longish, wild hair, looking down, intent upon his fingers as he played appeared in the publicity photo of Kalman run in the *Republican* in March 1934 preceding the show's launch. He was the draw. There was no photo of Norman.

Piano music was missed in many homes. After 1900 the rising number of pianos in homes reversed and the number of homes with pianos fell. The trend first went to phonographs and then to radios. Throughout the 1930s, many long-established piano manufacturers went out of business. With many thousands of radios and many fewer pianos in homes, Kalman as a pianist on the air enjoyed an automatic following. Kalman was the next best thing to their old piano.

Norman's strategy was poetic, as well as musical, variety. He banked on fans of Kalman loving poetry in general (not a bad bet). In selecting and editing poems for broadcast, Norman relied upon experience. Norman knew what held people's attention. From childhood and in Miss Lu's class he had recited poems. What pleased people he kept delivering, while discarding whatever did not.

Having also tinkered long hours to make news items sound right when read aloud—which he called "the tenets, properties and requirements of radio speech"—Norman was likewise able to distinguish what could go as is and which poems benefited from primping for broadcast. He was good and gave on radio for free what his newspaper paid him for, as did social clubs in the Springfield area. (He was often invited to lecture about poetry and to recite poems, speaking unaccompanied, appearing with no prop but a book.)[43]

His show worked. Letters arrived in praise of *Rhymes and Cadences*. Norman's program was never in danger of cancellation. A show that needed no sponsors and drew listeners was golden. Given repeated exposure, depending less on Kalman and Beethoven by the month, Norman developed a personal following. His ever-increasing, enthusiastic audience moved Norman to ever greater effort. While Kalman continued to hold up his end the show, Norman threw himself into shaking up the poetry part.

At first, Norman necessarily used his own mellifluous, melodic voice to bring out, alive and kicking, the words of books he lugged into the

WBZA studio from the public library a couple of blocks away and books from his own small collection. That he changed. Norman realized that there were plenty of poets in the hills that surrounded Springfield. Since the days of Emily Dickinson, many poets after that reclusive Amherst belle in a series to Robert Frost had marked Amherst as, in Norman's declaration, "the unofficial capital of poetry in the world."

Vital to Norman, one of them was an especially good reader: Amherst College Professor David Morton. Morton, in his fifties, had a slight native Tennessee drawl and a reedy, piercing voice that carried well. The professor drew out the clear meaning of his melancholic, rhyming poems of lost days and long-forgotten people. Norman scored a coup by booking Morton, at no charge, to appear often. Morton helped his show's prominence and ratings. Norman tried out other poets, too, but their delivery abilities were limited. (In fact, Norman said that he found no one to equal the obscure but audibly charming Morton until he ran into Carl Sandburg.)

Throughout his series, Norman presented Morton and the other local poets reciting their original works. Norman recited his own poetry only once, an especially curious decision because Norman always thought of himself first as a writer. Indeed, writing had been his job for years. Why he did not offer his poems to likely receptive neighbors he never explained. Perhaps he preferred that others shine in the spotlight he created, poets he sought to nurture at cost of airtime for himself.[44]

Or, at bottom, his Springfield radio show was, after all, a continuously increasing success that he dared not jeopardize. Although it is not a large jump to think that Norman had a high judgment of his own poetry at this time, only later—with an original rhyming script—did Norman became known as a writer of CBS radio scripts. Norman was an actor-producer-director on the radio. He would in a short time become radio's best-known writer but, when first hired by the CBS network in 1938, it was not to a write but to act as a producer-director.

Planning and presenting a weekly program with nobody's help (or interference), Norman discovered that he could produce and direct a 15-minute weekly program. Overseeing Kalman's two or three classical pieces or excerpts between recitations of two or three poems, and scripting a few words of introduction or a couple of questions of guests, Norman developed the basic skill set of a radio producer and director. He worked to perfect pace and timing, to figure out which poem went with which other poem and with which music. He nudged reluctant poems into readability and shy poets into felicitous delivery. Norman was not producing shows of the length, scope, and complexity he would finally handle but he was definitely learning by doing, making mistakes no one but he noticed, flexing the combination of skills he would need.

On top of everything, the public liked his voice. Norman, ever fond of a responsive audience, refused no group time at a podium. Word spread. He found himself in demand as a speaker. For example, late that spring, on June 1, without solicitation on his part, he was surprised to be invited to speak at the annual convention of Western Massachusetts High School Journalists. He was doubly pleased to be selected by the head of the English Department of the high school in Springfield, "a man I never met"—and to be paid.[45]

"Five bucks is five bucks," he told Em.[46]

What might he spend it on? In his Mulberry Street haunt, Norman continued to investigate the mysteries of radio. A dealer picked a ripe one and dropped off a shortwave set "on trial." Reviving the Eastie boy who maneuvered his cat's whisker to capture the sounds of a band in New York, Norman boasted about receiving signals "clearly" from South America and as far away as Germany. He wanted it. Badly. He wooed his frugal self into buying the $65 set at a discount.[47]

Trouble in Paradise

One earlier association with radio no longer interested him. By the time Walsh gave Norman back his old "Radio Page" job, Norman had outgrown it. The page was not closely enough connected to broadcasting. Norman wrote Em, "I'm not in love with my radio job, because it is too damned detailed. There is an awful lot of clerical work and not enough of the executive work which I enjoy."[48]

He was nearly 25. He had been through hell and back health-wise. He was conscious of what he was doing and what he was *not* doing as within him kicked a nascent radio producer and director. Still, the page was his. Norman took on the task grudgingly but compensated by upending a mess. He inaugurated a filing system, carefully proofed, and weeded "the morgue" of pre-written obituaries and any pictures that would not be used.

With those reforms, and the page itself reflecting improvement, Norman waited for recognition—in vain. Words of praise came from readers, but not from those in high places. Norman let off steam, venting to Em, "The trouble is that although at least two dozen people have commented to the editors, and although several letters have been received praising the WHERE TO FIND box, there is no expression of appreciation from the editors."[49]

He was so alienated from the Radio Page that he unlinked his name from it. The *Springfield Republican* Radio Page appeared thereafter under an ostentatiously fake pseudonym. It was now "by Vladimir Shrudlu."

To counter this bitter byline humor and overall mood, Norman's attentive editor, Walsh, approached him. The 1934 election was coming up. Would Norman emcee coverage from Springfield through the WBZ Boston hook-up? This offer in late October 1934 was recognition. It was even a possible giant step to something bigger. They both knew that Norman's visibility would soar.

"I go to Boston Monday to confer with BZ," he gleefully typed to Em soon after accepting Walsh's invitation. "It looks like we're in the radio racket up to our arses. Writing, editing, suggesting, broadcasting."[50]

In 1934, the New Deal, the results of the "First Hundred Days," were on the ballot as much as candidates. In this potential minefield, Norman succeeded in offending no partisans and in pleasing the public at large. Perks appeared. Suddenly the most eligible bachelor in town, Norman bragged to Em. He referred to "quandaries over paramours." He then teased Em by xxx'ing out the prefix and thus reshaping his problem as the more roguish "quandaries over amours."[51]

Mentally healthier than ever, instead of knee-jerk outrage, when not re-elected president of the local reporters' Republican, Norman exhibited statesman-like amusement. He was sure, and boasted to Em, that "it is recognized that I am the George Washington of the local guild, and the author of its constitution." He could see the bright side of the setback. He could "raise more hell from the floor" than he could in the chair of the Springfield Press Guild. His "amours" doubtless soothed him as well. Then Norman was approached by the other Springfield radio station, WMAS.[52]

Broadcast from studios at the Hotel Charles, its tall tower rising just beside the river, WMAS reached people who preferred local radio over Boston-affiliated WBZA. This small station was pursuing Norman to appear on its roster with *Rhymes and Cadences* or a poetry program like it.[53]

Norman's reaction was unbelievable. He suddenly felt overwhelmed. Upon receiving WMAS's clamor for his services, he got worried. He scheduled an x-ray as soon as he could at the hospital in nearby Westfield. Before he would take another step toward another project—he knew that his dedication would be uncontrollably excessive—Norman wanted his doctor's approval.

The doctor, following review and comparing the current with all earlier x-rays, cautiously offered the bland conclusion that there was "no suggestion of any new or increased involvement" in his chest. Relieved, Norman took it as a green light and made his last Pioneer Valley career move.[54]

Although only ambiguously cleared, Norman signed on with WMAS to do a series of weekly fifteen-minute spots for a variation of *Rhymes and Cadences*. With airtime on both Springfield stations, Norman was now audible to everybody in or near Springfield.

This begs a final question: Even for that prize, why did Norman tax himself to do these weekly programs essentially for nothing? The short answer was that Norman was enjoying himself. The long answer was that, again through the exercise of language, he was bonding with innumerable people. It had been his primal pleasure since childhood in Eastie.

Now he longed increasingly for an audience larger than he ever had. Norman was inching his way toward an exit from journalism into radio. By the end of 1934, Norman had made it only 85 miles from his birthplace. In a job he inherited in 1929 when his brother quit, he earned $ 35 a week. He lived in a rented room and drove a beat-up, old car while he banged out copy concerning fungible fires and interchangeably luckless litigants of criminal proceedings. Radio beckoned with its ever-expanding audience.[55]

To make the transition from local radio to a network would take luck and years. Ironically, in Norman's case, it would take *bad* luck. Even though Norman liked to emphasize luck—looking back in his nineties in Mike Kacey's documentary, he characterized his life and career as "a series of serendipities,"—on the contrary, serendipities were very nearly his downfall. Norman had to work hard to overcome his lucky breaks, which kept him in journalism and, repeatedly, back in Springfield. Norman's rut was too comfortable. As will be revealed shortly, he was saved from via a series of unwelcome and painful adversities. He was led to his larger audience and to the attention of the entire country in radio by a series of bumps and jolts.

Norman's Roller Coaster

Meanwhile, without leaving town and just doing his day job, Norman witnessed the Fascist and Anti-Fascist movements in conflict. They clashed in city hall in Springfield. An obscure organization applied to use Springfield's centrally located, large civic auditorium for a fair to benefit the Italian Red Cross. At public hearing over approval of the application, Norman learned that "proceeds were to alleviate the suffering of Italian soldiers then slaughtering Ethiopians for Mussolini and the King."

A modest group of unnamed Anti-Fascists, "a Negro pastor" and four others of unstated race, objected. A spokesman for the American Red Cross spoke in favor. Ultimately, permission was granted. This use of city property bothered Norman. Shaking his head over the city officials' "political immaturity," Norman attended the fair. Finding it well-attended, he was disgusted. One intuits words spoken in a tone of icy contempt: "I saw the Fascist salute freely given, and I watched old women and young mothers drop gold wedding rings into a kitty." Norman hated acts of mindless

One of the earliest images of Norman in New York: this rare "joke shot," doubt-less arranged by Em, who handled public relations for NBC, depicts Norman and mock-loud actress, Peggy Burt, on the set of *Magic Key of RCA*, a variety show broadcast 1935–1939. Image c. 1937 (courtesy American Radio Archives and Museum).

conformity. In Norman's eyes, Mussolini and his henchmen stole a bit of freedom—and gold—from hard-working Italians he knew in Springfield.

Intent on leaving Springfield, Norman took his first swings at the ball too early. He made a move almost as soon as he got back. Released from house arrest by his doctor, again wooed by swooning women and by both WBZA and WMAS, burning bright with almost irrational exuberance, Norman somehow convinced the editor of the *New York World-Telegram* to give him a two-week trial.

With New York in his sights, and two weeks off from the paper, Nor-man packed a few necessaries and took the train in mid-1934. He must have thought of Heywood Broun, who had been the *World-Telegram's* most famous columnist back when Norman met him. It might have been a good omen except that it was not. Soon after Norman's 1928 visit, Broun left the ranks of that paper's columnists. He had been making a spare living since by freelancing and making occasional appearances on radio.

New York newspapers were known as the best in the country. He idolized the *World-Telegram* as the best of the best. Despite this favorable prejudice, Norman, who rarely stumbled so badly, found this trial more than trying. He lost all confidence in what he had been doing for seven years.

"The change from Springfield was too sudden," he said in his unpublished memoir. He leaped from a city he knew "forwards and backwards" to getting lost on the subway. He found "(his) kind of yarn" only once, when a bear escaped from the Central Park Zoo. His bear story made the front page. Among other assignments, however, he recalled "tracking down a rumor, which turned out to be false, that hurdy-gurdy men had been banned from the city streets" and "an interview with a German writer named Bonsels, of whom nobody had heard and about whom nobody cared." Within days, he actually hoped *not* to be offered a permanent job. While waiting for two weeks to expire, still in New York, he stumbled into another stumble.[56]

By serendipity, it *seemed*, an offer arose that sounded—and was—too good to be true. WLW Cincinnati, one step below network radio, the "Nation's Station," the so-called "Brightest Spot on the Dial," was a 500,000-watt station, the first to reach coast to coast. WLW was auditioning for a news reader at the Hotel Park Central. *News reader?* Of course, Norman *was* a news reader, an *experienced* news reader. Of course, Norman went. And, of course, Norman was hired.

"[T]he job was mine before I read as far as the second dateline," Norman said with obvious pride. It was not luck. All of those hours on WBZ and WMAS paid off. He was no tyro, and it showed.[57]

Recognizing a Cinderella story when he bumped into one, bedazzled Norman swam in visions of the opportunity of a lifetime. The door to New York journalism might be closing but a staircase to the stars was opening. He went back and shook hands with the surprised editor at the *World-Telegram*, thanked him for his kindness and boogied back to Springfield.

There he paused only long enough to comb out the few tangles that still connected him to that city. He gave up his room, sold his car for $ 10, said good-bye to his friends, and gave final fond embraces to selected ladies before anxiety reclaimed him. On the threshold of the radio career Norman had long craved, as he shook hands with Walsh, something led him nonetheless to ask Walsh for another two-week leave. Softy that he was when it came to Norman, good old Walsh granted this favor without hesitation. No, Norman need not resign for another two weeks.

They probably both laughed.

Norman next went by train to Cincinnati. He said that it marked the first time he crossed the Hudson River. WLW was the best of stations and the worst of stations. Its reputation, its reach and its resources were all formidable. On the other hand, the WLW studios were ominously "so refrigerated that I had to put on a hat and coat." Its executives were set on icy, too. "It was a driving, profit-making, broadcast-fabricating factory," Norman sourly gleaned after getting settled on site, "as little concerned with creative programming as a laundromat."[58]

Nonetheless, Norman was on the air across America every night at 11 o'clock. It was too much fun to throw this job away by demanding creativity too soon. Besides, Norman cheated immediately. He managed some fun by offering spontaneous "Believe It or Not!" facts and off-beat human interest items, just the kind that he had always liked as a reporter in Springfield.

The microphone held no terrors for the pleasant baritone. Norman's easy-on-the-ears presence and ingenuity was noted by his superiors, his work was praised and, instantly upon Norman's request for a $10 raise, his pay became $50 a week, effective immediately.

Suddenly earning nearly twice his Springfield pay for less than half the effort without having to leave a radio studio, Norman floated in heaven. Meteoric success overwhelmed his common sense. Not even waiting, Norman excitedly pulled the last plug connecting him to his newspaper job in Springfield. He giddily notified Walsh: he was done with the *Republican*, "effective immediately." His notice led to an article saluting Norman in a congratulatory tone.[59]

In Cincinnati, a fiasco unfolded after an edict that nobody could refer to strikes—labor strikes, school walkouts, anything. Being a close reader who thought like a newsman, Norman saw a practical problem. As part of a five-page list of suggestions, he suggested that this rule needed attention. He noted that WLW listeners would be puzzled. Big strikes were covered by their newspapers, like general strike that closed the port of San Francisco. To higher-ups, Norman had raised a literal red flag. Feeling a threat from within, WLW reduced its personnel by one. Norman was given a two-week severance package.[60]

In the prior five years, his only published book had failed abysmally, his marriage proposal was rejected and, after he coughed up blood, Norman had faced fatality for months under a working diagnosis of tuberculosis. When cleared to return, he was not re-elected president of the local union he had founded. His dream job at the *New York Telegram* collapsed within days and now his breakthrough job in national radio likewise vanished. He was bounced off "The Brightest Spot on the Dial" into the street. He was jobless for the first time since he was seventeen.

Norman applied for jobs beginning where he was, in Cincinnati, knocking on doors. He was rejected by WKRC, the Cincinnati *Post* and the *Inquirer*. He sent applications out to Los Angeles, to Hollywood. Back in

Winthrop, he scavenged for anything in Boston, at WBZ, WNAC, WHDH, and the newspapers, the *Post*, the *Herald*, the *Traveler*. He felt terrible. He hated "the inglorious need to speak pushingly in your own behalf." His feelings of uselessness were "new and frightening." Finally, he had no real choice. He paddled backward. As he put it, "hat in hand," he asked Walsh to take him back.[61]

Walsh, bless him, did so.

"You're welcome when you show your face," he told his prodigal erstwhile employee.[62]

Humpty Dumpty could not be put back together again, though. Walsh no longer had a nightly broadcast to offer. All Walsh could do was fix things for Norman as reporter to have a less physically arduous, mostly stationary beat. Walsh assigned his now car-free man to cover the courts. Norman speedily found a new place to stow his gear within a fifteen-minute walk of the courts.

The room he rented at Avon Place was clearly nothing more for him than a pit stop. Although grateful to Walsh for a respite, Norman was still going to escape. He would be a reporter no longer than he had to. He renewed his no-budget weekly poetry programs, without a pianist, on both WBZ and WMAS—and audaciously opened negotiations with NBC.

He offered NBC *Rhymes and Cadences*. (Em *worked* at that network but Norman instructed him explicitly to "keep mum" and let him "fight it out alone.") Despite his up-and-down ordeal at WLW, Norman was now almost mystical about having a destiny beyond Springfield *and* on the radio. He was ridiculously right. His show could work anywhere. It later worked in Manhattan. Poetry was in. But at that time NBC had no interest in *Rhymes and Cadences*.[63]

That winter, Norman wrote Em shocking news. On January 10, 1936, he was so moved at a concert that he *opened* his eyes:

> For the first time in my concert-going it was impossible to shut my eyes and listen to the music. [Jose Iburi's] hands were too amazing, and I sat banjo-eyed watching him do some intricate tricks with Debussy and DeFalla. Equally exophthalmic was I when he marches through a Beethoven sonata which took three years off my life."[64]

Clearly, wherever he lived, whatever he did for a living, Norman's lifelong love affair was with classical music. The Iburi concert was only the climax of a marathon affair in Springfield. His encounters with classical music included concerts, Kalman up close, of course, and Norman had taken out every classical music album on the shelves of the Springfield Public Library—twice—then three times—then more. He began every day with Beethoven, Brahms and other luminaries, then, each night, he played such music softly at his machine's lowest setting. Classical music never got old, his love only grew stronger.

During that winter, 1935–36, Norman took on teaching journalism at the Young Men's Hebrew Association. He also continued to speak to any group that invited him. In Springfield, a liberal among liberals but also among apolitical or sometimes mindless and Fascist-leaning neighbors, he was pretty much waiting to leave for New York. In the interim, he continued to attend concerts and to find recreational opportunities in liaisons with local lasses.

Then, one spring day in 1936, Em called. Acting on his own, he had scheduled an interview for his brother in New York. He respected Norman's instructions to the letter, not to interfere at NBC. Leonard Gaynor, an executive of the country's newest major studio, 20th Century–Fox, was coming to New York briefly to hire a publicity agent. The job up for grabs was, thus, not NBC and it was not exactly radio, but it was a job in New York, where Norman could make many useful contacts, and it also involved a bit of scripting for radio delivery by other people. Norman's interview was set for the following Wednesday.

In response, Norman said thanks, but he had a date. If he took off for New York, he would disappoint the girl (and probably his *own* expectations?). Without listening any longer or arguing, big brother Em pulled rank, said, "Norm, be there," and hung up.

Left looking at his phone in Springfield, Norman then hung up, too—and broke his date. Walsh gave him time off on short notice, he caught the necessary train, made the interview punctually and found himself in the running. When he told Em, with whom he stayed overnight, Em argued that Norman could write and succeed by freelancing in New York, whether he was hired by Fox or not.

After Norman returned to Springfield, Em discussed the matter further with his new wife, Freda. With her blessing, he upped the ante. Em and Freda offered Norman a bed indefinitely, a key to their mid-town Manhattan apartment *gratis*. In a confirming letter, Em all but made the invitation an order "You should cut loose from Springfield to come live with us, job or no job."[65]

Norman had no reason to hesitate when Gaynor got back to him. It was a rich offer with but one imperfect term: Norman was not going to speak on radio. On the other hand, the job was *not* grunt-work reporting. He would work *with* newspapers but not *for* a newspaper. And, instead of running around the courts of Springfield, he would meet and greet Fox movie stars and starlets flying into New York, coming in from Hollywood by train, plane or arriving on ships from Europe. He would also attend premieres in a tux and show up on screens across the country in newsreels.

Norman could imagine people seeing his face in theaters in Boston, Winthrop, Springfield, Greenfield, and Cincinnati, asking, "Is that—?"

These dreamy perks were not all: the job paid well. It did not fully satisfy his inner needs, but neither did the $35 a week job in Springfield he was doing. Norman, who never did anything for the sake of a bankroll alone, could not turn down a job (1) in New York (2) that paid better than any he ever had, that (3) came with a huge expense account, where (4) he would see his beloved Em and Freda daily. Besides, as the Fox man about town, Norman would make auspicious contacts with stars as he reserved tables at the best restaurants and nightclubs and for hit shows, *concerts*, and ballet.

A final tickle was the job's one nominal *radio* duty. Norman was to rewrite press releases and photo captions for radio broadcast. It was fun with which he was familiar. He had been scripting for radio for his own delivery on WBZ and WMAS. He knew how words *sounded* on the air. That Norman would be handing over scripts for others to deliver may have felt like half a loaf, but still, it was New York, wasn't it?

Norman shook hands with Walsh and left Springfield, now for a third time, the charm. He was done with newspapers. Hello, his next job was pitched squarely between New York and Hollywood. Norman was going to be Darryl Zanuck's ambassador in Manhattan.

Em and understanding Freda, with their a two-room apartment, were true to their word. They literally opened the door to New York to Norman. Under the circumstances, their generosity was extravagant. They invited not only Norman but, soon, Al as well.

At first, the younger brothers slept in one room on a pull-down Murphy bed and, whenever they needed the bathroom, knocked politely on the newlyweds' bedroom door before walking through to the facility. Ever-practical Em scouted for a new apartment. Within months, and possibly with a new rent-sharing arrangement, Em leased a three-bedroom with some genuinely private space for everybody.

Norman was not in Springfield anymore. Almost weirdly, he was both back in the bosom of his family and escorting stars and hobnobbing his nights away at the most dazzling spots in the Big Apple. Norman was 25 in a city where anything could happen. That he worked for Tinseltown added luster. Magic was in the Broadway air. Norman's words were going out on air. If Norman could only get *himself* on the air, anything might happen.

Poetic License

Working behind the scenes out of old Fox studio's headquarters on the West Side, much of his time spent squiring celebrities at night spots,

Norman was cut off. He lacked the refreshment of two-way dialogues and instant feedback in the streets of Springfield. Celebrity escorting was over-rated, as was any pleasure in trotting around in a tux at film premieres wearing a forced smile. He was not in the job of his dreams. He was living with Em and Al and engaging in a routine that did not nourish his core.[66]

Pa knew. Either from their weekly phone calls or by analyzing Norman's letters, Pa gleaned that Norm needed a pep-up in late 1936. Pa told him, "If you are moody to write a novel or something, may I suggest you do it methodically, i.e., devote an hour or so 2–4 times a week, it will last lon-ger, give you more time to think and from my point of view it would make it more interesting."[67]

Pa was right in general, but not specifically. Norman's attempted novel had been a failure that he never tried to repeat. Writing was fine but what Norman needed was airtime. His poetry programs had enjoyed success. He was in the city of national networks. Brother Em worked for NBC, the biggest network in the world. Norman auditioned for NBC and earned a chance to go on air. Norman's recorded poetry show was broadcast in March 1938 on NBC's *The Magic Key of RCA* show for pilot programs. Prob-ably guided by the *absence* of a major public response, NBC executives con-cluded that Norman was not ready.[68]

Classical music came to his rescue. One day he found WQXR-AM, "1550 on the dial," a station at the end of his set's range. WQXR played classical music all day. Run by affable John V. Hogan, a pipe-smoking Yale-trained engineer and inventor, its "money man" and administrator was Elliott M. Sanger, a former journalist.

At least since his senior year at Winthrop High School, Norman had excelled in approaching strangers. He introduced himself at the station both as an admirer of its classical music selections and as someone who would like to emcee a poetry show.[69]

As he had already done for two stations in Springfield, he would work for free. He recited a bit of poetry for Hogan and Sanger as an *impromptu* audition. Both men quickly recognized that Norman had talent but his accent and diction struck them as inappropriate.

"Hardly a week went by when WQXR was not offered a poetry broad-cast," Sanger wrote. They told Norman to go home, to work on his accent and diction, and come back. He did all three.[70]

Hogan boldly offered a six-month contract. Norman accepted and Hogan scheduled twenty-six fifteen-minute slots for Norman's poetic selections, *Poetic License*, each week on Wednesday evening at 9:45 p.m. (Fifteen-minute programs were far more common than half-hour shows at that time.) Hogan was giving Norman a clear shot to gather momentum and a following. Six months after NBC's rejection, in October 1937 Norman began at WQXR. In an instant, all of New York was his potential audience. His listeners were a diverse but sophisticated and music-loving group far larger than any Norman had ever addressed.[71]

Norman enjoyed the show and its prep work. He recruited poets to recite their own stuff, rehearsing and directing them himself. He adapted poems by others. He wrote introductions and patter. Others in New York were better at these functions, but nobody was learning faster. He once said that Springfield was his higher education but vocationally, professionally for radio, New York and WQXR were his grad school.

Standing behind a floor microphone in a sound-proofed studio, signaled by a technician or two behind glass, simultaneously present in the unseen homes of thousands of people, he recited poems, as he had begun doing before radio existed. For fifteen minutes each Wednesday for five months, with or without guests, he flew through the air with the greatest of ease. Norman kept things fresh, even managing to get old David Morton down from Amherst. Professor Morton, blessed with a wonderfully mellifluous voice, sonorously recited long strings of Tennessee hill country poems from memory.

Not insignificantly, Norman proudly advised Ma and Pa when they could hear his show. *Poetic License* could actually be heard in Winthrop sometimes. Pa wrote Norman about it. He proudly told his son how "McKenzie walked over to my car in the yard to-day as I was taking the bookkeeper to the bank this afternoon & he told Miss Piper how he enjoyed the program, he damn near repeated nearly every word you said."[72]

Poetic License found fans in New York as well. One in particular changed Norman's life. Nearing the expiration of his contract to work for free, in March 1938, Norman produced his best WQXR program, a show without any music or sound effects, his hand-honed, deftly cut version of Edgar Lee Masters' *Spoon River Anthology*. For cast besides himself, Norman drafted Em—and his butcher—to join him and the poet Genevieve Taggart. A pastiche of soft and loud, nuanced and crude voices resulted. Norman's adaptation was well-scripted, well-paced, and partly raucous but overall professional.[73]

Anyone who tuned in was hooked. The characters' poetic bursts flowed into a heart-quickening narrative swirl of small town lives. It was the climactic highlight of Norman's unpaid WQXR career. Tuning in to hear the performance that particular evening was a new listener, Bill Lewis, the chief of programing at CBS.[74]

Lewis was listening because Em had gone to NBC's personnel man, Ted Church, on behalf of his brother. With Norman on the air now, and successful in New York, would NBC reconsider? Church would not commit to hire a young man who was still reciting poems for nothing, but he thought of Lewis. At CBS, cultural presentations were its pride. They hosted Shakespearean plays.

On the premise that CBS might be a good match for Em's poetic brother, Church called Kitty Crane, Bill Lewis's secretary. He asked Kitty to tell Lewis about this talented fellow on WQXR every Wednesday night. Soon after that, as he recovered from a cold at home one Wednesday, Lewis remembered and listened to *Poetic License*.[75]

Lewis knew when he heard the show. He acted. The next morning, Lewis passed the word. Kitty was to find out from WQXR how to contact Norman and then follow through and ask him to drop by Lewis's office.

CBS

Lewis's request was immediately and rightly understood: a *job offer* was coming. When Norman shared the news with Em, Em bound his brother with two nuggets of really terrible advice. They both actually originated from Church. First, Norman was to demand a high price for his services and, second, if hired, crazily, the novice was "never, ever" to reveal that he did not know what he was doing. Luckily, Norman stopped following both tips before either one killed his career.

At least he was not advised to demand a writer's slot or to go on air immediately. Either of those demands would have instantly killed the deal. CBS hired Norman to direct. He was not going on the air, nor was he to write. As he wrote Ma and Pa, he signed a contract "to serve as a director of dramatic programs" for the Columbia Broadcasting System to start on April 25 at a weekly salary of $125. (Fox had been paying him $50, plus expenses.)

He coveted other duties, and expressed his hope in this letter to the folks. As Norman put it, "I will probably direct two or three programs a week to begin with, and may not be on the air myself (i.e., with my own work) until after I have been there a while."[76]

But going on the air with his own work was his own wishful thinking.

He only got a contract by speedily shelving his salary demand. Lewis, former ad man and ever the salesman, persuaded Norman to accept the network's offer, unmodified. Lewis told Norman that he would get exactly what he demanded if he simply stuck around long enough. Without calculating the odds of his longevity at CBS, Norman signed on as the most junior of CBS directors.

Norman gave his notice, the Fox people shook his hand, Hogan and Sanger wished him well, too, as his contract with WQXR was at an end, and Norman started working for CBS beginning April 25, 1938.

A granitic refusal to admit weakness did not matter while Norman wandered, shadowing experienced directors to observe how things were done at CBS. He needed to do nothing more than watch. He spoke with writers, with technicians, sound effects men (they were all men at that time), generally absorbing as much as he could, interviewing like a reporter.[77]

How did he feel? Norman's mood that spring is impossible to reconstruct. Surviving letters and his memoirs leave out his feelings. For Norman, network radio was a rebirth. But—to what job? What was it like for him to *direct*? How did it feel finally, after months, to stand in the glassed-in box overlooking a cast and oversee a live show, signaling and gesturing much like a symphony conductor?

Later, certainly, after he had directed and produced and, above all, written scripts, he described CBS in glowing terms, its people as great and supportive. But, when Norman started, as CBS's newest and least experienced director, was he a kid in a candy store or a man drowning?

To understand why Norman could be nervous, one had best reclaim who he was on the day that he was hired. As he approached age 28, he had most recently been a movie studio greeter and publicity man. Earlier, for eight years in western Massachusetts, he had reported local news. His hobbyist after-hours poetry shows on WBZ and WMAS and a sample recording had not drawn any great acclaim. Lewis concluded that Norman might make a radio *director*. Truly, objectively, he had failed in writing (in New York journalism, with two unpublished novels, and a published book of epigrams that went nowhere). On the strength of a single professional-sounding show on WQXR, Lewis decided to give Norman a try at network directing.

Despair may have dominated him. Anxiety over his qualifications— and the stupid, strict instruction never, ever to speak of weakness—may have literally made him sick. He withdrew from any social life. He overslept. Norman had so little to report after his birthday in early May that Pa was concerned. "If I can read between lines, I'll wager you had the dullest birthday in a long while, if so, there must have been a reason for it or may be more than one reason, tired?" A couple of weeks later, Pa wrote, "You must be awful busy when we rarely get a word from you."[78]

In May, when Norman broke into directing shows on air, he did share with David Morton that he was too busy to be indecisive. "It is work which I love," he insisted, before saying that it was "far more demanding than any work I have yet done." He contrasted himself as "a person inclined, in the past, to be vague and indecisive" against a director, "Boss around the studio—over actors, over sound men, over the engineer, over the script."[79]

But neither to David Morton nor his family did he clarify how he *felt*.

His family's comments were well-intentioned but inane. Did their letters tickle him or ratchet up his alienation? Pa wrote after one show, asking, "How was the sound made of cows in the distance? There was a close-up sound of a cow that sounded like a human being imitating one, was I right?" His parents both shared how they got "quite a kick when 'under the direction of Norman Corwin' is announced."[80]

He was busy, he had to concentrate, he had to be sharp. Did he feel lonely? The rookie director's fan base wavered between small and even smaller. If Pa missed one of Norman's shows (working late for McKenzie?), Ma would tell him that she was sorry for him. Pa wrote about this to Norman, adding, "I don't remember when Ma got so 'nuts' about any program as she did with this one & she had a few women here to listen in."[81]

Norman sustained himself on such nominal feedback until he was tapped to direct a *Columbia Workshop* play. It was the call he had either been hoping for—or dreading. Norman recalled it with explicit pride some thirty years later, speaking to Bannerman, "I got the call from On High. There was a great cachet to being asked to direct a *Columbia Workshop* program. That was the prize, the main jewel in the diadem."[82]

Presumably after a nod of approval from Bill Lewis, Douglas Coulter entrusted their greenest director to direct a broadcast going out on the air live, as all shows did then. Ironically, the show was about the first time a young man came under fire. An adaptation of Stephen Crane's old novella *The Red Badge of Courage* was Norman's to do right or to mess up.

The result was pedestrian. Nobody was embarrassed, but neither was anybody stunned by its excellence or its awfulness. The few people in Massachusetts who noticed the broadcast and recognized Norman Corwin's name as director did not contact CBS. They called his parents and congratulated *them*.[83]

To Norman, the country's muteness was a huge disappointment. He had gotten more reaction from his local news shows. Likely, he sounded moody or absent, worried, during his weekly phone calls home. Pa, who had experience with a nervous breakdown that he blamed on overworking, wrote Norman in September. "Years ago I continually bit off more than I could chew & in time I dearly paid for it," he said. Perhaps not to scare Norman, Pa added some dismissive *caveats*, "well, my work was laborious in the 1st place & I worked 7 days & 5 days a week & at times it was 24 hours without quitting & on several other occasions even longer."[84]

Even so, Pa was not above increasing his son's workload, given its non-laborious intellectual nature. The next month, he asked Norman to send Dr. Abrams a response to "4 pages of poetry and a letter" that he sent Norman. "He is expecting some poetry also," Pa said.[85]

CBS reacted tolerantly. Coulter judged the show adequate and he gave

Norman another chance with another play, a light comedy, *The Lighthouse Keepers*. It went better but only because a very experienced vaudevillian actor pulled no stops to endow a somewhat lame script with broad humor. He carried the show.[86]

Norman had now swung twice and with neither show had he made a hit. Hired to direct, Norman apparently tortured himself over mistakes about which he could *not speak*. Fretful on the bench and, in part to stifle Pa, Norman scheduled a health check-up.

After the exam, he proudly reported himself to Pa to be in "perfect physical condition." Half-convinced, Pa made a 180 degree turn and wrote back, "Now if at any time you should feel that your throat or chest does not feel right, rest assured that it is mental & you must immediately turn away from that condition which is called neurosis & I suppose you know as much as I do about obsessions, etc."[87]

Certified fit but feeling boxed in by Church's advice—by which he was supposed to tough out his apprenticeship mutely—he finally refused to keep a stiff upper lip. He tossed away Church's advice and took a giant step.

An expert who knew it all, before whom he had made his mistakes, and who knew how radio worked, was also his savvy assistant. Her name was Betsy Tuthill. In mid–1938, Norman asked her to join him for dinner. Over a meal, he asked for her help during what became a confession.[88]

It took bravery. The confession was likely humiliating. It is uncertain whether they both knew then that he had been taken off *Columbia Workshops* and was on the skids, if not headed out of CBS entirely. Such was the track on which he had been placed. Norman's next assignment would be directing a little-remembered series entitled *Living History*.

Beginning with that dinner, Tuthill actively encouraged her boss. His assistant might be said to have saved him. Tuthill, who would have made a fine director but for board room sexism that excluded her from promotion, guided Norman up to the next level. But it did take guts for Norman to ignore Church's advice, and to go against his native self-reliance and habit of exhibiting confidence.

Living History is significant today only as the perfect vehicle for Norman to learn his profession. That is, few people were listening. Outside of prime time, through trial and error, all the while under Tuthill's close tutelage, the fledgling began to fly. Tuthill urged Norman to innovate while he also reined in his actors. She made him notice that actors more experienced than their director—which was all of them—were inclined to take advantages. Nudged by Tuthill, Norman gradually and consciously got them in line. Finally, they showed trust and did what he said or signaled (for much of radio direction was soundless, accomplished by waves and gestures of someone up in a control booth).

Tuthill had the patience, the compassion, and the savvy to identify Norman's mistakes and to go over with him, in each case, what he might do instead. In his memoir, Norman did not mention his stint directing the *Living History* series, although he happily gave general credit to Tuthill. Norman learned how to direct from a non-director, but that good woman knew exactly what she was doing.

With Tuthill's tutelage, Norman's skills grew. Coulter assigned him to direct a new series, *Americans at Work*. Manifestly, he felt inspired. Having survived his debut ordeal in full glare with two weak shows on *Columbia Workshop*, and then having learned to direct on the job with *Living History*, simultaneously eliciting what Norman tongue-in-cheek called only the public's "cautious enthusiasm" (his family?), Norman wanted—for a future with the network, *needed*—to make some real waves. Although we cannot read his emotional state,—he sealed that record—we know that he was pro-active. No longer mute, acting boldly on an impulse, he brought a long list to work. It is hard to believe that Tuthill suggested that he do this. Probably, Norman was a victim of spontaneous innovation.

Norman sought to shake loose some network funds to jolt his fellow Americans with the authentic *sounds* of their nation. He wanted to create and head a new unit. He envisioned crews roving nation-wide in search of sounds. He proposed that they record on site the roar of Niagara Falls. If CBS allowed him the money, the machines, the crews and the time, the Liberty Bell would peal, Times Square traffic horns would toot, and generators would charge up on the air. He would broadcast legendary clocks and the ticking of celebrities' watches. Airplane propellers would rev up and famous locomotives hiss and chug.[89]

Norman Corwin's Words Without Music

CBS executives were deaf to his pleas. His list of sounds went for naught. No sound trucks and crews were ever dispatched with bulky wire recorders in pursuit of any item on his dream list. However, Norman grasped a lesson in memo making. He was rapidly learning to ride the bureaucratic bicycle. He decided not to seek funds for an expensive project.

He began to write. Charles R. Jackson helped to mentor Norman in radio writing. In Jackson, Norman found a sounding board even more accessible than Em. Jackson's door was always open. High in "spirit and enthusiasm," Norman recalled dashing into Jackson's office "six times an hour with a new verse" to read it aloud for Jackson's opinion.

Norman came out of his apparent (but never acknowledged) funk. He reached a frame of mind that thrilled him, "aggressive and creative and confident," an attitude which inevitably underlay his best work. Jackson's 18th floor office was next to Norman's and they frequently took breaks to share their current projects and gab.[90]

Jackson was a great colleague, a generous and talented writer, a natural storyteller who would eventually write a best-selling novel, *The Lost Weekend* (which was made into a movie). He had also been bedeviled by hardship since 1916. That year, his brother and sister died in a terrible car crash. Soon after, Jackson was thrown out of college for homosexual behavior. And then he had been sick.

Like Norman, Jackson had survived tuberculosis. However, he was discharged only after five full years in a series of sanitariums—and after losing one of his lungs. Joblessness thereafter triggered severe alcoholism. With grit, Jackson wrote his way out of poverty. He married a fellow writer, Rhoda Booth. By 1938, at CBS, he was sober and happier than he had been in years. Though sadness had not done stalking Jackson, he was at that time full of life.[91]

Feeling writerly as well as having earned his director's spurs, Norman used his standing to suggest a different and simpler idea than a CBS sound crew: his own show. When interviewed years later, he skipped altogether any discussion of his sound trucks idea and quite casually presented his show as the next step in his evolving CBS career.

"After a few months of directing the work of others, I thought I would like to try an expanded version of *Poetic License*," Norman recalled in a 1966 interview. This sounds backward. One wonders which really came first, Norman's thought, or Lewis's interview with Norman. Between the bumpy uphill road to success in radio that he actually experienced and a fiction, Norman tended to see the past through rose-colored glasses as linear, smooth and ever upward.[92]

Certainly, Norman may have jumped up as a volunteer just at this time. In that case, to clear the way for Norman, CBS cancelled its poetry program, *Between the Bookends*. For four years CBS had carried this fifteen-minute show aired in many different time slots. Its famed announcer, Ted Malone, was the sonorous heartthrob of many women who never missed a show. Some of them mailed proposals, enclosing photos. With such a dedicated following, Malone quickly found another outlet. He made his debut on NBC's Blue Network on September 9, 1938. He remained on the Blue Network/ABC until June 1955.[93]

However, the reverse is more likely true. In late summer, 1938, Malone's departure left CBS without a resident poet. Had Lewis noticed earlier that Norman, the new director, was glum and in doldrums? Lewis did care about Norman. If Lewis told Norman of the imminent demise of *Between the Bookends*, his advancement opportunity would have been obvious. The possibility of a regular show of his own had just opened up. "I would like to try an expanded version of *Poetic License*," would be the *second* line of a dialogue with Lewis, in that case.

Lewis, who hired Norman to direct, had always paid close attention to Norman's voice. During an interview in the 1970s, Lewis credited his great radio writer's success to "that voice of his." Departing Malone's syrupy voice had virtually carried *Between the Bookends*. Norman's rich baritone and a delivery that was sharp and well-paced may well have motivated Lewis to approve Norman's own poetry program, though Norman built his career thereafter *not* on "that voice of his" to which Lewis credited his success.[94]

One would like to know the mindsets and the feelings of both Lewis and Norman as the clock was ticking. Malone was soon returning to the air over a rival network. To retain listener share, CBS needed a poetry show. And Lewis pointedly asked Norman to *experiment*. No argument ensued. With creativity, Norman never had a problem.

Network poetry shows were big deals at that time. Erik Barnouw reported in his classic history that poetry was then a "battlefield" between networks. Lewis gave Norman a little ammunition. He authorized a $ 100 budget for an audition recording (good enough when actors got $ 7.50 per half-hour for auditions, with unlimited unpaid rehearsal time at the director's call). Lewis then insisted on naming the baby, but Norman did not like Lewis's proposed title, *Words without Music*. To Norman, this was a highly deflating moniker for an audio showcase of rhythmic, musical verse. He protested.[95]

"*Norman Corwin's Words without Music*," Lewis then countered, instantly charming Norman's ears and stifling his objections. Ever the salesman and deal maker, Lewis offered Norman something he could not refuse. It was the glittering radio equivalent of his name up in lights on Broadway. Norman was to adapt poems for radio and no writer's name had *ever* adorned a network series. Lewis thus cordially ended all argument. *Norman Corwin's Words without Music* it was. (At the same moment, precedent was incidentally and casually set for Norman's name to be in the title of all of his later series at CBS.[96])

By this account, Norman left Lewis's office with a series in his name, a budget in his pocket, and the function of writer officially part of his duties. His life had changed in a few minutes. One wishes to know his feelings, whether butterflies in his stomach, tearful relief, a wave of adrenaline-boosted confidence, anything. Although the move was monumental, one has no way to answer the mystery of emotions. He seems to have repressed feeling anything in order to concentrate. Aiming to be outstanding, workaholic Norman promptly and ironically found his breakthrough in, of all sources, Mother Goose.

Norman did not have to wait until 1939. On Sunday evening,

December 18, 1938, Norman presented as his first show "Mother Goose," nursery rhymes with sound effects. It was a bit cheeky because the NBC audition that failed to take had been his parody of "Mary had a little lamb." In this show, sound effects dominated. Old Mother Hubbard's cupboard creaked, her dog yipped, etc.

As corny as it may sound today, the show was novel enough to move the needle. What Norman had hungered for happened: his show was all the talk of the next day. Some newspapers offered a few words of recognition, too. Nobody has ever topped scholarly Erik Barnouw's explanation of the spike in popularity of Norman's first national poetry show. It derived, Barnouw thought, from everybody's "submerged memories."[97]

His next show fell on Christmas Day and Norman told the story of a CBS publicity man coming by to ask what he planned. Norman was the writer, after all, the CBS poet in residence whose series bore his name. Allegedly "because he could not think of an appropriate Christmas poem to adapt," Norman said that he was writing—he instantly gave an arbitrary title—"The Plot to Overthrow Christmas."[98]

In his memoirs, he recalled having a week to write the show. Figuring a day or two for rehearsals, Norman wrote his first original radio script during a caffeine-fueled marathon. He recalled how, day and night, he "wrote in many chairs, a roof that we'd used to go up to even in inclement weather, in barber chairs, in transit. There was not a moment I was not making notes or writing or revising. I had to put that much time into it, otherwise it would not be done. There would be holes in it. I was rather ruthless on myself."[99]

Although he had only a week to put pen to paper, groundwork for this Christmas show went back to the previous summer. Norman knew what pleased people. In his turn at bat, Norman seized this, his great advantage, to knock out a hit. He would amaze his largest audience ever. Norman was going straight to Hell.[100]

Norman knew that Hell was hot. One of the country's and Norman's most admired role models was poet and radio dramatist, Pulitzer Prize-winning Stephen Vincent Benét. CBS had judged his property valuable and bought radio rights to his popular and patriotic 1936 *Saturday Evening Post* story (issued also as a brisk-selling book in 1937), *The Devil and Daniel Webster*. In 1938, Norman witnessed his friend Jackson adapt this choice piece of Americana.

Norman had grounds to marvel. Jackson's historical fantasy, with music by Bernard Hermann, aired on *The Columbia Workshop* on August 6, 1938. The Devil and the damned souls who were summoned up to serve on the jury electrified its national audience. Jackson had created an immensely diverting entertainment, loudly acclaimed by critics.

"The Plot to Overthrow Christmas" was finished in time to be rehearsed and aired live on December 25, 1938. Its setting transparently inspired by Jackson and Benét, Norman's rhyming story poem began:

> *Now it happened in Hades,*
> *Ladies,*
> *And gentlemen....*

Nero conspires with the Devil to end the celebration of Christmas. If Norman's show was more successful than Jackson's (and it was), it was in part because Hell worked better in December than in August. Also, the timing of his funny, original, rhyming show—broadcast on Christmas Day—could not have been more perfect to maximize an audience. Again and again, timing would help Norman. He clearly was walking on air that holiday. Novelty aside, its quality "made quite a few ripples." Norman relished to recall that CBS newsman and popular commentator Edward R. Murrow came by to congratulate him and stay in his office to chat for a good hour.[101]

Ed Murrow and Norman had much to say to one another. As Eric Barnouw pointed out, "The sustaining people worked by preference in the tensions of the time." What listeners heard on the news they could expect to hear amplified in their radio dramas. Norman's early contact with Ed Murrow was symbolic, if not important. Working as they both did within the sustaining (self-sponsored) programs of CBS, Murrow and Norman shared an infallible integrity and a view of the world informed by their basic decency.

Mother Goose and, more so, his Christmas show broke the ice. Poetry was in. A following developed, including among English teachers. Norman said that "in many high schools and colleges the program was required listening, and there was a note of evangelical zeal in some of the supporting mail."[102]

Norman's Christmas Day conversation with Murrow, a talk he said lasted an hour but did not otherwise describe, perhaps planted another seed. Or it may have had nothing to do with it, or more with the Italian war relief party in Springfield three years earlier. Something led Norman to weave the tensions of the times into his poetry show. For that, he need not rhyme. He could write free verse.

As Nazi bombs fell over Poland, Norman wrote another original script. He then directed his first war-based show. Entitled "They Fly Through the Air with the Greatest of Ease" (often referred to later as "They Fly Through the Air"), was a free verse poem embodying a mock-heroic narrative. At its core, a lightly veiled Italian bomber (one originally piloted by Il Duce's son, Vittorio Mussolini, over Ethiopia) goes down and crashes, killing all aboard. In time, Norman would become best known for shows with a contemporary accent but when he dug into the events of his day with "They Fly Through the Air" Norman was personally experimenting.[103]

This show, too, had a context. At CBS, he had been preceded by Arch MacLeish. CBS shows based upon current events might be said to have begun with a verse play of his called "The Fall of the City," aired on March 4, 1937. According to Barnouw, after that "a stream of verse plays began arriving at network offices," a flood that "went on for years." Thanks to MacLeish's success, the airwaves were virtually owned by the poets. Primed by the alternate breakthroughs of MacLeish and Jackson, an audience obtained that stood wide open to Norman's original efforts in 1939.[104]

Norman greatly enjoyed MacLeish's company personally. He loved to tell about meeting MacLeish for the first time in Jackson's office, where, delivering a monologue, MacLeish "tilted back in his chair and rocked on its hind legs" until the chair "shot out from under him, and he went over like a circus tumbler." After righting himself, MacLeish simply got back on his chair "and continued from where he had left off" until "an even more elaborate spill—arms flailing, feet flying." Catlike, Norman said in awe, MacLeish righted himself without falling.[105]

MacLeish caught himself on the air as well. After "The Fall of the City," he had gone on to write another engrossing verse play. His doleful verse play, "Air Raid," aired on the on October 26, 1938. Norman was determined to follow MacLeish's lead. He would tell a war story in free verse but in a different tone or mood. Unlike MacLeish, who had aimed to evoke sadness and pity, Norman wanted to arouse anger. He was personally outraged by two events of bombing by air, the infamous German bombing of Guernica, and one by Mussolini's son, Victor, who had bombed Ethiopian cavalrymen in 1935. In particular, Victor's boast, declaring the sight of fatal explosions "beautiful," turned Norman livid. In reaction, he wrote a poem.[106]

It was no easy task. Writing realistically in free verse presents frustrating challenges. During its making, Charles Jackson, the writer next door to him, acted the part of good friend and encouraged him to persevere. It was risky work. Norman thought that his job might be at stake. Jackson, an "unstinting" believer in Norman and what Norman was doing, checked "hourly to see how it was coming, and at intervals went through the program department like a herald, paving notice that an unusual show was on the drawing board."

In the end, Jackson promised Norman success. When the script came out as a book, Norman dedicated "They Fly Through the Air" to Jackson. In third person, Norman candidly acknowledged his mild-mannered friend as a man who "encouraged Norman when he came to CBS because Norman had doubts in his ability to hold onto his job."[107]

Besides Jackson, family appeared. His brother, Al, and wife, Sarita, made their living room his. (Al also loaned ties to his preoccupied brother.) Probably somewhat belligerently and grouchily, Norman ran through his draft of the new poem-play with them. Their feedback got him grounded. He thought that it would work. He later inscribed their copy to "The first audience this play ever had—in the living room at 510—with gratitude for your encouragement, for putting up with my tie-borrowing and your general patience with the *enfant terrible*."[108]

A large question loomed for a time. Would it pass the CBS censors and be broadcast in a country governed by a strictly neutral policy by a network that was emphatically and publicly committed to impartiality and which could not offend Italians or Germans or isolationists? But Arch MacLeish's "Air Raid," cleared and broadcast on October 26, 1938, had been a sensation. Network censors were okay with another "Air Raid" set in an unnamed country, an account of civilian bombing, in 1939.

For its success, as had been the case for his Christmas program, timing of the broadcast was key. The show went over well because people were getting ready to take sides. Norman brought the Italian invasion of Ethiopia home, literally, to bomb civilians in a large city. With sound effects but without music, "They Fly Through the Air" aired February 19, 1939.

A multiplicity of events comprised the context of his show. Italy's dictator, Mussolini, had just played a prominent part at the Munich Pact Conference of September 29–30, 1938. People were afraid of being invaded from then on. They panicked when Orson Welles used CBS news-bulletins in an adaptation of H.G. Wells 1897 *War of the Worlds*, broadcast on October 30, 1938. *Kristallnacht* occurred on November 9, 1938. By January 1, 1939, over 300,000 of Germany's 500,000 Jews had fled that country. In mid–January 1939 Hitler was demanding Danzig from Poland. Norman was credibly imagining the vivid nightmare of a foreign power bombing American civilians in city apartments much like New York City.

"They Fly Through the Air," unlike MacLeish's show, retains shock value to this day. Norman rightly characterized his script as "less abstract" and more "visceral" than MacLeish's. To guarantee its impact, Norman directed the show himself. The bad guys were finally killed by their own machines. Milking revenge in his last lines, Norman cruelly mocked the "supermen," urging them to call upon their leader for help. He depicted enemies unable to terrify gravity as they fell into a corkscrew that ended with an ear-splitting crash. The narrator then scanned the grim scene with greedy eye for blood, oil and bodies broken and burned.[109]

A lot was on the line for Norman. Unlike his 1938 stand-alone hits, "They Fly Through the Air" invited public comparison against a well-known prior hit. His big gamble paid off. The program was a success. The thin veil of one *unidentified* nation attacking another *unidentified* nation was offered, if not taken by the audience, at face value. Tuning in, Americans in their living rooms heard surrogates of a country like theirs in a city like New York. They heard voices in the cockpit and plane. Tense drama, as if overhead, jolted a wide audience awake and drew unstinting praise from reviewers.

For the first time, his mail was not all postmarked from Winthrop. Norman received letters from across the country vindicating his efforts. His show had seemed so real. The show's climax, the enemy bomber's spiraling crash, was itself so realistic that "four people in so many states wrote that they had heard the program in their cars while driving, and each had to pull over by the side of the road."[110]

His script, arguably his first *great* script, had avoided any softened nuances and belied simple sadness or stereotyped sentiment. Norman crossed a threshold. In his words, "people knew how to spell my name and the elevator man at CBS would say good morning." Suddenly famous not as a director but as a writer, Norman could now do anything but create more hours in a day.

In that, Norman continued to honor Lewis's request that he experiment. As might be expected, he adapted classic Victorian poems. But he also produced "an all-Negro program, from the writing of James Weldon Johnson, Sterling Brown and Irwin Russell." He created one show based entirely on Carl Sandburg's "The People, Yes." Sandburg himself sent word that Norman's radio adaptation carried "a touch of miracle."[111]

Spoon River Anthology had brought him to CBS. Now, by an act of what might be called poetic justice Norman brought *Spoon River Anthology* to CBS, along with its author. Norman got the network to sponsor Edgar Lee Masters' trip to New York.

Seventy-year-old Masters, who had been an early law partner of the famous champion of the underdog, Clarence Darrow, was a progressive devoted to representing the poor. For recreation and out of a sense of moral duty, he had fashioned an assembly of poems into *Spoon River Anthology* in 1915. Masters' simple device was to have each short poem by the speaking dead interrupted intermittently by a recurring, rhythmic chorus, "All, all are sleeping on the hill."

Before radio, Norman had seen the potential for the *Anthology*'s narration by actors. What Norman had done well enough on a shoestring at WXQR with Em, he delivered on the air in a grand way with a full cast at CBS. In the studio as the poem was broadcast on May 14, 1939, the old man granted the adapter the ultimate compliment: the production moved its original work's author to tears.[112]

A Book for Mr. McKenzie

Ma and Pa occasionally visited Norman, Em and Al in New York. The usually home-bound couple got a real kick out of seeing the sights, including (above) Central Park (courtesy Diane Corwin Okarski).

Pa was unrelenting. He kept demanding that Norman send a keepsake. Not to him but to his beloved boss, Mr. McKenzie. The demand grated sorely upon Norman. He paid no heed. Pa campaigned hard during the winter of 1938–39. As Norman was riding high, Pa hectored him repeatedly in letters, and, without any doubt, put in reminders each Sunday during their weekly phone calls. His father well knew the problem was the chosen recipient of the solicited favor: a man whom Norman unfortunately hated.[113]

Between Christmas Day's "The Plot to Overthrow Christmas" and "They Fly Through the Air," Norman's fame grew exponentially (or, as he noted, the elevator man at CBS started to greet him by name). Pa wrote the rising star imperatively and specifically. He urged that Norman "send a letter with a Columbia Broadcasting heading just thanking McKenzie for his interest in you & in suggesting things for your benefit & that you will look into it."[114]

Nothing daunted, Pa repeated his request intermittently for over five months. Under this peculiar torture as he rose in prominence, Norman came up with a way to satisfy Pa's demands without violating his principles. When "They Fly Through the Air" came out as a book, Norman sent *Pa* an extra copy, expressly to do whatever he wanted with it. Pa slyly and soon left the book on top of McKenzie's desk early one day, along with a disingenuous note saying, "With Norman Corwin's compliments."

Pa described in a letter to Norman how, to Pa's pleasure and dismay, "McKenzie walks in, puts his arm around my shoulder & said so as all in the vicinity could hear, how enthusiastic he was about getting the book ... then he asked me, did you or Norman leave the book for me. I at first left a note on his desk reading with your compliments & of course I had to stick to it."[115]

Possibly in fear that Norman would disavow the gift, Pa warned Norman to expect Mr. McKenzie's thank you note. Pa need not have worried. Fully enjoying his streak of success, Norman actually did send a nice letter "with a Columbia Broadcasting heading" to McKenzie, thus enabling Pa to walk on clouds.

Speaking of a fellow worker at the greeting card factory, Pa wrote Norman, "Turner called me over & after talking about an order or two said, 'Have you seen McKenzie recently?' I said, 'No.' He then said, 'Don't repeat this but your son Norman sent him a letter.' I said, 'Is that so?' 'Gee, Sam,' Turner said, 'McKenzie showed it to me, boy, that son of yours can sure write.' I said, 'That's nothing new, all of my children can write, whatever the contents of the letter may be its just another letter with him.' Turner: 'Don't let on, Sam, I told you about it.'"

Soon, the two men of this drama met. In the company's elevator, McKenzie took out the letter, showed it to Pa, and "if I would have had a girl who could have taken what he said in shorthand & sent you his very words, you would have been tickled. The good things he said about & for you made me feel glad."[116]

Norman's success within less than a year at CBS made radio heights look easy to climb. Pa became convinced that he, too, could write for the radio. He sent Norman several pages outlining an idea focused on refugees. It would have a happy ending. In Pa's summary: "The democracies have offered new lands for the masses, various scenes to show the different classes of people being happy, by singing, dancing & enjoying life in the new world."

Pa did not explain how dancing or happy scenes of smiling people might be conveyed over the radio. Probably, Norman was expected to work up the script from Pa's outline, crediting his old man for the idea. When Norman did not, possibly with a sigh, Pa ceased to send his son any more ideas for radio shows.[117]

"Seems Radio Is Here to Stay"

After three successive successes, "Mother Goose," "The Plot to Overthrow Christmas," and "They Fly Through the Air," the last two of which were original scripts, Norman took a risk. However, he was cautious and partly insured against blame: the risky show would not be his idea. The CBS top floor's executives had suggested the topic. By memo, they asked all CBS writers to consider something that would encourage radio listening in general. They seemed to be trolling for a show in some way telling how radio had come of age.

What ought to be said about radio listening?

Norman took an indirect path. He came up with a poem. He celebrated here-now collaboration. By apt choice, the perspective was as personal as any Norman had handled to date, or would ever propose in the future. How was it that listeners had anything to listen to? Behind the scenes was Norman's world. He recycled in poetry his first six months on the job, which he spent wandering around people invisible to radio listeners, observing and talking to technicians, engineers, sound effects people, as well as actors, writers, producers, and directors.

Norman knew first-hand that radio reflected a group effort. He revealed the industry's open secret that famous directors owed their successes to many other hands. Radio stars were likewise voices amplified by an invisible army, and supported, if not saved, by cavalry in the form of musicians and sound technicians. This clandestine coordination Norman simply made public. The risk was still there. Even if approved by the brass, how would such a show be received? Would it make waves?

The brass approved instantly and thereafter Norman's unique radio-adulatory show of April 14, 1939, called "Seems Radio Is Here to Stay" proved to be no dud. It was his fourth hit in a row. The show entertained. Norman's careful cadences and felicitous choices of words charmed critics. They declared that Norman was writing another chapter in his growing book of successes. Dinty Doyle, the redoubtable editor of the *New York Journal-American*, specifically labeled the program—really an original poem by Norman used as a script—"the best writing ever to go on the American air."[118]

Other ripples were equally gratifying. According to Leroy Bannerman, the industry itself broke into a buzz while the show was still on the air. Members of the crews in every local CBS station were hearing Norman tell the world what they had all murmured privately. Not having heard their functions celebrated on air before, they loved him for this one more than any earlier effort. Norman recalled mail from station personnel in Boston, Utica, Davenport and San Diego thanking him for making their jobs "seem more important and dignified." His boss, Lewis joked, "Seems Norman's here to stay."

But staying was not going to be easy. Competition was beginning its long race with radio. Shortly after the show's first broadcast, irony was also in the air. With the opening of the New York World's Fair on April 30, a television set went on display. Rival network NBC transmitted the first regular programs to Flushing Meadows and bulky wood-frame small-screen television sets could be bought in New York. The technology that would erase the jobs that Norman celebrated was trickling into selected stores.

(Executives at CBS long remembered the happy uproar. For a CBS anniversary show in 1945, they asked Norman to update this show and to produce it with its original cast—the last hurrah of "Seems Radio Is Here to Stay.")

Beyond "Seems Radio Is Here to Stay," that year's celebration of Norman seemed to have no limits. Praise from CBS executives was one thing, outside expert recognition was another. On Norman's 29th birthday, May 3, 1939, "They Fly Through the Air" won the Ohio State Award. This, the top award in radio then, reflected a consensus of academic, critical and peer judgment that Norman's free verse drama had been the best show broadcast on radio during the previous year. Officially acclaimed best, Norman was suddenly flooded with invitations to speak, to teach, and to write articles.[119]

His success had its costs. In Springfield Norman had been a bachelor whose hardest question was deciding which woman to date. In New York he had been the footloose and carefree man about town working for Fox Studios. He always had books, being the ever-voracious reader. Of 1938 and 1939, he said by contrast, "I had no love life. I saw no movies. I saw no plays. I read no books."

That said, in his heady, exhausting workdays, Norman sought—and found—compensatory or greater satisfaction. Happy in his isolation, talking as if he were serving a sentence, Norman described himself as "the prisoner of CBS—but a willing and happy prisoner."[120]

The prisoner had been careless with his writings. Em asked Norman what he did with his scripts. The answer was that Norman threw them away. He started sending them to Em, who thus became the custodian of the scripts of his brother, the *writer*. Norman's next gift to Em was eminently more practical. As soon as Em and his wife had their first baby (a son), Norman and his brother Al politely vacated and took an apartment themselves at 510 West 110th Street.[121]

At about the time of this move, Norman lost one of his very earliest idols, the writer Heywood Broun. Norman never documented his reaction. In his memoirs, Norman in his seventies fondly recalled Broun and their meeting at Broun's apartment when he was a teen-aged cub reporter.

Norman had also cobbled together his first book, with Hazel Cooley, largely by scrounging through Heywood Broun's columns for zinging quotes.

He retained his link to Broun, the book that Broun had given him on the morning they met, the book that Broun thought had been his best, *Gandle Follows His Nose*. Norman must have sided with Broun in the controversy. The copy that Norman gave to the archives, now stored in Thousand Oaks, California, has a slip of paper in it. The insert shows that, while still living in Springfield in the mid–1930s, just before he departed for New York himself, Norman trimmed a newspaper clipping and placed it into his copy. It was a critic's short but favorable reference to *Gandle Follows His Nose*.[122]

However, it is unreported whether the two men ever met after that first occasion. Not long after Norman had met him, Broun left deadline journalism for freelancing and occasional appearances as a radio emcee. Broun was ill as Norman rose in ranks at CBS. Broun died of tuberculosis—the scourge that had threatened and hospitalized Norman in his twenties—at age 51.

In December 1939, in New York, thousands of mourners paid tribute to Broun, the easy-going, articulate Brooklyn rooter for the underdog. Pathetically, whether Norman joined them probably depended upon the "prisoner's" workload at CBS. His participation in honoring Broun, likely though it was, is not documented either way. On it, his memoir is silent.

Curley and Pursuit of Happiness

Norman, now the famous CBS writer, wanted to think about war, not a caterpillar named Curley, after Hitler's Panzers and bombers invaded Poland and most of Europe was at war in September 1939. He came up against that choice, and had to pick Curley, after Bill Lewis asked him to a meeting in his office. Lewis offered his protégé a coveted sign of network favor. After a year and a half at CBS, Norman was tagged for commercial development.

Bill Lewis had obtained his superiors' approval to give Norman a variety show to script, produce and direct. CBS would fund the costs until the show proved itself adoptable by a rich sponsor. He asked Norman to preside over a completely new series that potentially promised popularity, profit, and permanence. Lewis the great ad man sold Norman on that cockeyed premise, although it was a series without characters, plotline, or any unity beyond general American pride. If the series had any theme, it was to celebrate the country at peace and ostentatiously to ignore overseas war news.

What Norman Rockwell provided in his folksy, charming images on the covers of the *Saturday Evening Post*, Lewis wanted Norman to do each week in sound. Way too optimistically, he foresaw an ever-increasing audience of millions of listeners loyal to Norman. Norman had hits, but nothing Norman had done at CBS suggested that he was the right pick to head a variety show. Lewis, who certainly meant no harm, was nonetheless convincing.

As the series got cooking, the plot thickened. Doug Coulter, who had green lit the new series, wanted a favor in return. More directly, it was a favor to a CBS staffer named Lucille Fletcher. Two years younger than Norman but years senior in CBS service, Fletcher had just married Bernard Herrmann, who conducted the CBS orchestra. Although unpublished, Fletcher wrote stories. Seeking a virtual wedding gift for her and Herrmann, Coulter wanted Norman to adapt for radio a rather goofy story Fletcher had concocted about a dancing caterpillar.[123]

This fat worm threatened to interrupt the linear arc of his rising serious radio career. Norman declined. Coulter badgered. At least read her story, he said, with an insistence unusual for anybody who worked with Norman. Norman, who (after all) worked closely with Fletcher's new husband, could hardly say no to that request. He agreed to read the story.

Thereupon, Norman not only read it, he heard it. In his mind, "My Client Curley" as a radio play would have to be a noisy rumpus. Its loudly beating heart was "Yes, Sir, That's My Baby" on piano played with a heavy hand. The story itself was a bizarre mix of crass self-seekers and fantasy. It was the opposite of Norman's goal of issue-relevant programs.

He reported back and told Coulter frankly, "I'm sorry, but with Hitler destroying everything in sight, I don't feel much like doing a show about a worm, however charming the worm."[124]

Having none of it, Coulter barked back gruffly, "Look, people all over are just as unhappy as you are about Hitler, and if you can write something to help cheer them up, it will do a hell of a lot more good than your brooding—for them *and* you."

Thus overruling Norman's objection and cutting argument short, Coulter demanded that Norman adapt Fletcher's story.[125]

Coulter *was* his boss. Norman started within an hour by making a phone call. He asked Fletcher for permission to modify her story. Helpfully, she immediately gave him *carte blanche*. Norman then gave himself but three days to knock out product. One imagines him writing fast with teeth clenched. A cast was put together to perform Norman's adaptation of Fletcher's story on the network's popular and long-running *Columbia Workshop*.

Even when Norman stooped, he conquered. What Norman spewed out on command was, to his absolute astonishment, acclaimed. Indeed, Norman's very image was transformed. Overnight, he went from being seen as some sort of poetic Ed Murrow to a verbal incarnation of Harpo Marx. In the *World-Telegram*'s phrase, Norman was "a pixie running wild in the CBS production department." Curley was featured on the cover of *Life* magazine. Few images more jarring to Norman can be imagined.[126]

The pixie was immediately seen as promotable. Taking heed of the catapulting caterpillar, Coulter concluded from that splashy hit that Norman had the common touch. Norman was an obvious candidate for commercial viability. Norman's upcoming vehicle, *Pursuit of Happiness*, was more anticipated than ever. CBS listeners would kick back and delight in the bright and cheerful things of life that Norman would bring. He would be "Mr. Happiness."

Norman ought not to have done the series. Blissful contentment was never his forte. He was not the Mozart of merriment, not even a black-haired Arthur Godfrey. But Lewis, to whom he owed so much, had asked him to do it and it had sounded good in general terms. After earning it with a caterpillar, Norman was to have—almost—a free hand over a relatively large budget and the use of CBS's 72-piece orchestra, conducted by Leopold Stokowski. His producer was to be Davidson Taylor, a tall, thin model of moral fiber, who had trained for the Baptist ministry, with whom Norman had always worked well. Equally important, recognizing the value of cohesion, CBS was to assign someone to series continuity. Individual shows only had to be entertaining. What could go wrong?

In a seeming coup, he got Burgess Meredith to emcee. Practically a prodigy, the Broadway star (who later enjoyed both a long film and television career) had been profiled by *The New Yorker* at only thirty, two years earlier. When the designated continuity manager, George Faulkner, fell ill, the star-magnitude brilliant Erik Barnouw stepped up to wrestle with the hydra-headed monster of disconnected skits and vignettes. Coulter authorized Norman to proceed for ten weeks at a time, subject to renewal for another ten weeks, and so forth. It was a natural, built-in stop-loss policy, but would it be needed?[127]

Weekly, the pixie pursued unhappiness as the CBS writer least likely to create comic sketches of domestic contentment. He tried sage small-town editors who spoke wisely, a black comedian who performed with broad humor, and actors who mouthed lines akin to a poke in the ribs with a smile, asking, "Ain't life good here?" Critics' reviews were not good. *Pursuit of Happiness* was panned. *Variety* typified the national take, needling that "the idea behind the show, whatever it was, did not manage to make itself known to the listeners." To carp was not to cure. What *Variety* complained about persisted. Missing cohesion was the series' forever flaw.[128]

A boost came from an unexpected quarter. In late October 1939, Norman unfolded a rare note from his sister, Beulah. She noticed the waves he was making. "Being the only sister of a celebrated brother," Booie humbly began, "has its compensations in many ways. To say that I am thrilled when I hear your name announced over the air is putting it mildly."[129]

His kid sister was not the writer that any of her brothers or Pa were, and she knew it. But she thought that Norman could use her opinion, and he most certainly could. She had been listening to his shows for over a year and now the show in particular that she found that she especially liked was his new series, called *Pursuit of Happiness*. Booie's words of praise were a boost to Norman at a difficult time.

In this context, Booie's spontaneous, short note meant something special to Norman. No one else in the family better reflected the voice of the average American. If Norman could reach Booie, his least academic and most fun-valuing sibling, then he was reaching and pleasing an audience like her. *Pursuit of Happiness* was worth pursuing and pursue it Norman did for as long as he was allowed.

For his part, Coulter kept gamely extending the series ten weeks at a time. Meanwhile, Norman could and did introduce some high-mindedness into the general swirl of this radio smorgasbord. For the first time, Norman tapped frequently and deeply into the vein that he would mine most in the future: the inexhaustible gold of American history. The authoritative historical vignettes Norman coordinated for *Pursuit of Happiness*, such as Raymond Massey's solemn, wise Abraham Lincoln and Carl Van Doren's witty Benjamin Franklin, were infinitely reusable and adaptable. The American historical components of *Pursuit of Happiness* remained the go-to arrows in Norman's quiver thereafter.

In the end, though, the whole experiment failed for want of experimentation. In his memo to Lewis, he scored the series for its "old and conventional and outworn elements." *Pursuit of Happiness* never found a sponsor. CBS could not market a variety show the content of which was, every week, weak. Erratic success was not enough. Big names were not enough. Meredith, "a great actor," was impossible as an emcee. He only announced acts, like a circus barker. With "no by-play, no surprise, no sense of fun in progress, no use made of the running device," Norman complained, there was no cohesion.[130]

Pursuing *ersatz* happiness for the better part of a year, he did none of his favorite things. Norman wrote a long summing up, lamenting in his memo the inherent limitations of a variety show. He made just one personal complaint: that he was "unable to apply his personal talents."[131]

During the series' run, Norman did bring on the air, "some for the first time on radio," fine actors and singers. One of these radio virgins was to become a close friend, Charles Laughton. Nobody admired Laughton's skills, or pushed them to their edge, more than Norman. Laughton was always willing to drop everything to take part in Norman's works. After Laughton starred in Norman's adaptation of Stephen Vincent Benét's "John Brown's Body," Norman got him back from Hollywood to narrate a script that adapted the works of Thomas Wolfe.[132]

Almost the best idea Norman came up with otherwise was to plug Meredith, the emcee, into acting some scenes. But there was one more, another bright general idea he got okayed. Pursued, it might have saved the series. He wanted to capitalize on two factors. No longer bound by the constricting title *Words Without Music* and granted a bigger budget, he wanted music, ever more music.

His show became an early showcase for folk singers, including Woody Guthrie and Huddie William "Lead Belly" Ledbetter. He also tried to line up composers for mini-musical segments. He aired a short operetta by Kurt Weill and Maxwell Anderson. Nothing similar followed. Although promptly commissioned, composer Marc Blitzstein could not hastily hammer out a musical based on an Ernest Hemingway story. His work would likely have resembled his famous rhythmic and percussive 1937 hit, *The Cradle Will Rock*.

In the end, one must credit Norman with wanting to produce a full-length musical. (This suggestion was especially masterful because *Pursuit of Happiness* aired on Sunday afternoons immediately following the weekly New York Philharmonic Orchestra broadcast, the millions of listeners to which would predictably stay tuned.)[133]

The clock ran out. In an internal exit memo, Norman lamented the invariable "Meredith to music to comedy to remote to dramatization" formula as boring rather than boffo. He accused himself of maintaining that in place, pleasing himself no more than his audience.[134]

His audition for a sponsor had lasted thirty weeks, however, and it did pay two dividends. For one thing, Norman always noticed what worked in failures. His historical dramas worked. He would do more of them. And the series also made one truly major contribution to American culture at large. *Pursuit of Happiness* tried in vain afterwards to scale the height it reached on the night of its third show, the night of the "Ballad for Americans."

"Ballad for Americans"

The "Ballad of Uncle Sam" had been the rousing eponymous centerpiece of a short-lived patriotic operetta. The show, developed as a Federal Theatre Project, barely opened in New York in late April before it was closed in June by act of Congress. The show itself lacked cohesion. Norman never saw this historical mishmash of Revolutionary, Civil War and other figures in episodic scenes. However, the song's composer, Earl Robinson, came to Norman. He obviously heard that Norman was open to musical ideas.

Thus, he cadged a few minutes from Norman by asking: would Norman like to hear a song? Music to his ears. A song? The busy CBS director and producer indulged his only known weakness besides poetry. He led Robinson to a studio with a piano, where Robinson played the melody and sang the lyrics.

Impressed, Norman nonetheless requested changes. It was too long. Make it shorter and less folksy, and slap on a new title. When Robinson fully (and quickly) obliged, Norman then went to bat for the inclusion of "Ballad for Americans" in his show. Sure, it would be controversial. Yes, it was a song salvaged from the ruins of the still-smoldering Federal theater. But it was *good*, wasn't it?

He made Lewis and Taylor sit and listen. It *was* good. No deliberation was needed. They approved. The ad man in Lewis actually saw the silver lining behind controversy. He was willing to buy *more* controversy. Wouldn't people talk about *Pursuit of Happiness* if "Ballad for Americans" were to be sung by Paul Robeson?

Norman was happy with the idea and Lewis got Coulter to open up the CBS vault. There were reasons to offer. This song might jump start the network's flagging newest series. Robeson's version of "Ol' Man River" in the 1936 movie *Showboat* had been a huge success. What he could do with this ballad might shoot *Pursuit* into the ethereal stratosphere.

Coulter agreed to pay the premium. With Robeson aboard, Norman's series was on a virtual shake-down cruise to test how many borders he could cross. He took the cast through extensive rehearsals not for a day or two, as usual, but for an entire week.

He wanted his actors and singers to have such command of their otherwise unconnected material that this show—broadcast live, as always—would be fast paced and tight. Perfection prevailed. On November 5, 1939, the song, and the show both ended thrillingly and literally on the last note.

Ironically, too late to go out over the air, the standing ovation of the in-house audience began like a gunshot and did not stop for twenty ecstatic minutes. Robeson took bow after bow. The switchboard lit up and network mail was incredible. Norman's creation, given Lewis's enthusiasm and his network executives' support, had stirred national attention.

(A couple of months later, the network engaged Robeson to reprise the song during CBS's New Year's Eve review. "Ballad for Americans," released as a record, was sung first by Robeson, then by Bing Crosby, and only made larger waves the next year, when it was sung [with modified lyrics] by the Republicans at their national convention, and by the Communists at theirs. The song was part of a successful 1942 Busby Berkeley movie, *Born to Sing*. NBC picked "Ballad for Americans" to be sung by Lawrence Tibbett. The song never lost popularity and was performed at ceremonies during the Bicentennial in 1976.)

However, "Ballad for Americans" stands as the only big national wave that this series made. Norman's variety show crested early, that night. A variety show format simply hindered him from doing his best work. Norman's later memorable shows typically developed a simple plot by unfolding it in short scenes, conveying content via careful lines that were idea-heavy by ordinary radio standards. In each instance—*Pursuit of Happiness* excepted—listeners were overhearing a debate unfold. Discussion was Norman's trademark.[135]

Pursuit of Happiness auditioned in vain for a sponsor. "The Oracle of Philadelphi," which Norman thought might possibly be his last words on network radio, was its swan song. In this show more than most, Norman scintillatingly celebrated sounds. Gale Sondergaard, as the Oracle, spoke lines that reflected Norman's articulation of what poets do. Behind her aural sweep of soundscape lay his lifelong passion for sounds and poetry:

> Come to think of it, our poets would have had a dreary time in a soundproof world. For they never could have gone on about ignorant armies clashing by night, or about the tinntinnabulation of the bells, bells, bells; nor could music, when soft voices die, vibrate in the memory; nor could there have been any meaning at the bar—and what would it have availed friends, Romans and countrymen to lend their ears?[136]

It was with this ringing ending that the curtain came down on *Pursuit of Happiness*. Not bad. Before it ended, Norman had raised for hearing the "tyrant's cannon" and "the roar of despotism." Unpredictably, his allusions to the war in Europe would only grow stronger and more frequent soon afterward and forward.

Norman did not document his reaction outside of his internal CBS memo, but the end of this series may have come as a relief. A world war was going on and Norman hated to be party to distracting attention from the real world. Regular listeners of Norman's shows were not the type to tune in for a hectic series of amusing skits, songs, and *pastiche* drama. They wanted to think, not to escape.

Norman, too, however, wanted to think. He had his agent, Nat Wolff, clear the way and carve out time for him in California, away from radio work and CBS deadlines. He was going to Hollywood.

Hollywood

In the course of *Pursuit of Happiness*, Norman met Charles Laughton. They hit it off perfectly. Admiration was both instantaneous and mutual.

Few more versatile and talented actors ever existed than Laughton and who quickly and permanently stood in utter awe of Norman's talents, which he thought that Hollywood ought to prize, too.

Back in California, Laughton persuaded his producer, Eric Pommer, that Norman was the person who could best adapt a new project, Elmer Rice's play, *Two on an Island*. To Pommer, Laughton's word was literally gold. Laughton told Norman and at Norman's behest, his agent, Nat Wolff, negotiated a lucrative contract.

He was to write, exclusively. For writing scripts at a far less exacting pace than required of him at CBS, he would be paid more. (During the time that Norman rode high in radio, 1937 to 1945, Hollywood was a money mill. The highest-paid man in the United States was Louis B. Mayer, who ran a Hollywood studio, Metro-Goldwyn-Mayer—and no industry was more glittering than making movies.[137])

But Hollywood money, easing up on work and glamour was not what drew Norman West. In fact, the primary lure was personal. After yeoman work in New York for the CBS network, he valued time off with people whose company he enjoyed.[138]

What attracted Norman to RKO Radio Studios in particular was the gifted actor who had become a great friend, and that actor's vivacious wife. Norman was not looking to gather fame and fortune with both hands. First and foremost, he arrived in Hollywood to be a house guest.

To reach the couple, Norman booked passage on the much-ballyhooed cross-country "American Mercury" flight, the fastest way to reach California from New York. Planes were new to Norman. Only once before, during an air show in Springfield, had he circled the city in a biplane as a curious reporter, going nowhere. This time, he flew across the country in style.[139]

In the big propeller-driven DC-3, Norman took off from LaGuardia and flew almost relentlessly to Burbank, only stopping four times to refuel. Norman discovered that he was not a nervous flier (although he preferred trains because on a train he could more easily read, work on scripts and, on a rented set, listen to the radio.[140])

Awaiting Norman at the Burbank Airport was the Bride of Frankenstein and Captain Bligh. The reigning king and queen of the "British colony" of Hollywood, iconic actors Elsa Lanchester and Charles Laughton owned any role they played. Lanchester, the plucky star who once played the bride of Frankenstein, was actually lovely, lively and comedically gifted. Her husband, who had not merely played Captain Bligh but also Inspector Javert, and Henry VIII, was indelibly these figures for millions of fans but was, to Norman, his highly *simpatico* friend.

The couple lived a comfortably domestic lifestyle in a secluded canyon mansion. Their mansion and the guest house that was Norman's for months were nonetheless only twenty minutes from Hollywood studios. Just as when Norman lived in a cottage on the Hudson about as far from CBS headquarters, he lived near his new workplace.

Both Laughton and Norman were relatively new employees of RKO Radio pictures. Laughton had cut his teeth on hits for MGM, but in 1939 took up the titular bell rope-swinging role of *The Hunchback of Notre Dame* and made it his own forever.

Laughton, a kindly, charming, and intelligent man, was a down-to-earth, urbane burgher and the most gracious and gentlest of hosts. Lanchester, equally personable, had a curious mind and active intellect. Their housekeeper was an expert ping pong player, whom Norman tried hard to beat. When the swimming pool was cooler, in the evening, they would swim.

For all that, he soon missed New York. He drove his sporty rented car to the top of a ridge overlooking the Burbank Airport, "then the *only* airport in the area," in order to watch the 5 p.m. plane take off for LaGuardia.[141]

Whenever he surfaced from the guest house to the main house, full of new and unused classical records, he was in a sound man's heaven. Norman was doubly enthralled when he learned to his absolute astonishment that Laughton, a brilliant raconteur, and cultured man, had not listened to the entire musical library he owned. Norman went into action. Ever the evangelist of sound, Norman aimed to change this but his attempt to fan a flame of interest in classical music failed miserably. Laughton listened but lacked the taste. Norman gave up, in favor of conversation.[142]

They were, all three, excellent and receptive conversationalists. Their wide-ranging conversations not only satisfied their intellects but also piqued Norman's curiosity. For example, when Laughton chanced to talk about an old murder case, Norman engaged in a search of his bookshelves for the right volume. Norman found the true confession of Herbert Dougal, a murderer whose account was published in a set of accounts of Victorian and Turn of the Century British criminal cases. What he read led him to pen his scariest script.

"To Tim at Twenty"

Norman not only read at the Laughtons, he also wrote. "To Tim at Twenty" had no reason to exist. Norman wrote it anyway. In Hollywood, residing in the Laughton guest house, he scripted a radio play starring his host and hostess.

"To Tim at Twenty" was written as a vehicle for the Laughtons. Norman, one of the best judges of radio talent going, used his ears (one imagines him closing his eyes) to confirm his sense of the couple's range. Norman thus discovered in this pair of film stars versatile and nuanced voices that could convey emotion without any visual cues at all.

The project itself was a clear signal that Norman missed radio. He certainly thought that he might. He had his agent have CBS keep his seat warm in New York. Although Norman's agent had obtained from the studio awesome monetary concessions and great future options for him despite an escape term—in Hollywood, Norman made four times what CBS paid him—Norman had insisted on a term that he could walk away any time after thirteen weeks. Shrewdly, by contract rather than by the grace of his old editor in Springfield, he had a job waiting for him, if he chose. The tall building on West 52nd Street was always his, only a few weeks away.

He was proving to himself that radio was his game. *Pursuit of Happiness* had swung and missed, failing to attract a sponsor. His stuff was not commercially profitable. Norman thus doubted his talent in radio, arranged for a trial separation, and only ended up proving that radio was his true love. Thus, "To Tim at Twenty" was no casual recreation and it was not merely a gift to kind hosts. "To Tim at Twenty" was going to refresh his name and keep his work on the air, too.

What Norman wrote was a stark monologue interrupted by several short scenes. As Norman was aware, few actors can do anything but bore with an extended monologue. It is one of the greatest challenges any actor can face, and yet that is exactly what he thought was needed. It would draw the best out of Charles Laughton.

He was confident that Laughton would carry off a show in which anybody else would fail. Norman wrote the longest part he ever wrote for one actor. Having lived with him for months, he knew Laughton well.

Next, Norman had to hit CBS up for a favor. When Norman begged Lewis to broadcast the 15-minute play, Norman was a screenwriter with only a future contingent possible reconnection. He sold the salesman, though.

What about *Forecast*?

Before he left New York, Norman had been helpful in the creation of *Forecast*. A quirky series little remembered today, *Forecast* was the CBS showcase for pilot shows by any writer, on staff or independent freelancers. The audition, if it appealed to an audience and a sponsor, might go further. *Forecast* was accordingly a "hodgepodge," as Norman put it. *Forecast's* arguably general openness to anything might provide a slot, might it not?

Although "To Tim at Twenty" was technically ineligible, not being a pilot of a series, Lewis nonetheless approved it for *Forecast*. That Norman's idea was also controversial, pro–British in a politically neutral radio industry, did not matter either. Lewis gave his favorite writer the high sign.

Moreover, Norman could not leave things for other hands to fumble. He got Lewis's agreement that he could direct the show and cast the Laughtons. On August 19, 1940, Norman took the reins of *Forecast* for an episode and directed "To Tim at Twenty." It worked. What might have been topical and soon outdated is not outdated even today. "To Tim at Twenty" was selected to be one of the Centennial collection's CDs. In the end, Norman collaborated with legends in one of radio's enduring masterpieces.[143]

True, the script might never have compelled attention if delivered by other actors, but Norman was responsible for that as well. The script's intensity, its unusual structure and its core of Aristotelian unities overall made it one of Norman's best shows, possibly the most immediate of them all in emotional impact.

"To Tim at Twenty" illuminates Norman's life. This memorable original play came to Norman exactly during his brief time away from radio. It was, in effect, a love letter to his jealous mistress, Lady Radio, penned while living with movie friends—whom he was simultaneously inspired to turn into radio stars. "To Tim at Twenty," a solemn cautionary sermon from overseas with an unmistakably British accent, was at bottom the daydream of a network radio genius who missed his intended profession when trying on the role of a restless Hollywood writer.

PART THREE

Norman to Age Forty
(1940–1950)

Requiem for Alfred Eisner

Hollywood was where they made pictures. Norman was a sound man. Through his agent's good work, by his contract Norman had a right to return to CBS. He exercised his right of return after the minimum time he had pledged to his studio, which was thirteen weeks.[1]

CBS welcomed their writer, producer and director back warmly. Despite his return to the air with "To Tim at Twenty," Norman still had to find his old footing. He familiarized himself with what was going on, being a gregarious gadabout and informal advisor for writers, techs, and directors, but as a writer, he lay fallow for a bit. He certainly did not reach his best level of writing immediately. A script for *Cavalcade of America* (essentially the History Channel of its time) was okayed for broadcast, but that was all.[2]

The network's executives could congratulate themselves on ducking one bullet. They had kept Norman from being snatched up by its rapacious competitors. NBC was not going to get him now. Even so, what to do next with their protected asset took them a few months of pondering. As Norman waited, evading depression and doldrums with other people's projects and writing scripts that nobody yet wanted, enter Alfred Eisner.

Eisner was a young man who left Hollywood for CBS in New York to work with Norman shortly after Norman returned to CBS. A new, college-educated screenwriter in Hollywood, Eisner exemplified the coming generation's feelings for Norman and for the potential of radio. To these bright folks, Norman was a hero and the spoken arts were being reborn on radio.

Unlike Norman's admiring public in general, however, Eisner had a relative—one of his several adoring sisters—who went to bat for him. This doughty woman, already in New York, made moves to pave the way for her kid brother. She wanted him to realize his dream and to work alongside his idol, Norman, before he died.

Eisner was dying and did not know it. Eisner, 24 as Norman just turned 30, was, like Norman, a self-consciously talented, outspoken maverick. Similar to Norman, Eisner had family to whom he was close, namely, his parents and four adoring older sisters. The two men also possessed marked differences. Eisner's family was rich, Norman's was lower middle class. Norman's education ceased with his senior year at Winthrop High School while Eisner attended Harvard on the Greenleaf Scholarship.

Compared to Norman, who found no great fun rooming with his cousin, Fred, at the Mohawk Chambers in Greenfield, Eisner got along famously with *his* roommate at Harvard, Leonard Bernstein. Eisner helped Leonard jam a piano into their dormitory. Like Norman, Eisner grew to become a dedicated anti–Fascist and a serious writer. At Eliot House, politically attuned Eisner triggered his roommate's activism. Leonard recalled their "all-night bull sessions; we marched, we demonstrated; I played the piano for strikers, for Spain, for blacks, for one cause after another."[3]

In their off hours, both Norman and Eisner loved classical music and jazz, while each man, when employed on their creative projects, was fully capable of concentrated work stints—as Eisner sonorously declared—stepping away from "all matters earthly and living the life of a hermit, yea, a veritable anchorite." Such monastic living, typical of Norman in 1939 and 1940, was only intermittently true of Eisner. Sandwiched between riotous escapades with wine and women, Eisner would withdraw suddenly and pump out a caffeinated 85-page movie treatment in "four days and nights."

Eisner lived in a Marathon Street apartment in Los Angeles that was, as he put it, "like a monastery"—except that he did not make it back to his cell every night. During the summer of 1940, Eisner lived as if each day were to be his last, devouring art and experiences, squandering money, chasing women, closely reading Hemingway's latest novel, and writing his own novel. Eisner's counterpart of Norman's patient brother Em was Leonard. Blessed by matinee idol good looks, Eisner wrote of having laid siege to a "would-be actress" with a glass eye who had, he claimed, "the most luscious body I ever rubbed against." Soon afterward, his heart throb was a rabbi's daughter. He reported to Leonard that she cooked as well as she made him happy in bed, "a duality of accomplishment not nearly as unimportant as it sounds."[4]

Just after Eisner had signed on as a junior writer at MGM for $ 75 per week, Leonard began studying composing at Curtis in Philadelphia. Eisner berated Leonard for not making a priority of writing him more often. By contrast, very happily squirreled away up at Charles Laughton's remote home while working for RKO Radio Pictures, Norman the script writer had no night life and asked nobody for more letters.[5]

Eisner's oldest sister, Eve, had contacted Norman. The CBS switchboard put her through. Although Eve was a complete stranger to him, Norman set time aside when she asked.

"The distress in her voice was so genuine that I could not refuse," Norman said in a bittersweet recollection for his unpublished autobiography.[6]

When they met up in his office at CBS, he saw that she had been crying. Eve brought a file. Before offering it to Norman, Eve shared the secret that distressed her so: her brother was dying but he did not know it. Her brash-voiced, tough-sounding brother, Eisner, had an inoperable brain tumor and only months to live. The family had kept it from him.[7]

"He told me a year ago that the thing he wished for above all was to work with you," Eve said. Her plan she delivered in the form of a series of instructions, "Call him up. Tell him you want him to take a job under you here, at $ 100 a week. I'm sure he'll accept. You pay him, and I'll reimburse you."[8]

Eve must have been a charismatic type. Norman, who customarily responded poorly to instructions, obediently looked through the file she handed him. It included a letter of recommendation from Leonard, with whom Norman had already worked at CBS, and some dark medical records. The documents, her woeful face, and his heart brought him to phone his immediate boss, Davidson Taylor.

When Taylor had no objection to such a humane fraud, Norman phoned Eisner. Over long-distance static Norman asked Eisner to come to New York as his personal assistant. Besides high pay, Norman baited the hook with creative opportunities. Norman promised to assign Eisner scripts to work on, and other duties, including reviewing and criticizing Norman's own radio scripts. Although ready for months to stop writing lines for Wallace Beery movies that would never be made, Eisner hesitated. He questioned Norman:

"Is it permanent?"

The unexpected question, which Norman carried in his head for decades, had an unintentionally sharp ironic edge.

Norman managed to duck answering by parrying, "Don't worry about that. We'll give you a better deal in every way than the one at Metro."[9]

As soon as he hung up—Norman urged Eisner to get the studio to waive notice and come to New York immediately—Eisner doubtless passed the incredible news on to Leonard. A few days after Eisner's death, Leonard wrote Norman gratefully that Eisner had felt about to reach the top, "with the world before him, wonderful jobs in his hands."[10]

The two young men brought up on the East Coast never seem to have met in Hollywood. They never drank together or enjoyed an extended conversation. Because of his sister, following Norman, Eisner took the train back to New York. Hollywood had disillusioned him, too. He lamented to Leonard that his movie studio had a "viselike grip around my economic balls." Done forever with Wallace Beery scenes, having gotten the call and the offer of a lifetime, to be Norman's personal assistant, he accepted with excitement.[11]

In New York by early November, Eisner was given an office and access to Norman's works in progress. When they met, he thanked Norman profusely and pledged his eternal indebtedness for the opportunity before telling his new boss blithely and specifically that he thought his latest script was "quite dull."[12]

Eisner's insouciance and verve likely threw Norman off. He left Eisner to himself for a lot of the three weeks that they were together.

"I thought there would be plenty of time," Norman said by way of excuse. The inverse truth was obvious: Norman had no time to hold hands with such an earnest critic. Similarly, he put off scheduling photos to stand beside and memorialize Eisner as a "CBS writer" until it was too late. Before Thanksgiving, the CBS photographer returned to Norman's office with news that Eisner was *en route* to the hospital.

"I did too little for the boy," Norman said in his memoirs. He called his good turn "the hoax" and spoke of feeling like "a cheat"—but at the time Norman was preoccupied, working more on Hollywood projects than on radio shows. Norman saw how Eisner, sick but walking on air, "busied himself in discussions, plans and writing. He was happy, and certain that the blood which occasionally stained the handkerchief he put to his mouth, was from varicose veins in his chest—a fiction told him by his doctors."[13]

Feeling very badly about promises he had not kept to his now-hospitalized assistant, Norman contacted *Variety* and *The New York Post*. After obtaining pledges of secrecy, he explained Eisner's situation. Reporters on both publications placed Alfred Eisner's name among other gossip items. The longest plug was from Leonard Carlton, the radio editor of the *Post*, who cooked up the following with Norman's coaching:

> Production executives at Columbia are more than a little interested in Alfred Eisner, who has been brought in from Hollywood to work on radio dramatic scripts. His first effort, *A Child Is Born*, is pronounced first-rate radio playwrighting and has been scheduled for early production.[14]

Tipped off that time was short as those presses were running, Norman went to Memorial Hospital on December 8, Eisner's birthday. He never forgot receiving attention and admiration that he did not feel he had earned.

"[H]is family and friends had gathered in his room," Norman recalled. "I was greeted like a potentate—here was the man who was going to catalyze the greatness in Eisner. The people made a path for me as I entered the room, and after a moment discreetly left so that I could be alone with my protégé."[15]

While he and Eisner were together privately, his bedridden assistant led the conversation. Eisner was on fire to get back to work. He conveyed his impatience and complained that he was supposed to be cured already. Instead, he told Norman, now the doctors told him "another month! I hate to lose time."

Saying that CBS was confident in him, wishing Eisner a happy birthday and advising him not to worry, Norman said that he was off to California. He had permission for a month off from CBS, from mid–December through mid–January. He would see Eisner when he got back. When they shook goodbye, Norman noticed how thin Eisner's hand was. Norman never said that he had a flashback back to when he himself had been but 23, spitting blood and hospitalized, but it is difficult to imagine he gave no thought to the parallels.

Once in California, he felt sorry in waves for Eisner and his family and regret over his neglect of Eisner. He described in his memoir that "the pretense of making myself fit the picture of princely benefactor weighed on me as hypocrisy, and I could not filter out a sense of guilt from my sorrow for him and his loving family."[16]

Norman was in California on January 4 when he got the news. It was not unexpected that Eisner died. Norman nonetheless mourned Eisner and continued to visualize this young man with whom he had had so little contact. On January 16, 1941, perplexed, he wrote glumly about Eisner to his CBS boss Taylor, "I find his memory lingering long after I thought I would have put it by."[17]

He first confessed. He quantified his neglect, writing, "I saw him only once after we (his boss, Taylor, and he) visited him together, and phoned him only twice." Norman then acted like a man given a second chance at life. He made an immediate and urgent plea that CBS give him something to do.[18]

"I hope, by Jesus and by lesser saints, to do some decent work in my lifetime," Norman, reaching for Whitman-like or Sandburg-sounding words and phrases at the beginning. As if the robust invocation of saints could produce a miracle in Manhattan, Norman suggested that he would write a script a week for half a year. This was a reckless gamble. Norman foresaw the danger and stared it down:

"Maybe it would be my swan song in radio, I dunno. Maybe I would rumble like a mountain in labor, and bring forth a mouse of rating. But I would just like to see," Norman told Taylor.

Norman's non-salesmanship of an impossibly one-sided deal prevailed. CBS endowed Norman with a series to be titled *26 by Corwin*.

Nobody had ever done before what Norman promised, even Norman would not quite do it (one show of his twenty-five was repeated). But, unlike *Pursuit of Happiness*, this series was his. The series would embody all of the coherence he could give it. He would be the singular author of every line of every one of the shows of a series that would begin broadcasting weekly starting May 4, 1941.

Because, in some mysterious way, Eisner seems to have led Norman to resolve to "do some decent work" in his lifetime—a sharp-pointed word, "lifetime"—the last word belongs to brother Eisner, Eisner the poet, the script writer who was once upon a time a radio writer at CBS with his idol, Norman Corwin. Once, when a sad mood struck him in his wild California days, he wrote a poem. The fragment he sent to his best friend, Leonard, reflected a dark but not a hopeless vision. In mournful, rich, bluesy words, Eisner expressed a glimmering moment in the form of a question:

> Baby, look down dat lonesome road: do you see the shining city, the purple hill?

One hopes that the young man who inspired Norman could answer the question by saying yes, that he saw it. Straining to see a future corresponded with Norman's primary motif. Such a vision informed all of his masterpieces. When successful, *26 by Corwin* brought its audience closer by one hour to the shining city atop the purple hill.[19]

26 by Corwin

Beginning this series, 30-year-old Norman had no scripts in reserve. The first installment of his planned six-month weekly marathon, "Radio Primer" (broadcast May 4, 1941, the day after he turned 31), was a rhyming poem. Much along lines of "Seems Radio Is Here to Stay," it went over well but it did not foreshadow a great and memorable or even a particularly novel series. "Radio Primer" only echoed a prior hit.

Intending original scripts, Norman made a bold move. For his art's sake, he needed isolation. Once before, in 1938–39, Norman had had no life outside work as one of the new directors of the *Columbia Workshop*. Solitude had worked well for him then. He felt even less resilient now, in his thirties. Getting out of the city would be good for his health. Distance from temptations to burn his candle at both ends would buffer his ever-precarious immune system.

As in all previous stages of his life, in New York Norman had been surrounded by circles of friends. This social life he now put on hold. Lunches, parties, theater, concerts, everything was dumped. Although his place was some twenty minutes outside the city, those twenty minutes insured his complete privacy. During the six months that the series ran, Norman lived in a cell with a waterfront. It seemed to him like a rural mental hospital. He called it "the Booby Thatch."[20]

"I lived a monastic life. I took a place up at Sneden's Landing, a little thatched cottage, and I worked there. I just worked, ate, slept, worked," Norman said. His seclusion was not total, however. Norman swore no vow of silence. He made unlimited calls, linked to producers, composers, technicians, and CBS higher-ups by a cottage phone that he kept in constant use. A secretary also breezed by daily to exchange paperwork.[21]

Then and there, in a cottage fronting the Hudson, surrounded by greenery, he began to produce his mature work. Just outside of the city, he quickly and regularly created sound-rich dramatic stories that lived and breathed. This series featured classic episodes that continue to hold listeners by their ears via recordings.

Meanwhile, beyond the cottage, radio ownership swelled. News-hungry Americans rushed their stores to buy more radios in 1941 than they had in any previous twelve months—or ever would again—13 million sets. It was a heady time for anybody on the air—especially foreign correspondents. Norman's good friend, Edward R. Murrow, along with William R. Shirer, Walter Cronkite, and many others in became voices familiar to most every American. They reported dreadful news from European, where countries fell like dominoes before Hitler's armies.[22]

Norman's goal was not heroic stories about war. He was not four years old reciting the poem about the French messenger boy. In the broadest sense of the word, he wanted to entertain. The storyteller who used to unfold his stories face-to-face with urchins in East Boston now considered which stories to spin between meals shared with an amusing mouse.

"The Sneden's Landing cottage was a joy," Norman wrote in his unfinished memoir. He took pleasure in its rusticity. Nothing irritated him. In the country, everything was novel. Accommodations that delighted him included "a mouse that appeared every evening at dinnertime and sat on a bookshelf watching me dine." Norman, who left the mouse a bit of cheese, was tickled to watch how it "would make much of manipulating" his gift, but never eat it in his presence.[23]

Given a longer association, the mouse may have inspired a radio version of Mickey Mouse, which Walt Disney claimed had been inspired by an actual Kansas City office mouse. Norman's rodent had enemies, however, who were not amused. The housekeeper was on the prowl. Unknown to Norman, she set a trap. The mouse thereafter enjoyed only a moment of posthumous fame. When caught and killed, Norman loyally buried it "with honors ordinarily reserved for a cat."[24]

With or without a fastidious mouse, in his idyllic setting Norman had no control over his weekly deadline. And, despite his precautions and isolation, neither was he in control of his health. By starting with no scripts in reserve, he played with fire, and as always, his body rebelled. His doctors grew concerned over his reports of indigestion. They suggested that he relax. He relaxed in his own way—by writing.

Lewis knew that he was witnessing something unique. He told Bannerman ebulliently and emphatically later that "only Corwin" could produce thirty-minute show every week. In fact, Norman could not. As Norman's doctors feared, his health broke. After three months, confined to his cottage with the *grippe* for several days, propped up pillows, sipping tea, Norman stayed up all hours and fought exhaustion to write.

Literally flat on his back, Norman made himself try his hand at radio fantasy. During his sickest, weakest week, he wrote an imaginative fable. He tapped into the vein of Curley and it worked. Virtually a poem brought to life, "The Odyssey of Runyon Jones," was well-received, well-reviewed. and well-remembered. It was, in fact, gossamer and sounds, more odyssey than Runyon Jones but its aurally pleasing atmosphere overcame any deficit in character development. (Norman turned it into a musical thirty years later.)[25]

He adapted a resonating trilogy of Bible stories—"Samson," "Esther" and "Job"—as well as the series' finale, which Norman himself narrated, "Psalm for a Dark Year." He wrote something light for Elsa Lanchester, whom he cast as Mary in "Mary and the Fairy" and science fiction, "Descent of the Gods," which became the series' single repeated show. From the works of Thomas Wolfe, he crafted an audio anthology. (It was more than good. In the *Columbia Presents Corwin* series, he did the same for Sandburg, Whitman and again for Wolfe. Given an author whose works he admired, or the Bible, he always excelled.)

Norman did not forget Ann Rutledge, Abraham Lincoln's first love, about whom he had written a script in October 1940. She is someone about whom almost nothing is actually known. The fog surrounding her only intrigued an imaginative writer who never ceased to carry about an agenda of sounds, poetry, and stories, in that order.

Sound effects, classical music, and poems were pleasures. His characters are shadowy, Rorschach-like, hidden within fragmentary lines and universal ambiguities. One would never listen to Norman's program about Ann Rutledge to find out the facts of her biography, but to live for a time in her aural world, hearing the dialect, the accents, the sounds of the backwoods, and to gain a sense of its overall atmosphere. In delivering that, nobody exceeded Norman. One was immersed in Ann's place and time as in a dream, not as in a history book.

Many other shows were not his best. Norman quickly and vocally admitted errors during this hectic season and claimed full responsibility for them. Nobody ever complained that Norman took credit that belonged to them or claimed that he blamed them for his failures. Norman won his co-workers' admiration and affection for the reverse habit—and pity from show business cut-throats of New York and Hollywood who did not know him, who thought he was a fool to criticize himself.

Given its high points, the series was so popular that Norman had reason to back away from self-criticism. Meanwhile, in Winthrop, in 1941, Pa was jobless. As Pa turned 64, the McKenzie Printing Company went bust and closed its doors. Paper shortages and shipping obstacles, with unpredictable markets ahead, at last proved to be beyond McKenzie's managerial skill.

Pa and Ma nonetheless had their house in Winthrop which, with tenants, was revenue-producing. Pa had savings and Social Security. Along with help from Norman and their other children, Ma and Pa were all right. For reasons of pride, Pa never officially retired. He claimed vaguely to be "in business on his own" after 1941.

Mostly, Pa volunteered his time. He was active at the Temple and in his lodge. But he also started and kept scrapbooks for each of his children. As grandchildren came along, he made scrapbooks for each of them, too. Norman was not the only Corwin busy making books that posterity would read and treasure. The difference between father and son was only of scale and skill. Pa's words, like the greeting cards he had run off for decades, were borrowed.[26]

Pa's scrapbooks, which he kept in secret for a long time, resembled his son's first book, the anthology of quotations that Norman worked on in Hazel's parlor. At his desk in Winthrop, scissors in hand, Pa cut quotations from the newspaper ("an education in themselves," Pa said of quotations), not excluding the comic section. He took up anything inspirational or humorous or potentially interesting to his respective intended recipients. Made one at a time by hand, the scrapbooks were slow labors of love. They were Pa's personalized greeting cards to his children and their progeny.[27]

Simultaneously tracking his son's path in print, Pa could hardly keep up. Published articles, photos and references to Norman formed a constant stream in print. Not only did Pa keep track in his own reading, others brought or sent him articles and pictures they clipped out about Norman. He ultimately made eleven scrapbooks for Norman.[28]

Norman was then in his prime in a country tightly linked by radio. His series for CBS, his best yet, was inarguably Norman's own product. He wrote all of the *26 by Corwin* shows. Many were good, some great and a couple were absolutely off-the-chart sensational. *Without* touching current events as his topic, he had made a splash. In short, the subject of resultant widespread, favorable attention, Norman had not expected to be fired—but fired he was, as too good, too big for CBS.

More specifically, CBS did not renew his contract. Doug Coulter, who had replaced Bill Lewis as the CBS vice president in charge of programing, called Norman to his office on November 10, the day after his series ended. Coulter told him, "You're so big in the business now that we can't just offer you any old show to direct. There's nothing in the house right now to hold you here."[29]

Norman was mute. Suddenly as jobless as his father, let go by an employer to whom he had been dedicated at risk of his health, successful but walking wounded, he gave in to a fatigue-driven numbness. He must have expected a congratulatory talk and hints of a new contract at a higher salary, but he experienced (he said) only fatigue when he got Coulter's courteous kiss off. He listened, nodded, wished Coulter well and then simply rose and left his office. Credibly, Norman said that he was just "too tired" to care very much.

Washington

Throughout Norman's life, bad luck frequently turned out not only to be good luck in disguise but even life changing good. When Norman was hospitalized for a long year, he practiced and made progress as a speaker. He failed as a novelist but that steered him to focus on other people's poetry. At the *Herald-Tribune*, a superficially great career move proved illusory and convinced him to exit journalism as soon as possible. When WLW let him go, he knew that he only missed personal misery. Such past experiences suggested that the loss of his CBS job would somehow result in something good.

Something did, something good. The same man who hired and helped him at CBS, Bill Lewis, sandy-haired, burly, bass voiced and energetic as ever—and once an ad man, always an ad man—had left CBS to captain the radio wing of the Office of Facts and Figures in Washington.[30]

Lewis had a project just then because his boss, Arch MacLeish, had spotted the 150th anniversary of the Bill of Rights coming up. It fell midway between the holidays, on December 15, 1941. MacLeish had given Lewis a free hand to come up with an appropriate radio program.

(MacLeish was a powerhouse. Norman remembered how he landed on his feet when falling from a chair in Jackson's office back at CBS. But MacLeish now not only headed OFF, he was also a personal friend of President Roosevelt's—*and* FDR had named him the Librarian of Congress.)[31]

When MacLeish assigned Lewis to sell the Bill of Rights, Lewis glowed with ideas. A radio special was justified—on all of the networks on prime time on December 15. Blockbuster was on nobody's mind but Lewis's at first. The networks balked. Lewis knew the key. What if the President would speak? He asked. Well, that would be different, they said.

Lewis promptly got MacLeish to get the President's commitment to speak. (FDR would only speak if MacLeish wrote the speech himself, but MacLeish agreed to do so.) With the President aboard, Lewis got the networks' attention, but each one presented the same problem. None of them wanted to broadcast a public service program while any of the others captured audience share with a comedy or a drama. Again, Lewis knew the key. It was an "all or none" broadcast. All networks to donate one hour at 10 p.m., December 15, or there was no deal, and word would leak out who to blame, not Bill Lewis. Accordingly, just as the popular Lux Theatre concluded on CBS, every regular program in the country would be pre-empted for the first dramatic program ever broadcast over all four networks.[32]

With the President of the United States a speaking member of his team, in a broadcast green lit by every network, and ready to set about borrowing top stars from Hollywood for free, Lewis returned to New York for his wife's birthday party, a small gathering that included Norman. Upon hearing the amazing news that CBS had let Norman go, he said mysteriously that he might have something to offer Norman, he would call him.

After checking with MacLeish back in Washington and finding his boss, who knew and liked Norman, only too happy to have him write and direct the show, Lewis called Norman. He had what he thought was a dream project. Norman had always been CBS's go-to adapter of historical events and historical figures. Norman balked. He did not recognize good luck when he heard it.

It was not a series. After *26 by Corwin*, *One by Corwin* sounded puny. Moreover, the ratification anniversary of a legal document sounded like a dud waiting to fizzle. Mashing people shuffling papers 150 years ago into a drama did not sound practical.

Norman firmly resisted. He was so tired. What he needed was a break. In the little cottage by the Hudson, he had put his life on hold. All of his doctors advised rest. He wrote in his autobiography, as if still convinced, "What I should've done when that series ended, was to go off to some Caribbean island and rest or, contemplate my navel in the desert, or something like that."[33]

As usual, Lewis kept talking. The resources of the Library of Congress would be at Norman's disposal. It was an intellectual adventure which he would enjoy more than an ocean cruise. He would be a nominally paid Federal employee but, hey, he could stay at a five-star hotel in Washington, room service, the works. Ditto in L.A. Trains, expresses, first class. Just like a vacation, only at no charge to him, and good for his mind.

When Norman still declined, Lewis asked Norman to meet him in Washington, please. As Lewis the *schmoozer* no doubt hoped, the capital's ambience would work its own magic. The iterated idea of the country's grandest library at his fingertips and President Roosevelt and all four networks and Hollywood stars, and his patriotic duty, eventually galvanized Norman. Maybe the Librarian of Congress would let him stay after hours, with the whole place to himself. What do you say to that? Norman finally said yes after all, perhaps he could do justice to the Bill of Rights.

Norman did not report if he agreed with a smile or with a sigh. He immediately and to his surprise put himself to dramatizing the story of the Bill of Rights. Both Lewis and Norman charged ahead with gusto.[34]

While Norman hit the books hard, Lewis launched himself to cast a show yet to be written. Before Lewis stepped back, he had promises of a stellar cast for free, including Jimmy Stewart, Edward G. Robinson, Walter Brennan, and others. Many had worked with Norman and, in most cases, his name was enough to draw them into the project.

Finally, the CBS radio studio in Los Angeles was reserved. It was Norman's exclusively for a week of rehearsals and for the broadcast itself on December 15. (Los Angeles was the only logical radio studio for broadcast because shows were broadcast live and so many of the show's stars were Hollywood actors engaged in shooting movies.)

"We Hold These Truths" followed, as otherwise described in the first chapter of this book. After its broadcast, Norman was never hotter. His producers received 22,000 letters. Publishers hounded Norman to turn out a book of the best of his *26 by Corwin* scripts. He did so. Norman wrote a "Foreword to the Foreword" at the beginning of *Thirteen by Corwin*, which came out two months after Pearl Harbor. It was a bold and open love letter to his former network.

"Now that I am no longer with CBS," he said, thus making certain that his millions of fans knew that CBS had shown him the door, "I am able to say what I think of that System. To begin with, Columbia is a nice place in which to work."[35]

His paean began with teakwood and cuspidors, indirect lighting and air conditioning on "the famed 18th floor at 485 Madison Avenue," which he loved as "the noisiest program department in the world" but he soon focused entirely on the abstract elements of creativity.

"The attractiveness of CBS to the craftsman lies in the attitude of its men and the unwritten policies of the organization," Norman said, any vocabulary reflecting the network's own gender bias. Norman said that he never encountered discouragement away from innovation and experimentation. At CBS, he vouched that instead of the "safe and accepted and sure-fire forms of art and entertainment" he found "an eagerness to tackle the untried; to explore; to promote the good and serviceable and courageous" that led to Irving Reis, Orson Welles, Edward R. Murrow, William Shirer, and plays and poetry in radio adaptations of William Shakespeare and Archibald MacLeish. Without crediting himself, or mentioning Paul Robeson directly, Norman elected to salute CBS itself for having "found 'Ballad for Americans' in an ashcan and transformed it overnight into a quasi-national anthem." Norman concluded that he would always be grateful to CBS for "its largesse, its free spirit, its boldness, its enterprise, its faith in its own men."[36]

Executives got the message. Even if success were actually generated by Norman or his cast, he would credit the network. Powerful insiders, whose names glowed for a few minutes of fame in the Foreword of Norman's best-seller, understood. Norman was wooing them. They responded. Behind closed doors, a vague offer shaped up into a lucrative inked deal.

However, Norman's return to CBS was encumbered. He had to do anything that the mobilized Federal government needed. Thus, his return to CBS began with a bump in the road, or thirteen bumps. He was to direct a series of thirteen programs (six of which he would script). Broadcast live on all stations of all networks for months at the beginning of 1942, it was the series not only least relevant today but also the one of which Norman was himself least proud. It was called *This Is War!*

This Is War!

Norman had an entire country as his audience. *This Is War!* was unique. The chance that was Norman's would never be anyone else's again: to address everyone, coast to coast, regularly each week at the same time for three months. During thirteen consecutive Saturday nights in early 1942, for one half-hour there was one program on all radio stations.

Enabled at last to realize an old idea, he roamed all around for real sounds. By means of verbal close-ups or voices overheard at a distance, explosions, machinery, silence, mournful music, Norman jolted listeners into a consciousness-in-common that *this is what is happening now.* Everything was done with sound, live, the sole images being those in the minds of his listeners. Duty, duty, duty was the theme.

As it happened, here-now sounds and strident calls to serve were not enough. The artistic creativity Norman needed to thrive was absent. Although it was from this series that *Life* magazine deemed Norman "radio's top dramatic genius" Norman's self-judgment was different. The propagandistic series in no way topped "We Hold These Truths." Comparing, Norman discounted his *This Is War!* shows in an understatement, saying, "I do not consider them among my better things."[37]

As doomed *Pursuit of Happiness*, this pudding lacked theme. It had no characters. His earliest shows were jaggedly joined pep talks. Norman sought to acknowledge common feelings and fears while generally (vaguely) encouraging united action. With that somewhat contradictory agenda, the series was tricky to write. A listener to the first episode of *This Is War!* could pick up a dissonance between two voices—voices that were Arch MacLeish's and Norman's, respectively. *This Is War!* began and remained a schizophrenic production.

First, MacLeish read a brief letter from President Roosevelt. The President recommended a highly rhetorical, inspirationally Churchillian program to carry "a fuller comprehension of the nature of the war in which we are engaged and of the nature of the labor we must undertake, the sacrifices we must undergo, and the dangers we must endure to win it."

Norman's segment followed suit. His doleful, dead-serious narrator, Lieutenant Robert Montgomery, United States Navy, baldly announced a new way to spend a half-hour on Saturday nights. "What we say tonight has to do with blood and bone and with anger," Norman had Montgomery say, "and also with a big job in the making. Laughter can wait. Soft music can have the evening off. No one is invited to sit down and take it easy. Later, later. There's a war on."

In a hodgepodge of propaganda next, Montgomery asked mockingly if Adolf, Benito, and the Son of Heaven (Hirohito, a.k.a. "the poker-faced Mikado") heard the sound of a new airplane in the background, a secret new weapon of some kind. He spoke about shedding blood before he proposed the mildly Freudian remark that "It's only people with a thumping inferiority who go around convincing each other they're a superior race."

Vignettes of Axis atrocity were alluded to, one of which was especially cogent: Norman seized the opportunity to pull the veil off of "They Fly Through the Air," his first celebrated war drama. The villains were now identified. The country that bombed was Italy and the bomber pilot was Mussolini's son, Vittorio. Norman was relieved to quote and name Vittorio Mussolini for writing, "I still remember a group of Galla horsemen, blowing up like an unfolding rose as one of the bombs fell in their midst. It was exceptionally good fun."[38]

Highlights of the first program included we're-all-in-this-together passages, Sandburg-like invocations as if from *The People, Yes*. After a stanza of the Depression hymn, "Brother, Can You Spare a Dime?" Norman had Montgomery list common denominators that "we like opera and symphony and swing, but still a song about a jobless worker can sweep the country; we like Cinderella stories and The Tin Man, but still a novel about a dispossessed Oklahoma family named Joad, can become a best-seller and be made into a movie."

Only one moment of magic happened. An eerily prophetic song called "Round and Round Hitler's Grave" was sung by children in a sort of hillbilly folk song manner. That song would be heard again. In 1945, on the day the war ended in Europe, this very song would almost begin Norman's most famous radio program, "On a Note of Triumph."

Norman did his wartime duty and, on schedule, each Saturday at six for thirteen weeks, beginning February 14, 1942, he dutifully offered an average of about 20 million Americans a dose of inspiration, information, and fright. The audience was too easy to achieve. There was literally no competition. With *This Is War!* for the first and only time, a Government-sponsored *series* was carried by all of the networks. Between February and April 1942, any radio anywhere in the country between 6 and 6:30 p.m. on Saturday, Eastern War Time, would only receive *This Is War!* Millions turned off their sets.

Behind the scenes, required to give the people something, the writer on the spot was mostly Norman, who required a broad margin for creativity and suffered, stifling. Under the twin constraints of tight deadlines and a government agenda, especially the latter, Norman wilted. Moreover, the series' bizarre-sounding prospectus listed three contradictory aims—"to inspire, to inform and to frighten the people of the United States."

At his best moments, he repeatedly filled the air with sounds rather than defining the war with words. For instance, the sounds of machinery precede and form the sonic background of this text:

> We singing people sing a different kind of tune now: a Battle Hymn made up of strains of music from a thousand whirring dynamos and working locomotive bells and tractors groaning in low gear; an orchestration all the world will listen to: a hundred thousand airplanes for wind instruments; heavy guns for tympani. The melody you know already; Song in the Key of V—V for Vindication, V for Victory.

He next cut to the opening of Beethoven's Fifth, "the 'V' theme attenuated for emphasis," followed by a ten-second segment of that symphony. Other programs bulked up on music, song, and sound, and he injected humor, often wry and sarcastic. In effect, Norman himself muted Montgomery's solemn opening words that "laughter can wait. Soft music can have the evening off."

In the end, although Norman's huge captive audience did not hear his finest work, there was one exceptionally good program. Norman both wrote and directed an episode entitled "To the Young" which was as good as anything ever broadcast on network radio. "To the Young," topically the tightest play of the series, was also outstanding in terms of concise but plausible characterizations.

Norman crafted a show that swung like a pendulum between idyllic peace (and romance) and grim reality (sacrifice and risk) in wartime. Simple but effective theater, a kind of nostalgia and reality stew, "To the Young" was the credible and sympathetic presentation of life as experienced in 1942 by young people everywhere. "To the Young" is a stand-alone work in which Norman, age 32, of draft age but medically exempt, caught his breath.

Overall, *This Is War!* was an uneven production. Besides being pulled in three directions by an inherently impractical agenda, he was writing on the fault line between his lifelong idealism for human solidarity and demonizing the enemy. In three out of the six shows that Norman wrote, he argued for hatred's necessity. That was Norman arguing with himself, and losing his argument in the currents of the time, became obvious. That internal argument soon ended, trumped by Norman's core compassion and humanitarianism.

Not so for the creative dean and head fantasist of NBC, Arch Oboler. Oboler, Norman's next-nearest rival in radio history books for the title of best American radio writer, known for his *Lights Out* series, had begun on air work more than five years before Norman did. He was writing radio plays, mostly science fiction, and enjoying a large, cult-like following when Norman was still a print writer in Springfield. He, too, had admired classical music beginning in his childhood. Oboler idolized radio as "an art form as unique, as image-provoking as music itself." To Oboler's mind, the listener "gave of himself as he listened; in his own mind he built pictures evoked by the sounds of words, and effects, and orchestral accompaniment."[39]

Norman and Oboler differed in other ways but one thing they apparently agreed on absolutely was to ignore one another's existence. Although both radio figures often in New York, they seem never to have socialized. It was an oil and water thing. Born only months apart, each of them the sons of European immigrants, after childhoods spent in urban environments, Oboler and Norman grew up to become different people. Norman did more reading and he wrote and published books. Oboler's first book, a collection of his radio plays, came out only in 1944, years after Norman had published several. Personal differences were likewise obvious to anybody who worked with both men. When Dunning interviewed Irene Tedrow, a long-time radio actress, he found that she "remembered Oboler as a 'fascinating, brilliant man' who in his writing liked to stretch the boundaries of reality, while Corwin 'dealt with things as they are.'" They were, she further recalled, even more different personally. While Tedrow said of Oboler that he was a neurotic who yelled, and who was sometimes difficult, she remembered Norman as the exact opposite—"a very dear, gentle man, such a loving person."[40]

It was natural that when the country went to war, Oboler would tool up a wartime series at NBC. Entitled *Plays for Americans*, Oboler's patriotic "message" shows drew on big name stars like Jimmy Stewart and Bette Davis, stars whom Norman often used as well. In one show Oboler beat Norman to the punch. With *Adolf and Mrs. Runyon*—Norman could never bring Adolf Hitler into any of his shows, especially in any kind of comedy or fantasy—Oboler took on *der Fuehrer*.

Norman, an idealist, as a writer was objective, clear-sighted, wrote up the world largely as he saw it, and often directed criticism to himself. Oboler was mainly a fantasist, a builder of alternate, often desolate, dystopian worlds, a writer who never strayed far from his ego. If one of them was destined to explode during a broadcasters' convention to urge hate speech, it was predictable that that one would be Oboler, and it was.

In his speech, delivered at the Radio Institute at Ohio State in May 1942, Ohio State being the academic source of radio's highest awards and the medium's most reputed overseer, Oboler called for radio shows that stirred up hatred of the enemy. Oboler's address to station managers, reprinted as an article that was widely quoted—and one that Oboler stood by and repeated—called for propaganda. Some heard what he said as a call for the same kind of racial hatred that the Axis was advocating. Oboler was not alone. At the time, Americans of Japanese origin were being resettled in isolated camps under military guard far from the Pacific coast. "Asiatic hordes" and "Huns" were hoary go-to propaganda devices.

He pled for hatred in vain. Oboler was, in fact, bounced off the air, not to return with a propaganda series for the rest of the war.[41]

Although Norman had penned some acidic lines into his own 1942 scripts, his conscience always saved him. In general, Norman strove to send a different message and he found the perfect way to do it. He stigmatized the *enemy* as being the haters, and insisted that we not follow them in hating.[42]

One Nazi in particular Norman thrust forward to serve as the personification of hatred: Joseph Goebbels. Whenever and wherever Goebbels appeared in Norman's shows, it was always in a rat-like guise, or as a literal rat. A stirrer-up of racial hatred, Goebbels incarnated this evil and Norman used Goebbels at every opportunity to speak up about equality. "We Hold These Truths" was ironic in being relatively mute on point of racism in late 1941. This changed. Norman countered the Goebbels gospel of a dominant Master Race by speaking to the unity of all races and the equality of all human beings both expressly and by implication.

In "It's in the Works," Norman expressly scorned people in this country trying "to keep that race hatred stuff going" when "that race-against-race line is old Nazi stuff." His narrator continues:

> "That's one of the main things we're *fighting* this war for!"
> MUSIC: (*Parenthetical motif in and behind:*)
> "In the town of Boston once, in a time of trouble, some patriots gathered in the street to protest the tyranny of a despot King. Soldiers of the King raised up their guns and fired upon them; and the first to fall—the first American to die for Independence—was a boy named Crispus Attucks. Attucks was a Negro."
> (*Music surges, then comes down for:*)
> "Race against race? Not on the day [of Pearl Harbor], a day later, when a bomber roared out of Luzon and headed for the open sea. The officer commanding her was Irish—by the name of Kelly. His bombardier—the boy who took a bead on the *Haruna*, got it pretty in his bombsight, pressed the button, sent the bombs away—he was a Jew named Meyer Levin. Race against race?"[43]

This point Norman considered essential to repeat. It was a point made even if it stepped on a story line or narrative. The White House program (co-authored by Norman) made no attempt to stitch seamlessly into the script the line, "One American who hates Jews or Negroes or Catholics is worth a whole trained staff of experts in the offices of Propaganda Minister Goebbels." Spoken as a voice-over at the program's very end, unrelated to the White House and only loosely linked to the preface that this show was intended to answer specifically: "What can you do?" Norman had a point to make, and he made it prominently, aesthetics be damned.

Other episodes were weakened by flattened characters who were, in effect, walking war slogans. The worst of the shows ended the series. "Yours Received and Contents Noted," the crankiest, most meandering and irritating of Norman's products, provides nonetheless the clearest x-ray of Norman's feelings at that time. Written and directed by Norman, this show indulged in on-air revenge. That is, here Norman took care of that German he met at Partenkirchen in 1931, the one who stopped speaking with him after he revealed he was Jewish. He makes his German puppet die with this confession:

> I have been made a fool of; I have been robbed ... of the earth and all the things upon it.... I am a German of the town of Partenkirschen, where I was born, where I belonged—but I died for nothing, for less than nothing, on a plain near Staraya Russia, far from Partenkirsche—I died of the bayonet of a Red soldier fighting to defend his home; I died for a thing of shame, for a hopeless cause....

In an unconscious extreme caricature of his constraints, Norman created not only straw men but straw boys. Addressing "the messenger boy who stops on the street to watch a construction job" Norman has the announcer, Raymond Massey, thunder:

Chances are he's carrying a message that has to do in some way with work, and therefore with the war. And in that case, he has blood on his hands.

It was an ironic scene to be constructed by the man who in his earliest days portrayed Napoleon's messenger boy dying in parlors on Bremen Street. He was angry at messenger boys who did anything less than their duty. By proxy, Norman also let loose on himself. Airing what was doubtless his own personal frustration, he created and faced down a straw man critic. Embodying public resentment over being a captive audience to government programming, the last letter he scripted was:

> Don't you think it's about time you jerks put a stop to the baloney you've been handing out? Why don't you get behind guns or do something useful? You've done nothing but waste the Government's dough and stir up trouble in the country. Get off the air, bums.... Unsigned.

Narrator Massey—who minimizes this letter as a "rare one," from "a crank"—replied first (with relief that Norman fully shared): "You will be happy to learn that this series has only five minutes to go before your specific wish comes true. This is our last program. We are going off the air."

Then Norman has Massey (whose most memorable public *persona* was as a near-saintly Abraham Lincoln) impute hatred exclusively to the Fascists:

> There will be more of the same kind of talk which has irritated the homegrown Fascists in their newspaper towers, which has confused the little critics who aren't sure there's a war on. There will be more of hate, no doubt, if only the men of radio explain why we are fighting, and what Fascism consists of.

Norman had struck out and he knew it. Self-deprecation is an occupational hazard of perfectionists, and Norman, being a perfectionist, could be self-deprecatory. When Norman had Massey say that "(m)any hundreds of Americans have written us, encouraging, advising, making valuable comments and suggestions, cheering the word they knew and felt needed to be said," the "many hundreds" who wrote in a country possessing 40 million radios has a tinny ring.

No ratings system existed then. Mail and phone calls were the measures of successes and failures. If a few hundred of supposed millions of listeners wrote, then the show was so much dead air. Content Analysis revealed even worse news. Peppered and salted with "advice" and "suggestions" rather than to compliments or praise, the mail for the series signaled a level of dissatisfaction unique among all of Norman's shows. Massey's was the best face that Norman could put upon his greatest failure.

England

Norman always expected to be drafted. It was a good bet. Although Em, married with children, was exempt, his brother Al was reached and drafted. Norman was still younger than many others called into service, like Leon Edel, 35, another New York author and intellectual, who was drafted on July 12, 1943. When called, however, Norman failed the physical exam, due to the vestiges of his bout with TB in 1932 and 1933. Norman went overseas to serve his country nonetheless, just not wearing a uniform.[44]

Three months after Pearl Harbor, Norman was going to England. Duty-bound, Norman headed for imperiled London on his first transatlantic plane ride. The *Luftwaffe* had bombed England mercilessly, London worst of all, day, and night, in late 1940 and by a terrifying streak of night raids in the first half of 1941. (Indeed, V-1 rockets or "buzz bombs" would rain down over London beginning mid-1944.)

Norman's close friend and CBS associate, Ed Murrow, who favored understatement, had broadcast news of the Blitz in tense, lucid and understandable reports. The worst days of the Blitz, as it had become known, were over by then but only Hitler knew that. When Norman traveled, danger loomed in the North Atlantic and just off the coast. Anyone in England knew that German forces at land and sea maneuvered not far beyond the white cliffs of Dover—and the Channel Islands themselves were enemy-occupied territory, with guns facing *west*.

Flying was not only quicker but considered, most often, safer. At sea, Nazi subs reigned. U-boat "wolf packs" roamed the Atlantic to sink any Allied vessels they could hit, military or civilian. During 1942, Allied losses (by tonnage sunk) grew larger every month. When he could get a place on a military plane, he left for England.

He did something else before he left. It may have been a move stimulated by thoughts of the hazards ahead for him or it may just have been an exercise in practicality. He turned over his most valuable and valued property, a 1941 Buick convertible, to Al. Thus unencumbered, he departed for London from Washington on an American Export Lines North Atlantic Clipper.[45]

His flight was uneventful. The fun began after he landed.

"I was the last of fourteen passengers to clear through customs and censorship and the only one to miss the special train that carried clipper customers to London in a nonstop run," Norman said.[46]

Norman actually arrived sick. As he put it, "A bit of food poisoning (probably nothing more than a virulent dose of typhoid) laid me flat and dragged the floor with me, after which I caught a low grade grippe," which, he joked, made the "cold and draughty rooms" of English homes a small pleasure.[47]

Expecting hardship from the first, Norman found rationing and scarcity made for some discomfort, but his accommodations at the Savoy Hotel were astonishingly good, even excellent. "The bathroom alone is practically a club," he wrote his parents, "mirrors, marble, one of those incredibly long bathtubs, super-gadgets for all kinds of little conveniences, a beautiful ivory telephone set in a niche, and in the room proper, a buzzer-set for summoning valet, waiter, maid; air conditioning,; special light controls, etcetera." Ed Murrow could not have been treated more royally. (Murrow was the producer of *An American in England*.)[48]

Appreciating the "quiet and clean" more than the "tinsel and plush" of the place, Norman worked hard in the Savoy and nearby Broadcasting House but what he accomplished was nonetheless nominal. As happened to others in war, and many in uniform, his sacrifices were largely in vain. Little relevant remains from the two series that Norman oversaw while in England or when just back in the States, collaborating with BBC.[49]

For both series, *An American in England* and *Transatlantic Call*, Norman literally lost sleep. Broadcast live in the wee hours of the morning over there for reception in early evening in the United States, they were marvels of technology. Sometimes, however, technology failed. Given atmospheric conditions, some transmissions went unheard outside the studio in London. A technician had to deliver the bad news afterward, that Norman had been talking to himself. He had a right to feel frustrated and, for just once, not to blame himself.[50]

Although the informative and less imperative tone of the British shows was better than *This Is War!* these shows, in style and content, are today manifestly the productions of another era, topical and soon outdated. Neither drama or poetry, in which Norman's talents were unsurpassed, they were instead a sort of cobbled-together documentary presentation sweetened with a bit of snarky humor and sentimentality.

Although he never reached England in his autobiography, one wishes that Norman had. The little that is documented reveals a Yank charmed by old Blighty and its beleaguered people. He loved the country, no doubt. At his best moments, Norman conveyed affection for his father's old home, London, while exhibiting a strong Anglophile bent. Suffering also drew him to write. A little shore town that faced more than its share of bombing, Cromer, he turned into two shows.[51]

One other sacrifice he made, besides fatigue, he noted after the fact, "In England I had been reluctantly and at times irascibly celibate." One Kate Locke cheered him up from afar, however, and sent him letters, peanuts, dried apricots, Hershey krinkles, some sort of butter and eggs, and "canned marmalade."[52]

In the end, although his transmitted documentaries were thorough and no British institution, icon or favorable stereotype was omitted, too transparently, what Norman needed to excel, with which he rose to the heights of radio whenever he had it—creative freedom—he lacked in 1942 in England. He was only in a position to reclaim it in the spring of the next year in New York, when he fell severely ill, sicker than he had been in ten years.

"The Long Name That None Could Spell"

Norman spent the months between March and July 1943, in dry desert air, as prescribed by one of several doctors he consulted. He had returned to the United States for the American side broadcasts of *Transatlantic Call*, which were broadcast from stations all around the country. He both wrote and narrated. He also got increasingly more ill. By his third program, he could barely breathe. In early March 1943, bedridden and medicated at the Drake Hotel, he wrote a last episode for broadcast out of Chicago station WBBM. At the last minute, another narrator substituted for Norman.

He struggled, wheezing home to New York by train, where doctors discovered that, on top of a bad cold, Norman had abscessed ears. As an infection treated with the relatively new drug penicillin, it was cured but Norman was completely exhausted. After a week with help to prepare his meals each day, he recovered enough strength to take another train West. In Palm Springs he breathed in hot, dry, clean air.

Getting away from it all was the idea. He had been in a similar situation in May 1933. Upon his release from the TB sanatorium to Winthrop, he promptly strolled up to the sea wall to gaze at the Atlantic. Salt air and isolation then worked wonders. Some ten years later, natural surroundings, sun and quiet again exerted a profoundly healthful impact. Within weeks, Norman discovered enough pep within himself to undertake something he had never done: a play for the New York stage.

Having recuperated to the point of being unable to rest quietly, he responded instantly and affirmatively when solicited on behalf of the Czechoslovakian war relief. A play sounded wonderful to his ears. For the first time in too many constricted years, Norman was invited to indulge his unfettered creative mode.

He was asked to supply an original drama to be performed at Carnegie Hall. Although a volunteer, he still faced a deadline. The group's biggest fund-raiser had to be ready for casting and rehearsals a month before its public performance in late May. Only by doggedly writing and revising for weeks in April could Norman wrestle with multiple obstacles inherent in the project and complete the play, his first.

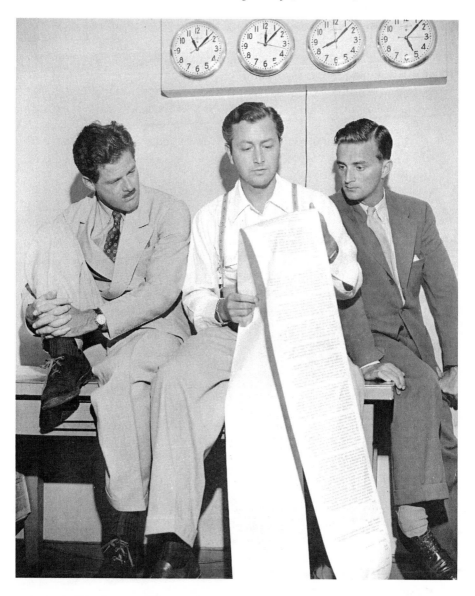

A tired globe-hopper, after Norman got back from England, he recuperated from illness until mid–1943. Still wan here (at left) when photographed in about August 1943 in the newsroom of KNX, Los Angeles, he is seated beside Robert Young (holding a teletype), and another script writer, Ranald Mac-Dougall. Young played the dashing lead of the short-lived series "Passport for Adams," for which Norman wrote the pilot and later resumed writing, taking over completely from MacDougall (courtesy American Radio Archives and Museum).

The tale Norman took up—during a period of extended illness, the second-most severe respiratory setback of his life—was tragic. Lidice, a small Czech town, was eradicated on Hitler's specific orders. Its population of some 200 men, women and children was all but exterminated in a single day on June 10, 1942. Lidice was destroyed in reprisal after one of Hitler's murderous favorites, Reich Protector Reinhard Heydrich, was assassinated in Lidice.

Playwrights soon learn, if they do not already know, that any true story is too balky to adapt into a playable script. In turn, stage plays are notoriously difficult to adapt for radio. "The Long Name that None Could Spell," both based on a true story and a play, was finally a radio show nonetheless judged to be awesome by public and critics. Dealing with innumerable narrative difficulties for a stage presentation reflecting these events, Norman used the question *why* as his focus.

Norman was always critical of writers who captured a moment of heroism to the exclusion of the reason why. When he wrote to Hollywood producer David O. Selznick early in World War II—brashly telling the director of *Gone with the Wind* how to tell a war story—he advised Selznick against seriously considering making any movie that highlighted a brave hero. Norman told him that heroism "is an old staple of drama. The quality of heroism, if isolated, can serve to defeat your purpose." In capital letters, Norman next emphatically asked Selznick not to show merely a brave man in his film but "WHY he enlisted, FOR WHAT he is fighting, what his people can expect from victory and what from, defeat."[53]

In writing this play, which honored both intentional and accidental heroes and wartime martyrs, Norman developed the specific stakes in play and the motives behind the risks taken. This was especially important because more civilians would die during World War II than civilians. Many of them were classic innocent bystanders. How could they be answered? Justice to them required careful and compassionate handling. On May 28, 1943, before a full house at Carnegie Hall, Norman's play was performed for the American Friends of Czechoslovakia. The play was the organization's most successful fund-raiser of the year. Norman's free verse play won tears and cheers and received a standing ovation, after which Czechoslovakian President Eduard Beneš spoke.[54]

The play's future, if it had any future, then rested in Norman's hands. As the war went on, expanding globally far from Czechoslovakia, and more civilians died, the play and its theme haunted him. As new events and more deaths overwhelmed the memory of Lidice, Norman had to decide whether this atrocity of 1942 retained relevance in 1944. Deciding yes, Norman put himself to this play in between other deadline CBS projects for what was his final—and some say finest—radio series, *Columbia Presents Corwin*.

Columbia Presents Corwin

Norman's creative career resumed in 1944. His creativity smoldered for all of 1942 and for most of 1943. He was in *Life* magazine, he was famous, he was known internationally, no doubt. But, fretting and frustrated, Norman had his agent negotiate a contract for twenty half-hour shows to do what he wanted in 1944. Correspondence from that the time reveals that Norman pressed his agent to make CBS yield. He was to push back any demands by the network executives for control. He wanted to take risks and, by refusing anything less, he finally got his chance. Rising phoenix-like as the war went into its stretch run, Norman's name went back up on the marquee of a series broadcast by CBS. This was the remarkable *Columbia Presents Corwin*.

Early on, Norman created not only one of his most moving wartime shows but one of the most moving radio shows by anybody ever about anything. His prophetic paean to a soldier killed in action, called "Untitled," was broadcast on April 18, 1944. "Untitled" was so good that popular demand required CBS to repeat it. Thus distinguished, "Untitled" was selected as one of the CDs for the Centennial collection. Attempting to characterize this show, Norman called it a mix of "integrity combined with a great deal of passion."[55]

In "Untitled," Norman again tapped into one of his most powerful devices. His awareness of its power went back to the best show of his otherwise lame 1942 efforts. In "To the Young," the one great segment of *This Is War!* Norman had empowered the dead to speak. (This was, of course, also at the core of the WXQR adaptation of *Spoon River Anthology* that opened the doors of CBS to Norman in 1938, and of Norman's adaptation on CBS, which had moved its author, Edgar Lee Masters, to tears.)

As befit the mood of that awful and bloody year of 1944, in *Columbia Presents Corwin* Norman mostly covered the war with a steely-eyed steadiness. When he did not, he offered adaptations of high literature (Sandburg, Whitman, Wolfe) or of high escapism.

Among other war-themed dramas, Norman took up "The Long Name None Could Spell." He modified his original play for radio. It had been arduous. The adaptation had taken intermittent time over almost a year. One imagines many cumulative days and nights translating facial expressions and actors' gestures into words. His persistence paid off. The show's immediacy and intense drama reflects the height of radio achievement to this day. How good was it? The show was so excellent that Norman had no doubt. The perfectionist said that this show was "one of my favorites of all my things."[56]

"The Long Name None Could Spell" aired over CBS stations on March 14, 1944, with an unusually gifted cast. Chief among them was Martin Gabel, the radio play's core, its narrator. Innovatively, one real-life newscaster, William Shirer, was cast to reprise his own war news bulletins.

Broadway actress Giuliana Taberna, a key incidental figure in Norman's life (in late 1941 Taberna had introduced Norman to Katherine Locke, his future wife) was in the cast, as well.[57]

Much as for "We Hold These Truths," the timing of this show's broadcast added to its impact. Civilians were dying at a rate higher than military personnel and, more than any other program since "They Fly Through the Air" in 1939, this one in 1944 concerned civilian deaths.

Ironically, having fought for a series in which he could write what he wanted, winning independence, it was in this series that Norman took up another person's suggestion for a show. Charles Laughton clued Norman in on the case of Herbert Dougal, a confessed murderer. Apart from the CBS executive who forced Norman to adapt a young bride's story about a caterpillar back in 1940, nobody, not even his own father, had pitched a story that Norman chose to adapt. However, in 1944, "The Moat Farm Murder: The True Confession of Herbert Dougal" became one of Norman's few mysteries, and easily the most chilling. Broadcast as a rare high escapist episode of *Columbia Presents Corwin* on July 18, 1944, with suspenseful and creepy music by Bernard Herrmann, it starred, appropriately, his favorite Brits, Charles Laughton and Elsa Lanchester.

Original gems like "Untitled," several adaptations of great American literature, "The Long Name None Could Spell," and the Raskolnikov-like horror, "The Moat Farm Murder," were individual achievements which, in aggregate, constituted a monumental accomplishment by a writer. It may be argued that no radio writer has ever done better, then or to date, than Norman in 1944. Norman had almost every reason to be proud.[58]

However, Norman was not a money-maker. He was part of "sustaining programs" that drew down on CBS funds. As his series won kudos, the trend in networks was away from sustaining programs. *More* sponsored shows—more than ever in the history of radio—was the rallying cry of executives.

In Norman's case specifically, during their last round of contract negotiations, CBS had sought to compensate itself. Norman had then—and would predictably always—rebuffed his network's demand for a share of his income outside CBS, such as sales of his script anthologies. He thought the demand unfair in principle, but he had to expect it to be raised again. Nearing the end of his war-centered *Columbia Presents Corwin*, in a changing radio business world, with the end of the war itself imminent, Norman had to anticipate the end of his run as well.[59]

He was not worried. Nor was he stoical. Having worked with a monkish dedication for six months, from March to August, he was more tired. Despite success, it was only natural for him to anticipate a meeting soon. In his mind's ear he could hear courteous but cold words. They were likely to be the same ones that he had heard before from Doug Coulter when his original and also successful *26 by Corwin* series ended in November 1941: that CBS had nothing to offer that was worthy of his talents.

"On a Note of Triumph"

Orson Welles, with cigar, and Norman, on the day World War II ended, August 14, 1945. After an all-night vigil awaiting news of the Japanese surrender, Norman completed a soliloquy about the war and its costs. (That V-J Day special was expanded, retitled "God and Uranium," and publicized as a "Day of Prayer Special" starring both Orson Welles and Olivia DeHavilland on August 19, 1945) (courtesy American Radio Archives and Museum).

In August 1944, CBS vice president Doug Coulter asked Norman to speak with him. It was to be a private meeting, at Coulter's office again. One can imagine Norman's thoughts and heavy steps up to Coulter's door.

Almost as soon as Norman arrived, Coulter got down to business.

Commencing, apparently looking Norman square in the eye, Coulter said, "It looks as though we're going to have victory in Europe very soon. Will you therefore knock off what you're doing and begin to write an hour's commemorative program, to be done on CBS the night of victory in Europe?"[60]

Astonishingly, Norman only felt tired. Again, as in 1941, after Coulter spoke, fatigue overwhelmed him. To this glorious opportunity, he reacted internally just as he had when Bill Lewis had offered him the program about the 150th anniversary of the Bill of Rights. "It was very hard for me because I was weary from all the war radio," he said in his memoirs. A sense of difficulties overwhelmed any delight.[61]

"Weary" was an understatement. Since his slow recovery from bedridden illness in mid–1943, Norman had been writing, revising, rehearsing, and directing almost every week to meet the inflexible deadlines of live shows. Norman did not speak about being tired. Nor did he refuse, as he had refused Bill Lewis. After all, Coulter revealed understanding. Coulter himself set the condition that Norman "knock off" what he was doing.

Thus, he was not fired but freed of other responsibilities. He accepted the invitation.

He would try to compress thoughts about the war and the coming peace to fit the space of one hour. After he left Coulter's office, he wrote one more script for *Columbia Presents Corwin*. Broadcast on August 15, 1944, it was ironically titled "There Will Be Time Later." In that show, Norman was like Washington composing a farewell address. Norman explained in a note when the script was published after the war:

> I did not expect to be on the air again for a long while; hence the program was to be a sort of valedictory. If consequently, it has moments of bitterness, if in places it has a valedictorian air, you know why.[62]

The writer who at age 31 had come up with "We Hold These Truths" in less than a month, who not long ago had pumped out 25 original scripts in 26 weeks, after a similar series of twenty shows, was 34 and tired. His deadline, though indefinite, seemed imminent. Allied troops were in Rome and marching into Paris. The *Wehrmacht* was in retreat. The Red Army was on the border of Poland. Hitler's generals had just tried to assassinate him. Would the war be over before Christmas? Good bet. Neither Coulter nor he knew that Norman would have the luxury of nine months.[63]

"I was fed up with writing," Norman said of this period, "and wanted nothing more than to pick up a gun and join in the fighting. That, however, was an old conflict within myself and basically attached to my intermittent doubts as to whether my programs were in any way helpful to the war effort."[64]

America's Prince Hamlet was wobbly, hobbled, virtually at stop. Succinctly summing up his fugue state in August 1944, Norman said, "I was a tired man." Just how soon Norman put pen to paper is unclear. It seems that he tried in vain to start. He could not relax his exhausted body and vacuous mind.[65]

"The script did not come, and I was in despair. Ten days I gnashed my teeth, paced the floor, walked the park, listened to music, did some reading that I hoped might switch on the ignition," he said, characterizing his agony for the first week or so. "My mind was vacuum, abhorred by Nature and the Muses."[66]

Norman's network of New York connections and contacts then came to his rescue like the cavalry. Publishing giant Simon and Schuster's Jack Goodwin offered him a favor. No space better suited creativity, Goodwin urged, than his hideaway by Long Island Sound. Goodwin would loan it to Norman. The Goodwin house in Rowayton, Connecticut, proved congenial to the city-bound workaholic. Words began to flow, if only in sporadic spurts. Norman took advantage of good days that fall by sailing and writing simultaneously. As always, water called to him. He recalled first scenes that came to him "in a sailboat out on the Sound."[67]

It was slow work, nonetheless. Norman said, "It took a lot of effort to get myself going again." Uniquely, he sailed and let his unconscious drift but, on shore, he found writing sites everywhere. Ashore, he was back in his earliest days and first series with CBS: he found himself scribbling "everywhere—in barber chairs, in bed, in taxicabs."[68]

He took one extended break. It was, as usual, to California, but for an unusual event. In Hollywood, Norman oversaw a once-in-a-lifetime broadcast. On the night of November 5, 1944, a whole galaxy of stars under Norman's direction spoke up and sang in favor of a fourth term for President Franklin D. Roosevelt.[69]

Norman's grammar school days may possibly have come drifting back to him. Certainly, the First World War did. Seeing troop trains, Mrs. Hoffman, and experiencing Armistice Day's euphoria were transparently experiences that made it possible for him to write lines of "On a Note of Triumph." The paired themes of the admitted great past failure to end all wars and the hope of potential lasting peace *this time* were dynamic twin keys. Norman spoke to two generations, those who recalled the First World War or had taken part in it, and those who were younger. Both had relied on Norman since 1941 to tell them about this war in an honest way. Norman shaped his script as someone who was himself quite consciously a member of both groups.

He may even have recalled high school. Twenty years before in a play, Norman at fifteen stood as one of four benumbed war veterans, a mute prop in a comedy. A faint possibility arises that he had pondered even then, as he waited in the wings, the point that wars went on after hostilities ended. Victory of one's side did not guarantee those who served, or the people back home, a smooth postwar life. Working these premises, personal or not in origin, Norman wove an indelible pattern in his most memorable show.

The script was incomplete when the Battle of the Bulge suddenly erupted in mid–December. Norman soon realized the war would not end until the next year. Current events prevailed. He "dropped the script" and took up other projects. Not until mid–January, as the Allies approached the Rhine and the inner Reich, did Norman start again, and make what he called "daily progress."[70]

Though he recalled "it was not exactly a hayride," he had a complete first draft in hand by the end of January. It had flaws, some never fixed. None of his Fascist foes had recognizable faces. (When he tried to punish Hitler, Norman always failed. Unlike Oboler's "Adolph and Mrs. Runyon," the enemy in his wartime works was never Hitler.) He solved the "hatred" problem ingeniously. In this show, children singing around Hitler's grave was a masterful touch. Thus juvenilized—and only juvenilized—could he take unalloyed and very atypical delight in anyone's death, and then only briefly.[71]

He revisited and resisted, a moth to flame, Oboler's sort of hate radio. The focus of "On a Note of Triumph," despite its title, was *not* triumph but the high costs of war and the road ahead. Norman's show unfolded as a thoughtful, provocative invitation to think about what to do. He strengthened a powerful series of questions by putting them into the mouths of average fighting men, *including* those in hospitals and some suffering lifelong losses for—what?

Norman offered a vision of action to make a prosperous and peaceful world. He looked to the people, the millions, the masses, to answer. Gradually, Norman, with time on his hands as well as a script, uncertain as usual about his success, reached out for feedback.

First, he made the rounds of his family. This was common for him, but next was unusual. He shared what he had written with a few friends. Their feedback was incredibly helpful. On his clipboard, he made revisions *in situ*. By late March, as the Allies crossed the Rhine, in a move unique to this show, Norman took to the road. Faculty members, students, cafeteria, and custodial workers of a Virginia college heard him recite his complete draft. He learned that he was not there yet. Anonymous written responses showed that his large and diverse audience was respectful but not overwhelmed.

By the time Germany surrendered, radio's war correspondents, led by the most respected of them all, Edward R. Murrow, had taken the gloves off. Murrow broadcast the raw and unvarnished facts in sight from the Buchenwald concentration camp in mid–April. He concluded that, "If I have offended, I am not in the least sorry." Americans were ready to listen to accounts besides optimistic news and hometown boys' anecdotes.

Norman's smaller audiences, while encouraging, never brought him to think that a legendary show was in the making. He did not realize that a new, hardened national mood was coalescing. Norman's goal remained modest. The show eventually entitled "On a Note of Triumph," he hoped, would stimulate "lively and intelligent discussion." He would be glad if most of his regular listeners tuned in. Norman never dreamed of ratings like comedian Bob Hope's. Indeed, Norman made an awful pun, saying of 1945 that he had by then "given up hoping against Hope."[72]

The author of the show was off-the-charts wrong. Prince Hamlet deadpanned, "It is most pleasant for a writer's estimation of his work to be revised upward by others. Too often it works in exactly the reverse pattern."[73]

On May 8, 1945, V-E Day, anybody near a radio was in his audience. They came in under anybody's radar until some sixty million people were listening. Numbers grew as the broadcast went on, as people called their neighbors to tune in and listen. The country's response astonished Norman and CBS by its depth, breadth, and duration.

Immediately, thousands of calls came into the networks. Beginning the next day, truckloads of sacks and boxes arrived containing almost five thousand cards, gifts, letters, and telegrams. CBS executives hyperventilated over the network's triumph as they scanned reviews for any hints of flaws before approving an encore performance.

No radio critic was unsatisfied. Dozens of glowing reviews flowed into and overflowed CBS desks. Norman's spell-bound radio audience was not satisfied without a complete live rebroadcast on all of the country's 500 stations the following week.

What was true on the air proved equally true in print. Norman had entrusted Simon and Schuster with a copy of his script after word was out, in early May, that Hitler had shot himself. Quickly set in galley proof before the radio show aired, Jack Goodwin gambled precious, rationed paper on his sole judgment that Norman had a hit. Beginning the day after the broadcast, Goodwin had his company run off 50,000 copies.

Goodwin was amply rewarded for the big risk he took. Demand was even greater than this huge supply. Those 50,000 copies sold out in two weeks. Incredibly, the reprint of a radio show was the best-selling book in the country. Norman's small, plainly bound booklet, the first radio script ever to make the bestseller list, was reissued in a second printing of 25,000 and several more times and it did not stop selling until the end of the year.[74]

As a phonograph record, "On a Note of Triumph" likewise sold out. In this instance, Columbia Records was unlucky, however. Its records sold out in record time, but there the records ceased: the company could press no more. A shellac shortage pinched production. The problem proved insoluble and capped the number of LP records of the radio show sold at only 13,000 copies.[75]

As a program, "On a Note of Triumph" serves to this day as the gold standard program of the Golden Age of Radio. Professional print and broadcast journalists thereafter pared phrases from this broadcast for titles of their own later works. People played the record in their homes and teachers in schools had their classes listen to it on V-E Day for years. Some carried Norman's words of that night in their hearts for the rest of their lives. Flying to Rome in 1966, Norman met one of them, an admiring TWA pilot who knew and accurately recited his show's opening and concluding lines for their delighted author.[76]

What was the secret? Certainly, timing. Broadcast at a pivotal point, Norman's mixture of free verse, Biblical cadences, folk song, streetwise, slangy narrative and "sharp questions" articulated both the current meaning and the future potential of the Allied victory. His script matched the nation's somber mood exactly. The message matched the moment. The electric tension that earlier surrounded "We Hold These Truths" crackled again. As the Allies triumphed over land, sea and air in Europe, Norman triumphed on the air for one entire brilliant hour.[77]

Notwithstanding, the show was Norman's swan song. Few scripts remained to be written, few shows to direct. He was right about the end being near. The same factors that buoyed Norman to the heights, the saturation of radio, the hunger for patriotic pieces, public openness to his kind of serious realism, were ebbing along with the war. A taste for the intellectual fires he always sparked was fading even as network radio faded into history.[78]

Norman nonetheless remained capable of surprising audiences. The most extravagant escapade Norman ever designed followed a couple of months later. Norman gave himself a temporary dispensation from rectitude and solemnity. His madcap and over the top, completely original "The Undecided Molecule" featured the ostensible trial of a wayward molecule for deviance from standard.

Broadcast July 17, 1945, "The Undecided Molecule" was a comic operetta. It only got weirder—and more farcical—by the minute, as anything should that starred wisecracking Groucho Marx (the judge), hilarious Robert Benchley (the clerk) and other talented comic actors of the time. For a national respite, Norman had created a rhyming romp, simultaneously one of Norman's own favorite pieces. Though still at its core a debate over ideas, it was funny.[79]

Norman's eleven scripts in 1945 included a much less celebrated or remembered short program commemorating Japan's surrender. A fifteen-minute soliloquy was spoken by Orson Welles on the evening of V-J Day, August 14, 1945. (The script actually had two lives. Expanded to a half-hour, retitled "God and Uranium," and voiced by Orson Welles and Olivia de Havilland, it was broadcast as a "Day of Prayer Special" show on Sunday, August 19, a day designated by President Truman as a day of prayer. Wild public acclaim and critical adulation followed neither show.)[80]

Unlike "On a Note of Triumph," his script for Welles had been rushed. As Michael Kacey wrote in his program notes for the Norman Corwin Centennial CD collection, "This CBS special was hurriedly created due to the suddenness of the war's end." Norman had been in California polishing off a script called "L'Affaire Gumpert" when a CBS executive named William Fineshriber called from New York to ask him about a V-J Day commemorative program.

"I was against doing it, especially on such short notice," he said.

However, Fineshriber was, in the term Norman used, "persuasive." Perhaps he wooed him by conjuring up past success. After all, Norman had done V-E Day justice, hadn't he? But that had been given months to write and time to test audience reactions to each line of that work. This was hastily assigned to be dashed off in a few hours.

No matter, for V-J Day, Norman "sat up all night hacking at the order and came up with a fistful of lines for a single voice, to be supported by a single sound effect" (a cannon shot). It was not a shot heard 'round the world.[81]

Kate

Norman once said emphatically that he thought it was *logical* to marry. Whether Norman would marry anybody had been touch-and-go since Hazel rejected his proposal but kissed him in Forest Park in Springfield in 1929. Cool and independent, possessed by an awesomely ambiguous mindset, Norman had paid no attention to Kate when he first met her during the last half of 1941. In the street, in the shadow of the CBS building, brief greetings unfolded in a few seconds. Norman was clearly on his way to or from work. Being a preoccupied man, Norman did not remember it. His words to Bannerman were, "Katherine tells me that she first met me at a street corner outside CBS, 52nd and Madison Avenue."[82]

Hamlet and Ophelia. Kate's performances were critically acclaimed as "definitive" in the role, which she played opposite Maurice Evans in 1930s runs (courtesy Diane Corwin Okarski).

Their first meeting was not the first time Norman had ever seen Katherine "Kate" Locke, however. He saw her in her original hit with top billing, *Having Wonderful Time*. The latter play, almost five years (and four other roles after her debut on Broadway as "Girl Tenant" in "Firebird"), literally made her name. In his review the next morning, legendary theater critic Burns Mantle paid tribute in the New York *Daily News* by saying simply, "Ladies and gentlemen, I give you Katherine Locke." She later played Ophelia, and Norman saw her again.[83]

Finally introducing them was another actress, Giuliana Taberna. Whether Taberna was walking with Norman and spotted Kate or Norman encountered Kate with Giuliana is unclear. Norman had not only directed Taberna in minor radio roles but had worked with her then-boyfriend, composer Deems Taylor, frequently for CBS. (To Norman's immense satisfaction, Taylor composed the musical background of *Samson* and *Job*, two of Norman's three Bible-based shows.)[84]

Perhaps close associations with too many stars had jaded him. Norman once attended a play specifically to see Kate on stage but of this he

Kate Locke with Ralph Bellamy, stars of "Johnny Gets His Gun," 1936 (courtesy Diane Corwin Okarski).

made no mention to her. In fairness, at that time Norman had little time to spare. His high-pressure weekly series was nearing its end. His CBS contract was about to expire. Working to earn renewal, Norman was overall an exhausted man.

Of their brief encounter in the street, Norman summarized, "Nothing came of that except a nodding acquaintance, but Kate said that she was impressed at the time but dared not be too impressed because she was married."[85]

Whether Kate was technically married with divorce pending or Kate was divorced pending a final decree is uncertain, as is the date of their meeting. (Bannerman in his book gallantly guessed that Kate's divorce had just become final.) Kate's first marriage to Maurice Helprin, a movie director's assistant from New Jersey, was at or near its end as 1941 ended. Norman and Kate seem to have avoided discussing her first marriage. Norman once told Bannerman that Kate "may not have been happily married, but you'll have to check with her on that."[86]

For his part, Norman's last passionate relationship, in Springfield with Esther, had ended in 1936. CBS had become his engulfing long-term relationship beginning in 1938. Between 1938 and 1941, Norman spent time with women during brief escapes from CBS. To Bannerman, Norman confided that the "years between Esther and Kate" were filled by "other women. And much travel. Experience." With that final word, spoken in an off-key doleful way—presumably, *bad* experiences or a creeping revulsion for shallow relationships—he implied some finality before he summed up in forgiving defensiveness, "So one changes, you know?"

After 1941, after CBS let Norman go, and after he came triumphantly back to CBS in 1942, he directed Kate and Henry Hull in an episode of *This Is War!* During his otherwise regrettable series, their proximity moved Norman to be unusually expressive. During a break in rehearsing, he asked Kate if she would marry him, literally in passing. (Kate recalled it well. Norman recalled nothing. It was possibly a bad joke on Norman's part.)[87]

Something was developing emotionally, sputtering between them. After England, especially by late 1943, Kate was the "very smart" woman he kept coming back to. It was not her glamour, he emphasized to Bannerman. Although Kate enjoyed a celebrity aura on Broadway, Norman told his biographer in an indignant tone, that he had dated plenty of rich and famous

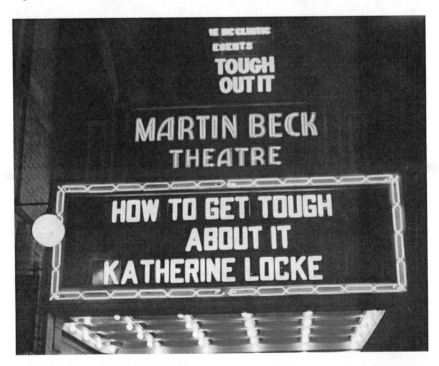

Kate Locke's name was up in lights on Broadway (1938) before CBS hired Norman (courtesy Diane Corwin Okarski).

women. He said that "had (he) been interested in wealth and celebrity (he'd have been) married once, and perhaps three times before" he ever met Kate.[88]

By 1944, their feelings were mutual and deep. Norman waved Bannerman off from closer scrutiny with highly formal wording, saying only that they "knew each other for quite a while" and referring to a "number of years this had been going on … on and off and on and off, beginning in '44 in an important way." He told Bannerman that it was not that they went places together ("I didn't go places even with myself. I put myself in a chair and worked."), but they grew close.

When Bannerman at another point asked Norman to specify *when* they became a couple, Norman identified the year of the hit "El Capitan, and the Corporal." Norman wrote it about (and on board) the El Capitan train. In 1944, perhaps by a felicitous choice, perhaps by a whispered hint, another CBS producer than Norman selected Kate for the starring role. But by about then—the show was broadcast on July 25, 1944—apparently Norman only had eyes for Kate.[89]

When they began courting Norman loved radio and was married to CBS. Contradicting himself later to Bannerman, Norman insisted that he did not remember exactly "when I began to 'go with' Katherine in the sense of 'going with.'" Norman adverted to spats—"two or three estrangements"—absences and frequent travel. Kate had to wait. "I was much separated from her by projects on the coast that took me here and there," Norman told Bannerman. The period of 1942 or 1943 seems too early but, despite the confusion and contradictory reckonings during interviews, it seems likely that by 1944, Kate had bested her big rival, CBS.

The radio networks' run was nearly over by the time that CBS executives, having decided that radio's origins went back to 1920, faced an anniversary in 1945. As the war ended, in a virtually superstitious ritual, CBS decided that the occasional piece that Norman wrote, "Seems Radio Is Here to Stay," dubbed "the finest" by a radio critic in 1939, would be repeated live with the original cast and music by Bernard Hermann. "Seems Radio Is Here to Stay" was a more ironic title in 1945 than it had been in 1939, broadcast the week that television sets first went on sale in New York City. The tide of American radio was now ebbing fast. "Seems Radio Is Having a 'Last Hurrah'" might have been a better title.

CBS did not hold Norman so tightly in its arms as Kate. Norman glimpsed her as CBS released its thrall. Kate, a sophisticated and extroverted cosmopolitan of Hungarian Jewish descent who had marked Norman from their first meeting, was unfailingly dedicated to him. Norman had become increasingly keen to have her in his casts and, although their relationship was not necessarily one of impassioned romance, he brought her home to his family. A match seemed to be gelling.

Kate's immigrant family, the Lockes (Mendel and Jenny, here with son Sam) were cosmopolitan New Yorkers compared to Norman's Boston area work-ing-class parents, Sam and Rose (courtesy Diane Corwin Okarski).

Norman said in a somewhat confusing syntax that, although other girls "knew Emil and Al and the folks [when they] came into town, we'd have dinner with Kate, she'd be my girl to have dinner with." He seemed to mean that his family saw him in passing with a lot of other women, who knew them and whose names they knew, but the one woman at his side when the Corwins sat down for a meal was Kate.

Her place at his side, a wordless image, symbolized a tacit affection

Kate seems to have had to guess existed. What her guarded date was feeling he did not say. The "poet laureate of the radio" did not find passion particularly easy to express. Even after he courted and married Kate, he declared that he had never written a love poem. (One wonders. Is it plausible? The likelihood seems greater that Norman wrote many, was dissatisfied with all and sent none.)[90]

Norman's face was not particularly expressive. Most surviving candid photographs and newsreels capture a reserved demeanor or a fixed smile. For lack of details, one guesses that their fights probably derived from frustration over communication. The same unflappability that made Norman a great director hindered the leap of sparks between candid and trusting hearts. In between heated spats, they eased into a comfort zone in one another's presence. A rocky but loving relationship between different temperaments evolved. They came to rely on one another. It is hard to imagine Norman happy with anyone but Kate, or someone very much like her in personality.

Norman's closest friends of those years described Norman as a workaholic. Kate's solution exhibited a stroke of genius. Kate left Norman alone when he picked up his faithful clipboard and began to write. Whenever possible, radio got them together. She rooted for his success through the big project that took him farthest away in 1946. During the "One World Flight when Norman went around the world, she was at his side mentally.

He explained his continuous priority to Bannerman, "(B)y the time I took the world flight, she was important enough in my scheme of things that I phoned her from various countries abroad. I remember telephoning her from Australia. We weren't married then. And for a while we thought that maybe she could fly to Honolulu and I, on the way back, from the Antipodes, could meet her in Honolulu." (This rendezvous plan failed because Norman was not staying in Honolulu long enough.) Norman further recollected that "when I came back to New York, and [from] then on, to the point of our getting married, we were together a great deal of the time."[91]

Today, one knows none of this from the journal he kept as he flew. Kate's name, their planned but ultimately impossible rendezvous, and all of those phone calls are not in Norman's journal of the world flight, which ends:

> When we arrived at LaGuardia, I was met by about 20 reporters and cameramen, and a group of family and friends. My brother Al drove us home in my car, and as soon as we were established in the door of 38 Central Park South, I phoned the folks to say that the trip was over, and that I was safely home.

He did not say that Kate was there, although she was. He had yet to propose. Until he proposed in 1947, Norman had long exhibited skittishness about acknowledging a relationship. That he pined for Kate the whole of his world trip was a secret shared only with Bannerman about thirty years after that trip, and apparently excised from at least the published version of his journal.

Norman was dreamy rather than detailed in discussing Kate. In a mix-up reminiscent of his father's London-and-Poland nativity, Norman told Bannerman that Kate, a quintessential cosmopolite, had been born in New York. Then, he promptly realized, "No she was not. She was born in Russia. I think near Odessa." Norman told Bannerman that Kate's father was a teacher in religious schools, a Hebrew teacher and a cantor, and a scholarly man, before he awarded the old man his rarest accolade: her father possessed "a great knowledge and passion for music, especially opera."[92]

Kate was incredibly patient, contenting herself with discontinuous and erratic waves of close attention, stubborn argument, and absolute affection. Kate's tolerance was key to maintaining a relationship. His exclusive devotion to her came only after the war and as radio's glory days were ending. Then Norman very consciously looked to Kate for wholeness. He told Bannerman that "she had a very good pragmatic head for a great many of the things that I lacked. That she complemented me, so to speak." He referred to a comfort zone. It was simply possible for him to be more relaxed with her, he said.[93]

Norman wanted Bannerman to understand that he was a different man when he proposed than he was when he first met Kate. He was not only not a playboy; he was not head-over-heels in love. He had good sense.

Norman and Kate burrowing into scripts. The couple had an extended up-and-down courtship until, finally (in Norman's phrasing), "it made sense" for him to propose (courtesy Diane Corwin Okarski).

With Bannerman, he went overboard in *not* describing a passionate decision. To listen to Norman, he worked his way to a conclusion that marrying Kate was *logical*. Sounding like Robert Benchley coming to something surprising in his Treasurer's Report, Norman told Bannerman that his spontaneous proposal one day "astonished" them both. As in a Benchley skit, however, he did not want anybody to think that his heart had run away from him. He insisted that his marriage proposal was the product of long and sober reflection. Norman mansplained his rationale. It was a line that he would only script for a guy resisting saying how crazy he was over a girl. He said, "I just became so accustomed to having her around that it seemed to me that something would be missing without her, and at that point, I'd decided that getting married made good sense."

He further suggested that Bannerman ask Kate about it. In a boastful understatement, he thought that "Kate would probably deny that I became impassioned and lost my cool." Norman's ideal after the war was sound judgment or decisions based on "good sense." This hallmark of maturity distinguished their marriage from his previous trysts. He told Bannerman to expect Kate to confirm "that I was too cool too long, that it took us longer than the actuarial figures would propose, for me to propose."[94]

Delightfully, their madcap wedding was anything but logical. Its logistics were ludicrous. It was a tale of travail. Appearing before an appropriate official in New York one Friday, the couple discovered that Norman had not obtained the necessary license one week in advance. But, they learned, no advance license was needed in Maryland. Maryland it was. Taking along Kate's friend, Mabel Schirmer, they then raced by train on Monday morning for Elkton, on the eastern edge of the Maryland border. In Elkton, they married in a ceremony quickly performed by a Justice of the Peace in order to catch the first afternoon train back. Coming and going, Kate and Schirmer sat together and chatted while Norman worked alone on a script spread out in a small compartment. Togetherness got a slow start.[95]

However, after the war and after he left CBS, Norman was no longer alone. No longer constructing cathedrals in air, the art he began to master in his evolving relationship with Kate was the art of living. In that art he excelled entirely—though never exclusively, and never without Kate's help—outside of the public's gaze and media awareness.

Nothing like Norman's career ever happened before in radio, nor would it ever happen again. When Norman reached forty in May 1950, he had already lived a packed lifetime. He had done his part to heal emotional war wounds and to prepare a lasting peace. At the same time, he made "poet laureate of radio" his honorific forever. Best of all personally, he found love. After running a long gauntlet of relationships, he found family.

What could be better than that?

Postwar to 1950

Standing, left to right: Charles Laughton, Paul Robeson, Norman and Robert Young at Norman's testimonial dinner, held in the Florentine Room of the Beverly Wiltshire Hotel in April 1946. Laughton was a versatile actor with whom Norman enjoyed a close friendship and who he cast in more of his shows than any other actor, Robeson (who, in 1939, sang Norman's revision of "A Ballad for Americans") introduced the guest of honor that evening, while Young, star of Norman's "Passport for Adams" series, served as the dinner's emcee (courtesy American Radio Archives and Museum).

Norman's postwar life and career was also nearly post-radio. That is, the presence of radio shrank, increasingly replaced by unblinking eyes of television sets in the country's living rooms. And as television expanded, radio trivialized. More and more, disc jockeys, ad jingles and traffic and weather reports filled the air.

The loss or greatly reduced presence of network radio is tragic for a number of reasons, one being that it took place at Norman's prime. He was yet to turn forty and could reasonably anticipate many more productive years. His skills had never been sharper *and* appreciation of his work remained high, if not higher than ever.

Proof of the latter arose from old material, from when Norman sought and found ideas in the Bible. He devoted one of his *26 by Corwin* to Samson. (He also took on Esther, then Job.) The show had gone over well enough in 1941 but the words he wrote for it in one week flat were so rhythmic and right that they might be lifted, unmodified, to become the libretto of an opera.

They were. A composer, Bernard Rogers, promptly appeared at Norman's door asking for permission to write an opera based upon his *Samson* libretto. Norman casually agreed. Rogers thereafter did not change a word. (Norman criticized the composer later for being "far too respectful of my original script. It was as though he was dealing with the Bible or Shakespearean text"—but Rogers's instincts were sound.)

Rogers titled the script and score *Samson*. The League of Modern Composers selected it for first prize, which entitled *Samson* to be performed and aired as a special presentation by CBS, the score conducted by Bernard Hermann and played by the CBS orchestra on a program called *Invitation to Music*.

In June 1945 Norman was invited to the piano rehearsal of the opera by singers in a studio at CBS. Norman found—with his eyes closed, no doubt—that the opera was "disappointingly atonal" and "quite modern" when "it should have the desert and the night, and that quality in it."

Equally dissatisfied, Hermann killed the broadcast. Although the League's award winner, *Samson* was withdrawn from the schedule.[96]

Norman "commiserated with Rogers, not for myself because I hadn't done a lick of work and there was no custard running down my face from a pie thrown into it, as far as the public was concerned, whereas there was for Rogers."[97]

Revived enough to rebound, Rogers asked Norman if he would "mind awfully" his submission of the opera in another competition. This was the Alice M. Ditson Fund Contest, winning which meant a cash prize and production by the Metropolitan Opera. Rogers explained that the opera would be submitted anonymously, so that the judges could not be influenced by the name of the composer or librettist. Norman agreed.[98]

Retitled *The Warrior*, the opera won the Ditson competition and it was performed at the Met in January 1947. Underneath this double award-winner—the music of which had disappointed Norman's own trained ear and which the CBS conductor had vehemently rejected—was Norman's script. What people heard *in words* worked. Norman breathed new life into a figure so well-known and so often portrayed on stage and screen. Writings by Norman pleased expert judges and the public in the air, on stage, whether in 1941 or 1947.

(Norman's inadvertent operatic adventure confirms that he really probably could have saved *Pursuit of Happiness* series by adapting a Hemingway story or a Whitman poem or other texts into musicals.)

Newlyweds Norman and Kate, 1947 (courtesy Diane Corwin Okarski).

In October 1947 for ABC, Norman took part in the writing of a special on the First Amendment, "Hollywood Fights Back." The only other shows he did in 1947 for CBS were mixes or culls from tapes made during his One World flight. Unfortunately, the One World award and adulation, CBS's accommodation, contract waiver and leave of absence, his four-month around-the-world journey finally only resulted in a big box of leaden recordings which, transcribed, ran to 3,700 pages. The belated broadcasts turned into a victory lap without an audience.[99]

The ballyhooed One World flop, as it were, could not have escaped the attention of Norman's higher-ups. The same crew had decided not to renew his contract once before, in 1941. With Bill Lewis long gone from CBS and face time with his successors scarce, Norman had to wonder about CBS chief William Paley. In the early Forties, Paley and his wife had dropped by the control room "just to watch and listen" to Norman's broadcasts, after which they would chat. Likewise, Norman mentioned town house parties to which he was invited by Paley. How accurate, though, was it to call Paley a friend of Norman's?

We have evidence of their possible closer bonding during the war. In England, Paley entertained Norman and other journalists with parties in London that were likely uproarious. In another mood, Paley and Norman stood together at the RAF aerodrome in Cambridge awaiting the return of Sterling bomber crews from a raid on Wilhelmshaven. Paley's public tribute to Norman at his public send-off, held at the Waldorf Astoria the night before he left on his One World Flight, had been glowing.[100]

Still, in 1948, on a train outside Pasadena, 38-year-old Norman stared out the window. For his memoirs, he sketched a gloomy stream of consciousness:

> [T]he resolves aborted, opportunities missed, works released too soon, scripts, speeches, scenes, words irrevocably printed or spoken, blunders in my personal life, stupidities, obstinacies, neglects of education, impetuous decisions, excesses of brashness and caution, all came together like a tweedy TV pattern, blurred and blobbed, a hail of dried bird-shit.[101]

Amid such dark thoughts, he ran into Paley in the train's dining car. When he did, Norman said that he discerned "a different Paley." Paley was outwardly embarrassed. Their mutual (and admired) friend, William Shirer, had hastily departed from CBS, so hastily that it was widely believed he had been fired for his liberal opinions. As Paley went on to deny having fired Shirer, he mused aloud about drawing new lines. He finally told Norman that the survivors at CBS had to "face up to the fact that we're a commercial business." He blandly asked his most thoughtful writer, "Couldn't you write for a broader public?"[102]

It was certainly not a question that made Norman's day. Back at the window that reminded him of a TV screen, handwriting was now on the wall. Norman saw not only a new Paley but foresaw 90 million radio sets, sets filled with "soap operas or gags or programs of towering innocuousness."[103]

About six months later, on May 3, 1949, Corwin turned 39. He had been almost 15 years in broadcasting, over ten of those years on the top rung. Radio churned with changes below during this time, however. For one thing, the number of sponsored shows doubled. As Barnouw recounted in his history of broadcasting, "Before the war approximately one-third of network time had been commercially sponsored; by the end of the war, it was two-thirds." In another development, fewer newspaper readers meant more radio listeners. Advertising dollars formerly earmarked for the print media went to radio, and most of that money flowed into the networks, which competed to broaden its listener share. The lowest common denominator type of programming was understood to reach the broadest possible audience.[104]

Write for a broader public? Curley, the dancing caterpillar, was an act he could never repeat. To write another W.S. Gilbert rhyming show like "The Undecided Molecule" without the inimitable Groucho or the urbane sophistication of deft Robert Benchley was soul poison to imagine. Of course, Norman might captain another *Pursuit of Happiness* and win a broader public with a variety show a bit more musical than that series, but that was not going to fulfill him. Besides, Paley had not stated the obvious: radio overall was dying.

After a single 1949 show of which he said nothing later, Norman left CBS. The contract offered by the network was "strikingly inferior" to both of his two earlier contracts. Not only did CBS want his services, the network wanted half of anything he earned from anthologies of his scripts or movie rights to any shows.[105]

He had some regrets. He felt losses. Although not expressed at the time, when Bannerman asked what he missed "of the old days," Norman stated immediately, "The camaraderie." Perfectly right. After all, rounding up circles of friends on verbal magic went back almost to the beginning of his life as his chief joy. At CBS with colleagues like Ed Murrow, Bill Lewis, Betsy Tuthill, Charles Jackson, and Max Wylie, he was in Paradise. His other regrets were a workaholic's list of what he missed, "The pride CBS took in its cultural accomplishments, the sense of eagerness to do good work, to expand artistic frontiers, to rush in where fools and NBC feared to tread."[106]

He had to move on to do anything good. His first show for the U.N., "Could Be," broadcast on September 8, 1949, was top rank. Not only did Michael Kacey select it for inclusion in the centennial set of CDs, it was the subject of unusual fan mail at the time. A note came in from a listener who said that he had just put on his coat to take a walk when he heard the ear-snagging beginning of "Could Be" and stayed in for an hour to hear it to the end. Admiral Chester W. Nimitz went on to congratulate Norman for "one of the best radio dramatizations that has ever been my good fortune to hear."[107]

Although radio no longer addressed Mr. and Mrs. North and South America and all the ships at sea, Norman could still call an Admiral to attention. And the United Nations. After its broadcast live over the Mutual Broadcasting System on March 26, 1950, six weeks before Norman's fortieth birthday, "Document A/777," a show about the adoption of the universal declaration of human rights, a recording of the show was introduced by Mrs. Eleanor Roosevelt and then played to the United Nations Assembly.[108]

Clearly, Norman had a lot more to offer radio, only radio had no more to offer him. There were too many television sets and too few Admirals and U.N. Assemblies to keep him writing, producing, and directing radio shows. Now married, still-young Norman had to work. If he could not exercise creative freedom, and do his best work writing for radio, what ought he do?

That was the question Norman faced as he entered his forties.

He needed not stay too glum too long. It would work out. He would live long and prosper. Had he a moment of reminiscence in 1950, he might have imagined reporting the news over the great "Herberts-Harkins Howling Hetrodyne" radio he set up on stage at his senior class show in Winthrop.

The first bulletin, of Norman Corwin departing from his big job in New York radio for new adventures at age forty, might have brought smiles.

Norman thinks he'll get a big job in the Big Apple? The heckling might begin, "I know for a fact that kid has never been north of Lake Winnipesaukee or south of Coventry, Rhode Island."

The next prophecy, that Norman would be named by critics as the "poet laureate of radio" would have sounded impossible even to his great admirer, Miss Lu. Who would place a ten-cent bet on that? She could not imagine her student doing that.

Then, with the climactic prophecy that tens of millions tuned in to hear Norman just after the beginning and nearly at the end of the next world war, the audience would say sarcastically, "A likely story." First, there would be no Second World War and, second, Norman was never going to address a hundred people.

But the bulletins came true.

You have just witnessed "Whatever Happened to Norman Corwin." We hope very much that you enjoyed hearing his unlikely story. *(Chimes.)* Once again, broadcasting to the Winthrop High School Class of 1926, this is Station YAP, from the tower high above the Rollins-Rowe Stores in downtown Philadelphia. We now sign off from our broadcast day while wishing all of you out there the very happiest of good nights.

Good night.

Epilogue

After CBS, Norman had his family, his material needs were covered, he never lacked for affectionate and familiar faces and his fan mail never entirely ceased. He made his mark with an eventual 17 books. Most of all, friendships occupied Norman. Several wide circles of friends across a spectrum of his interests, and the many around Kate, enabled Norman to demonstrate greater empathy and broader, more active understanding than he found possible (or time for) in his earlier, busier days.

For a longer time than either would have wished, Kate and he had no children. At his most laconic, Norman noted to Bannerman, "I

Like father, like son. Young Tony Corwin on the beach, 1950s (photograph by Lotte Nossaman, courtesy Diane Corwin Okarski).

think there were two miscarriages." Their wait seemed forever. With Bannerman, he estimated "seven years" passed before their children, Tony and Diane, arrived before counting out the actual five years. Longing for children seems to have pervaded them both from March 17, 1947, through the summer of 1952, when they joyfully filled out forms to adopt Tony. Their blessing doubled; at the time Kate was, as Norman boasted, "big with child," a child they would name Diane.[1]

As with affection, Norman did not find admiration easy to express. Also, Norman's admiration for Kate's professional skills may not have equaled hers for his. Not only had she not (like him) been internationally celebrated, he was born before women had the right to vote, and had grown to manhood within a patriarchal and chauvinistic nation. Such experiences may have narrowed his perceptions and limited the extent of his celebration of Kate's movie roles. He sung no praises. Of her professional work, he told Bannerman only that her film work after they married "was never a problem" for *him*.[2]

Diane Corwin at play, 1950s (photograph by Lotte Nossaman, courtesy Diane Corwin Okarski).

Small things pleased them both, Kate more than Norman. They excited one another conversationally, in which endeavor Kate was more often the initiator. Kate joyfully shared her most special mail with Norman. On the day that Kate received the old Burns Mantle review of her debut from a fan in New York, a woman who had saved it for decades, she proudly and promptly brought it to show Norman. In his turn, he thought it remarkable. She likewise shared with Norman any proof she encountered of his continuing influence. For example, she noticed someone on a bus reading one of his books. He lit up when she told him. Evidence of

Tony Corwin and a feline friend, 1950s (photograph by Lotte Nossaman, courtesy Diane Corwin Okarski.).

their glory days, whether of hers or his, pleased them mutually. They were a couple. They were one. They were married with children.

Any biographer who visits the Special Collection department of the American Radio Archives at the Thousand Oaks Library in California consciously works in the shadow of RE ME. A security box stored there contains some 400 double-spaced, typed pages of an incomplete autobiography. Norman jocularly explained to UCLA Professor Mike Kacey that he stopped writing due to "I-strain." In 1986, Norman had made a similar remark when writing a note to the biographer of William S. Paley, saying, "I just got tired of writing about myself."

Another book, with which Norman cooperated, noted that Norman "abandoned" his autobiography. His life story threw him off. It did not satisfy him. He was the proverbial cat chasing its tail.[3]

Norman wanted to be remembered. He gave over 10,000 documents to the Thousand Oaks archives. He gave the travel journal away for its publication in 1972 and helped *gratis* in the production of a book of his letters. He took part in documentaries, even suggesting a spin-off film just about him.

His first forty years lived within him to be revived, if only in memory.

He published four radio books, writing detailed prefaces for each of his scripts. He cooperated with a biographer in his sixties. And there was RE ME.

In his memoirs, Norman stopped short of the most personal of his big fights. During the period of McCarthyism, Norman battled the blacklist. He stood against a toxic stock "patriotism" unworthy of that label. An entire book could be written on Norman's role in that important struggle. Within a few years of spectacularly shaping and leading the country's response to the defeat of Hitler, perhaps the country's most publicly idealistic wartime writer,

Diane, in the 1950s (photograph by Lotte Nossaman, courtesy Diane Corwin Okarski).

Norman was being battered and smeared. The currents of American politics had turned into rapids to negotiate carefully. Writing radio scripts for the United Nations, which Norman did, sufficed for a time to mark a person as "unreliable." However, few at the time endured and counterpunched better than Norman.

Nothing thwarted him for long. His career extended to eighty years, during which he wrote three cantatas, one of which was performed in the Assembly Hall of the United Nations. Besides the radio script of "Samson" mentioned earlier, which became the libretto of an award-winning opera, his stage plays included the musical version of another wartime radio play, "The Odyssey of Runyan Jones," a Lincoln-Douglas confrontation, "The Rivals," and (in his nineties), "The Strange Affliction," his lyrical and light rhyming romance. For television, he scripted the first and last show of ABC's twenty-six part "FDR," which aired in 1963. In 1996, National Public Radio digitally remastered and then ran a collection of his radio shows as a series called *13 by Corwin*.

William Shatner played in that PBS series. Although perhaps best known for playing Captain James T. Kirk on *Star Trek*, Shatner was an active partner in several theatrical productions with Norman. In a preface to a collection of Norman's last plays, Shatner, a classically trained Shakespearean actor, wrote about his excitement when acting "parts of the play I thought rivaled Shakespeare."[4]

Norman regularly asked Shatner to fill in as the virtual substitute for Orson Welles. In the 1990s, after cameras had been packed up and on a "dead set," Norman directed his actors for a *faux* broadcast with such vigor and verisimilitude that they were, in their imaginations, swept off magically and on the air.

"We're shaking, we're nervous," Shatner admitted, as Norman conducted the play.[5]

Activity alone was no stay against loss. Norman gradually lost people and institutions close to him. Of the *Springfield Republican* and his former comrades, Norman wrote in the 1980s, how "it foundered and sank," as good reporters died or, some like Bill Walsh, "left before the end." He regretted losing contact with his former colleagues, reporting that "when I became nationally known for my radio work, I heard from only two or three of the score from whom I had worked for so long," although one of these was Walsh.[6]

The Corwins in the early 1950s. Left to right: Em, Booie, Ma, Norman, Pa, Al. The members of the family were close lifelong. Beginning 1927, for example, Norman and his father spoke long distance each Sunday until Pa died in 1987 at age 110 (courtesy Diane Corwin Okarski).

Ma Corwin died in 1961. When his best friend in high school, Barney Zieff, died in 1965, Norman wrote, "As we get older we lose friends and loved ones, and try to be philosophical about it. But the passing of Barney is a hard test of that philosophy." Pa lived until 1987. The old plate maker and scrapbooker was then 110, and the oldest person in Massachusetts. Norman's ever-loyal brother and admirer Al passed in 1990, in his eighties. Kate died in 1995 at age 85 while Em lived until 2011. Just as Em was uniquely Norman's "big brud" and his closest friend, Kate was Norman's one and only.[7]

Wisely, Norman never remarried. He could not have found another Kate. Although, statistically, men who live alone do not tend to live long, second bachelorhood did not hurt Norman. Never the average American man, Norman did live long. Besides genetic advantages (his father and Em being centenarians), Norman lived within the social nourishment and renewal of many friendships, both old and newly formed.

These friends were people he spoke and listened to, sounding boards as well as sources of fascination to him as they talked and shared. Celebrity alone never cut weight with him. Many of his friends were publicly unknown. Their connections he treasured no less. For example, in 2007, Norman got an unexpected update on Jumbo Tranghese. The old Springfield "barrel bouncer" had died but his five children survived. The youngest of Jumbo's three sons, John, wrote Norman a note. That one short note triggered a waterfall of notes, advice, referrals, and newspaper clippings of the Springfield barrel-rolling competitions from Norman's files, and reciprocal gifts, as well as phone calls and a memorable visit.[8]

Between 2007 and 2011, John told Norman about growing up poor, sleeping on the kitchen floor with his brothers in a house with two beds, one for his parents and one for his sisters. Norman had to have considered his own experiences in Eastie as John told about growing up in a three-family tenement that his father inherited.

When John was old enough (age 8) he rose early in any weather, cardboard covering holes in his shoes, when freezing wearing anything he could find to walk six blocks to peddle newspapers including the *Republican* at a street corner. He brought that money home before he started his classes at the School. (Small world: the "barrel bouncing" contest during which Norman met Jumbo took place in the schoolyard of the Howard Street elementary school.) John and his brothers took any odd jobs, shining shoes, running errands, shoveling snow.

At seventeen, to John's horror, reviving Norman's own youthful trauma, in his last semester of high school, which included poetry, he technically failed that course and was in jeopardy of not graduating.

"I should fail you," Miss Maurer, his English teacher told him, giving him a pass. "But I have trust that you will pick up poetry and I know that you've got plans."

John, who did have plans to get right to work, apologized, took the pass gratefully and told her, "I'll write you a poem."[9]

That summer, John mailed Miss Maurer a poem about persistence and got a happy acknowledgment from her. It was with his last poem for over fifty years. John penned his next rhyming verses for his fiftieth wedding anniversary, when he composed a lively polka for his Polish first wife, a bouncy, triumphant song he titled "I've Got Nancy." When Nancy died of cancer not long afterward, he mourned by writing songs again, some sad, some happy. John finally met Patricia, with whom he experienced a second chance at love.

John and I were in the Student Prince, a well-known Springfield German restaurant two doors down from what used to be the editorial office of the *Springfield Republican*. Up those stairs John's father had bounded in 1931 to ask for Norman. We were eerily close to where Jumbo and Norman had met. We were on the street where a relationship began that took both Jumbo and Norman into radio and into headlines, Jumbo only briefly but Norman for much longer.[10]

Norman confessed to John that he had never written a song, although one adapted poem set to music was broadcast. Norman explained in one letter to John, "I did not trust myself to write them, but I took poems written by others for my texts. The best of them was a piece called, 'Go Down, Death,' which is the only piece of mine that made it to a radio broadcast. There used to be a black quartet on CBS, and they arranged a version of it, and, by God, it was broadcast."[11]

On invitation to Thousand Oaks, John flew in from Massachusetts to see one of Norman's stage productions. Norman met John in a Jaguar, driven by his helper. John, as guest of the author, then saw the light romantic comedy partly in rhyming verse, "The Strange Affliction," performed by a cast of stars, friends of Norman, headed by Carl Reiner and Nanette Fabray. Touched finally to meet his friend, Norman inscribed John's copy of the Thousand Oaks program, "Live forever—that's an order."[12]

Norman also arranged for a surprise professional studio recording session for John while he was in Thousand Oaks. John, who did not sing, declined, but he was inspired. When back in Springfield, his dormant poetic side was stimulated, really jolted into high gear by Norman's encouragement. He hired singers and musicians for a recording session to cut CDs of his romantic ballads and country songs. He joined ASCAP and became active in the Connecticut Songwriters Association. He worked earnestly with an agent and corresponded with others in the song industry, including Arthur Hamilton ("Cry Me a River"), all contacts he made through Norman.[13]

Although without commercial success in music—and, being a great salesman, John had manfully tried—John said, "I cannot *not* write songs," when I met him in his seventies. After reprising Norman's consistent enthusiasm for what he was doing, and following a minute reviewing his CDs, John said softly, "My grandchildren can play those when I'm gone and know about me."[14]

John's words in the restaurant fit Norman, too, whose radio shows like "They Flew Through the Air," "To Tim at Twenty," "We Hold These Truths," "To the Young," "Untitled," and "On a Note of Triumph" were recorded so that we can still hear them—and know about him.

There were movies as well. Norman's script, "Lust for Life," the story of Vincent Van Gogh, was nominated for an Oscar in 1956 for the Best Adapted Screenplay.

Norman served as a member of the Academy of Motion Picture Arts & Sciences, including as chair of two of its committees. As the writer in residence at the USC Annenberg School for Communication & Journalism, for many years Professor Corwin taught communications and wrote a monthly column about the media.

"A Note of Triumph: The Golden Age of Norman Corwin" won an Oscar for the best short documentary film of the year 2005. Many witnesses spoke about Norman's radio show, "On a Note of Triumph." Their memories of it remained vivid after more than 50 years. As some spoke, like Studs Terkel, their eyes lit up in recalling an exciting and moving event. To hear Norman, they did not go out to celebrate but waited at home on V-E Day to tune in.[15]

In an incidental demonstration of his ongoing acuity in his nineties, Norman discerned potential before an accomplished filmmaker did. When Mike Kacey got "good answers" to "good questions" during an interview of about an hour and a half on videotape, he was pleased. Just after they stopped, however, Norman spoke up. Norman sensed that their interview—actually made to cannibalize for a longer documentary about radio's Golden Age—could stand alone.[16]

On-the-spot impressions are notoriously erroneous. Judgments quickly made often err, especially in show business. However, piqued to consider Norman's suggestion, Kacey followed up. He reviewed the tape later.

"When I watched the interview in the editing room, I decided it would, indeed, hold its own," Kacey said. The old *maestro* was right. His ears worked. He knew a good story when he heard one. The video needed but little editing. "The Poet Laureate of Radio" came out to critical praise in 2006.[17]

Norman lived to be 101. He remained sharp and mentally active until his final few weeks. Before that, Norman gave interviews, whether short or long, readily on request. Although Norman died in 2011 after a brief illness, and although he had been afflicted by several medical difficulties that bound him to a wheelchair, for a long time, he enjoyed the giddy sense of defeating mortality. Humorously, he claimed to be waiting to die on a slow news day. (In the end, he did.)

His children, Anthony and Diane, survived him, as did his radio plays, books, and film work. He changed the world in ways that cannot be precisely traced or ever proved. Almost subliminally, his Bill of Rights show informed the country what was at stake that first week that war was declared. Finally, on V-E Day, he, and not the President, asked the hard questions that were due for answers after Hitler was dead and the German military had surrendered.

The citizens of his country turned to their trusted Norman at critical moments and heeded what they heard from him as closely—if not more closely—than they did most anybody else during the war. Norman, the poet, writer and music lover, the producer, writer and director, his eyes closed, merely on "sounds coming through the air," first heard by him on earphones on Harold Marchant's crystal set in Eastie, Norman on CBS brought Americans to stop and to think—and, if he did not make things happen like world brotherhood and perpetual peace, at least he planted those flags and staked a clear verbal claim to them for future humanity in appeals that were lyrical, high-minded and Biblically cadenced.

His epitaph might have been, "People listened to him."

For so they did, for a long time.

Norman mirrored quite fashionably in about 1970 (courtesy of ARA).

Chapter Notes

Preface and Acknowledgments

1. Norman spoke of network radio as a horse that had carried him far and was then "shot out from under him." See the documentary film by Les Guthman, *Corwin* (University of Southern California School of Journalism, 1996), at about 53:23.

2. See the documentary by Michael James Kacey, ed., "The Poet Laureate of Radio, An Interview with Norman Corwin," Anthracite Films video (2006).

3. The thirteen-part early 1942 series *This Is War!* was directed by Norman, who also scripted six of the shows. The show after Pearl Harbor was "We Hold These Truths." The V-E Day show (his most famous, considered his masterpiece) was "On a Note of Triumph."

4. Lillian Ross, *Picture* (1952; DaCapo Press, 2002), 191. (Spencer Tracy and Gregory Peck were considered, too, but James Whitmore was ultimately chosen to narrate.)

5. Norman's later close friend and acclaimed television writer Norman Lear wrote that he always thought of him as "the patriots' poet laureate." *Norman Corwin's One World Flight: The Lost Journal of Radio's Greatest Writer*, Michael C. Keith and Mary Ann Watson, eds. (New York The Continuum International Publishing Group, 2009), ix.

6. NC letter to Elspeth MacDuffie O'Halloran (December 7, 1933), NCL, 18.

7. In Kacey's documentary, at about 6:00, Norman said, "I am the beneficiary of a whole series of serendipities," and that he was lucky, although he promptly added, that he worked hard to capitalize on his "lucky breaks."

8. Norman Corwin, letter in reply to a fan, actress and friend Joan Alexander (January 12, 1941), in A.J. Langguth, ed., *Norman Corwin, Norman Corwin's Letters* (hereafter, "NCL") (New York: Barricade Books, Inc., 1994) 52–53. Decades after this letter, Norman's reaction to a proud daughter's praise was identical. Diane Corwin Okarski recalled, "As a student, to fulfill a classroom assignment, I once wrote a glowing essay about my father. I showed Norman my writing expecting his approval. He liked what I'd written though he had one caveat: 'You must include my flaws.'" Letter from Diane Corwin Okarski to the author, April 25, 2020, unpublished, used by courtesy of Ms. Okarski.

9. *RE ME*, 8, unfinished and unpublished, is today part of the Norman Corwin collection at the American Radio Archives in Thousand Oaks, CA. Excerpts used by courtesy of Diane Corwin Okarski.

10. *Norman Corwin Centennial* (Radio Spirits, 2010) (hereafter, "*Centennial* CD"). A select set of eighteen of Norman's shows originally broadcast live between 1939 and 1949. Program guide by Michael James Kacey.

Norman's December Surprise

1. Erik Barnouw, *The Golden Web: A History of Broadcasting in the United States, 1933–53* (Vol. 2) (hereafter "Barnouw"), 152. (The dinner went on as planned—"They would have to eat anyway," Eleanor told Murrow. "At midnight he and the President had a long talk…He used nothing of what he had learned.")

2. Bannerman, 77–79. Norman Corwin, *RE ME* (hereafter *RE ME*), 242–45.

3. These and other details in this chapter are drawn from *RE ME*, 242–45, and from Diane Corwin Okarski, who invited the author's attention to *More by Corwin*, 350. See also Bannerman, 235.

4. The Welles program elicited over 20,000 letters requesting a repeat of the repeat performance. This demand for a *third* broadcast of Norman's "Between Americans" in six months is a sign of the country's appetite for something as good, fast-paced and idealistic as Norman could produce.

5. Norman Corwin interview, Radio Pioneers Group IV, Columbia University Oral Archives (April 28, 1966) (hereafter, "NCI/Columbia), 24. Norman had overlapping but somewhat different versions of whether he got a telegram or a call. A telegram seems more likely. In 1966, he recalled it as a phone call from Lewis, during which Lewis said, "Certainly, we're going on. It's more important now than ever. That's the way the President feels about it."

6. *RE ME*, 245.

7. "Em" was Emil Corwin, a publicist in New York in 1941 and many other occupations into his late nineties, the oldest of the three Corwin brothers. Al Corwin letter to Ma and Pa (December 16, 1941), ARA. Norman was informed, he remembered in 1966, that his show had "the largest audience in world history to have heard a dramatic program." NCI/Columbia, 23. The audience actually increased by the minute as people called one another urging them to listen. *Ibid.*, 25. The show may finally have reached 80 million people.

8. *Ibid.*

9. R. LeRoy Bannerman, *Norman Corwin and the Golden Age of Radio* ((The University of Alabama Press, 1986) (hereafter "Bannerman"), cast list, 237. Full chapter on the show, 73–88.

10. Al Corwin to NC (12/28/1941), ARA. Al was then a civilian employee. He was inducted into the Army on September 10, 1942, was eventually promoted to Captain in July 1945, and was discharged that year after the surrender of Japan.

Part One

1. NC to Anna Neethling-Pohl (May 23, 1984). NCL, 370. Norman Corwin

interview, 8B, ARA. Transcribed by Kevin Soini.

2. Emil (hereafter, "Em") and Frieda Corwin interview, 8A, ARA. Transcribed by Kevin Soini

3. In his college yearbook, in 1925 Em was described as "a little man with quick steps and pensive brow." Ancestry.com, U.S. School Yearbooks, 1900–1999, online. Al was "the tall boy" in letter of Em to NC (December 20, 1941), ARA.

4. Corwin, 8B. "Peck's Bad Boy" was a character featured in a comedic stage play and series of books by George Wilbur Peck which were popular from the 1880s into the 1900s. Em and Frieda Corwin interview, 8A, ARA.

5. Em document, "Reminiscences of Pa," (January 4, 1968), 2, ARA.

6. Em and Frieda Corwin interview, 8A, ARA. Also, *RE ME*, 9. (He recalled that "tank cars, cattle trains, coal gondolas" shunted "night and day." He also recalled an exotic sight in the harbor, of "vapors of the city dump." *Ibid.*, 10.)

7. Norman's exposure to diversity had limits. Eastie was not an integrated community and African Americans were not encountered every day. The jazzy rhythms and trilling jive and deep bass hymns of African Americans, the bountiful, cascading flow of dialect that informed Mark Twain, were not part of the sound palette of young Norman. Norman was out of Massachusetts and in New York before he was deeply in those living, rich sounds. For a long time, from geography and demographics, they were necessarily unfamiliar.

8. Whether by deduction or from an unnamed source, Bannerman stated this conclusion. Bannerman, 14. ("As a child of four, Norman learned poetry by listening to Emil's arduous recitation of rhymes assigned in school.")

9. Of them, David Hoffman, about Em's age, was an athletic type. He soon joined the Navy. Younger Albert Hoffman, one of Norman's own schoolmates, was a go getter who became the head of the fabulous Masabi mines. Ultimately a multi-millionaire, he funded the building that bears the Hoffman name at Harvard College.

10. Em and Freda Corwin interview, 8A, ARA Transcribed by Kevin Soini.

11. Either these satisfying childhood experiences or some innate confidence

becalmed his nerves permanently. On public speaking, Norman told Bannerman that, "for some odd reason, in an area where many people are nervous and have stage fright because they have to get up to speak to a big audience, I never had the slightest quiver. Never. And perhaps I should have. Even when I came unprepared (there) was never stage fright." NC interview, 8B, ARA. Transcribed by Kevin Soini.

12. Famously, in April 1912, eight of its properly attired musicians played "Nearer My God to Thee" on the deck of the *Titanic* as that ship went down in the North Atlantic on her maiden voyage.

13. NC to Em (October 18, 1991). NCL, 430. ("When I was eight or ten years old... you took me to Symphony Hall to hear my first symphony. You paid $ 2.50 for the ticket, and I just remembered that I never reimbursed you for it...[What I owe you with] interest compounded over sixty plus years comes to exactly $ 501.87.")

14. Norman Corwin, *Thirteen by Corwin* (New York: Henry Holt and Co., 1942), Preface, vii.

15. NC to Carl Van Doren letter (February 15, 1942), NCL, 64.

16. *RE ME*, 23.

17. Bannerman, 218. Walter Winchell, the gossip columnist who debuted on radio in 1930 and continued to broadcast into the 1950s, adopted and used as his opening the tagline, "Good evening, Mr. and Mrs. North and South America, and all the ships at sea—let's go to press!"

18. Em and Freda Corwin interview, 9B, ARA. Transcribed by Kevin Soini.

19. McKenzie's primary product line was greeting cards. In nearby Worcester, the George C. Whitney Company, the largest and oldest manufacturer of valentines in the world (going back to the 1860s), closed in March 1942, also due to paper shortages.

20. While Em said bluntly that "Norman hated McKenzie," he offered no explanation and Bannerman chanced not to ask why. Em and Frieda Corwin, 8, ARA. Transcribed by Kevin Soini.

21. Pa was uncertain whether he had been born in Poland or London, although he was certainly raised in London and had no memories of Poland. On January 22–23, 1977 Em interviewed Pa, an interview of which a transcript was made now in a folder at ARA. At Transcript (hereafter "TR"),

3, Pa told Em, "Well, there was always a question between Poland and London. My father was in the Russian army or Polish army, I don't know which one. In those days, the orders were given by bugle. And he was a bugler. He got wounded and he couldn't do anything after that...(M)y dad had relatives in the U.S., and they asked if he wouldn't come to Boston, that the opportunities here were greater than in London." Poland was part of the Russian Empire when Pa was born in 1877. When he met foreigners, Norman played with the ambiguity, "I tell Englishmen that my father was born in London, and Continentals that my mother was born in Hungary." He also told Russians, "My grandparents were Russian." NC to Em (5/8/1932), ARA. *RE ME*, 13. Pa was about 13 when he saw "Boy wanted" ("not a professional sign") in front of Samuel Ward & Co., Franklin Street fine stationers. TR 32. He was hired at $ 3 a week to load stationery packages and boxes onto a hand truck, hauling it through the streets for delivery. *Ibid.*, 33. When he was older and bigger, he was paid more to work on the third floor, "where they did plate printing" at Ward's. *Ibid.*, 34.

22. NC interview, 1, ARA. Transcribed by Kevin Soini.

23. Norman's ill feelings about McKenzie may also have involved a perceived connection between Pa's thirst-inducing heavy labor on a machine on a poorly ventilated third floor and drinking during breaks. Pa himself told Em about "working for McKenzie" when beer was five cents a glass, ten cents for whiskey (apparently at some place near work). TR 80. Ma once smashed three consecutive bottles of liquor he brought into Bremen Street. TR 82. As he grew older, Pa drank less. He did advise Norman to stop colds in their tracks by taking "2 or 3 oz. of likker." Pa to Norman (September 15, 1938), ARA. Well before Pa ever turned 100, his special, rare drink was a lightly spiked orange juice. See also "Year of the Electric Ear," interview of NC by Douglas Bell (undated), 2, in COR03875, Folder 3, ARA.

24. Em and Freda Corwin interview, 9B, ARA.

25. Pa lived to be 110, Em to 107—he only retired at age 96—and Norman to 101, active and writing almost up to his last month. *L.A. Times*, Pt. VI, 8 (March 1, 1987).

26. U.S. Census (1920), accessed on Ancestry.com.

27. Em was very conscious of the importance of "big bruds" to great men, especially great writers. The only book he wrote of aspiring to write was on the theme of big brothers. He asked Norman his opinion of a "study of the brothers of Ed[gar Allan] Poe, Jeff[erson] Davis, Will[iam] James, James Whitcomb Riley. In each instance the big brud had plenty of influence. There may be lots of other big shot brothers, but there is not a bad quartet I have. Wot you think, Joe?" Em to NC, COR03877, Folder 4 (2/23/1931), ARA. Em had by that year already striven, with modest success, to get review copies of Norman's first book into good hands.

28. Memoir by Rose Corwin, copy and permission to quote received from Diane Corwin Okarski. Also, Em interview, ARA. Transcribed by Kevin Soini.

29. Em and Frieda Corwin interview, 8, ARA.

30. Untitled memoir notes by Rose Corwin, copy and permission to quote received from Diane Corwin Okarski.

31. The inserted word reflects a judgment call. All other informants report that Pa was a constant reader of newspapers and books, a highly literate man (who in turn spread the choicest epigrams from what he read).

32. RE ME, 13. (Norman struck another description, one that referred to his parents' clear diction and nicely modulated voices.) He praised public libraries and seems to have, very early, selected his own reading matter.

33. Em and Frieda Corwin interview, 8A, ARA. Transcribed by Kevin Soini.

34. Norman wrote of looking from the third floor over the train-yards across the street, past "vapors of the city dump," beyond which was Boston Harbor, where he could make out Governor's Island and, on a clear day, just make out the railroad trestle of a short line connecting Boston to Lynn. RE ME, 10.

35. Pa also saved money by making lots of wet, tightly rolled newspapers for slow-burning fuel in the stove. TR 90. His attempts at ingenuity stopped short of making any use of a cobbler's last, hammer and leather that he brought home. TR 91.

36. "On hot summer nights, the boys used to come out in[to] the streets." Em and Frieda Corwin interview, 8B, ARA.

37. This is as Norman recalled his childhood neighborhood. RE ME, 10.

38. Quote from the Norman's third person autobiographical "Introduction" in Michael C. Keith and Mary Ann Watson, eds., Norman Corwin's One World Flight: The Lost Journal of Radio's Greatest Writer (New York: Continuum, 2009), xiii.

39. Untitled memoir notes by Rose Corwin, copy and permission to quote by courtesy of Diane Corwin Okarski.

40. Bannerman, 15.

41. Ibid., 14–15. Norman's first illustrated "novel" is not among the archives in Thousand Oaks and it is not known whether it still exists.

42. Em and Freda Corwin interview, 8A, ARA. Transcribed by Kevin Soini.

43. MAC awarded Em a Bachelor of Science in 1924.

44. Al and Sam Corwin interview, 24, ARA.

45. Facts concerning the Oliver and its repossession problems are derived from a spritely, detailed online source. See www.typewritermuseum.org/collection/index.php3?machine=oliver3&cat=kid-

46. COR 0077. ARA. Al Corwin to Norman (January 14, 1975). Al, who recalled its Quaker oats box core, believed that the crystal radio "had a farther reach than Medford Hillside. We also pulled in WBZ Springfield, WGY Schenectady, and KDKA Pittsburgh."

47. RE ME, 14.

48. See Donna Halper, Boston Radio: 1920–2010 (Arcadia Publishing, 2010), a well-researched, well-written, profusely illustrated review of the rise and fall of radio in the metropolitan Boston area.

49. RE ME, 72, ARA.

50. For example, see Boston Daily Globe, July 5, 1924, p. 3, article headlined "Convention Minutes by Radio to Globe."

51. See Robert K. Murray, The 103rd Ballot: Democrats and the Disaster in Madison Square Garden (New York: Harper & Row, 1976).

52. New York Times, July 8, 1924, 1.

53. The boy's fatal condition derived from an infected blister on one of his feet. By contrast to the Madison Square Garden convention broadcasts or this sad breaking news story, the 1924 Presidential campaign was

not the tinder of radio fire. The Democratic candidate, corporate lawyer John W. Davis, spoke formally as if addressing the court, unwilling to attack his grieving incumbent. On the Republican side, President Coolidge delivered a few sober, mournful-sounding lectures on good government.

54. NC to Sam Corwin (May 5, 1928), NCL, 2.

55. NCL, 16–17.

56. NCL, 418–20.

57. COR03864, Folder 2, Em to NC (10/31/1930), ARA.

58. *RE ME*, 15. Suffolk County Registry of Deeds, Thomas Ambrey sold the Perkins Street property to Samuel and Rose Corwin for $4,527 on November 28, 1923. The house was well-maintained, a "fine home," as Norman termed it, and not a "needs work" project for fixer-uppers. Presumably in need of a stream of income for a while, the Corwins did not immediately move and occupy the house. They continued to pay rent on Bremen Street through April 1925. They moved away from Eastie on Friday, May 1, 1925.

59. *RE ME*, 15–17.

60. Em and Frieda Corwin interview, 8, ARA.

61. *RE ME*, 18. NC letter to Gerald Kean (February 6, 1986). NCL, 382. Of his early diary, he stated, "whatever entries I made were grudging and barren." NC letter to Em (February 27, 1994), NCL, 441. No diary survives at ARA.

62. The Corwins moved to Winthrop in 1925, when Em was 22 and Norman was 15.

63. NC interview, 6, ARA. Transcribed by Kevin Soini.

64. E.g., COR03864, Folder 2, NC to Em (penciled "1930," dated only "Friday…12:01 a.m."), ARA.

65. COR03872, NC to Em (8/1/1933), ARA.

66. Information on Barney A. Zieff is from ancestry.com, accessed 11/20/2015. When Em and Norman went to Europe in 1932, Barney was with them on the ship to Hamburg from New York on October 2, 1931 and the trio visited Paris and other places together. ancestry.com. See also U.S. Census, 1930, ancestry.com. Although likely, it is uncertain whether his brother was a pharmacist in the same store.

67. Their friendship stuck well beyond their senior year, until after Barney married. Barney somehow found the love of

his life in faraway New York. He and Esther wed in Manhattan in 1933. After the ceremony, the couple lived in Winthrop. Barney continued his 50-hour workweeks as a drug-store clerk at a time that love was easier to find than a good job. See also NC letter to Esther Zieff, then Barney's widow (March 7, 1965). NCL, 229. ("Barney was the best friend of my school days…I always felt an enormous quality of loyalty and dignity in Barney, and an inexhaustible capacity for giving and receiving affection.")

68. Norman emanated innocence during his lone beach walks. He described in his memoir of feeling like Adam "not yet suspecting the idea of Eve and a snake." *RE ME*, 19.

69. The Winthrop home was purchased, mortgaged, in 1923 but the family delayed moving. See footnote 55.

70. Per Norman's mother, he was 13 in the ninth grade in East Boston, i.e., 1923-24, when his teacher was Emma Bates Harvey, who had also taught Rose and all of Rose's younger siblings. Undated memorandum entitled "MRS. HARVEY- TEACHER," courtesy of Diane Corwin Okarski. *Perhaps* Mrs. Harvey (and his mother?) enabled Norman to skip tenth grade; school records have not survived. In any case, immediately after moving to Winthrop in May, 1925, Norman spent only a few documented weeks in eleventh grade. Then, in September, 1925, twelfth grade began with Norman as the youngest member of Winthrop High School's senior class.

71. Untitled memoir notes of Rose Corwin, copy and excerpts used by courtesy of Diane Corwin Okarski.

72. *Ibid.*

73. Em and Frieda Corwin interview, 8, ARA. Transcribed by Kevin Soini.

74. One speculates that Norman's trademark "theater of the mind" presentations, where ideas predominate over plot or characters, may in part have roots in chemistry, given his sustained and even impassioned awe before that hard science's disembodied ideas, logical analyses and the indifferent operation of laws of nature.

75. When Miss Lu met the newest student in school, she had been teaching at Winthrop High for eleven years. She was unconventional, a maverick who flouted rules, especially arbitrary deadlines. She originally came to Winthrop with an

unusual recommendation from her former employer, who wrote "'Miss Lu' is not
the most conscientious teacher, but she gets
results." Mrs. Lucy Drew Steutzel interview,
12B, ARA. Transcribed by Kevin Soini.
  76. *Ibid.*
  77. Untitled memoir notes by Rose Corwin, copy and permission to quote from
Diane Corwin Okarski.
  78. *Ibid.*
  79. *Ibid.*
  80. *Ibid.*
  81. An essay he (age 16) wrote for Miss
Lu, called "WORDS," was a "deep poem"
including an anti-war theme, a phenomenon which he termed then "the human
abattoir." *RE ME*, 19. "WORDS" may be
Norman's earliest anti-war writing.
  82. When Dr. Shapley sent him a letter in
1949, Norman savored "moving in 25 years
from being a fan of his to him being one of
mine." *RE ME*, 22. Also, NCL, 121–22. Norman spoke with tongue-in-cheek affection
of the "little entrechats and pirouettes which
I learned from my distinguished career as a
debater in high school." NC to Kate Locke
(March 8, 1946). NCL, 93.
  83. "Smooth" was about the escape of a
smooth "con man" inmate from the electric
chair. *Echo*, 64–67.
  84. *Echo*, 64–67; also, see *Echo*, 26–29.
ARA. The radio in the Class Prophecy play
was a "Herberts-Harkins Howling Hetrodyne," a large, "grotesque" radio set. Its last
signal, from "Station YAP, the Rollins-Rowe
Stores, Philadelphia" was a clear homage to
WNAC, which broadcast from atop a store in
downtown Boston. WNAC was the first station Norman heard over the small crystal set
put together by his brother, Al, back in Eastie.
  85. Em said, "My father took some of his
poetry in to show it to Mr. McKenzie, his
boss, and McKenzie had enough perception
to see that there was an unusual talent there.
He had somebody else look at Norman's
poetry. I don't know who it was or what it
led to. It made that kind of a ripple you see."
Em and Frieda Corwin interview, 8, ARA.
  86. Em and Frieda Corwin interview,
8A, ARA. Portions of a transcript made by
Kevin Soini of Bannerman's interview with
Em on this point are quoted below:
BANNERMAN: [Norman] never finished
high school…
EM: Yes, he did. He graduated from high
school.

BANNERMAN: Well, he told me he didn't.
He never finished Latin, or something. And
he never went back.
EM: He didn't get his diploma?
BANNERMAN: No.
EM: I didn't know that.
BANNERMAN: I didn't know that either.
EM: I think he went through his four
years, though.
BANNERMAN: Yes. It was only, perhaps,
Latin. And he was supposed to go back
but, I don't know, he said he was never very
good at it or something of the sort and he
had to go back and retake an exam or retake
something.
EM: Well, I think Norman decided that
he was not going on to college and he didn't
think that I, who had just graduated college,
was such a great success, so he didn't see any
point in going on to college. So my father
got him an ancient typewriter. And on that
typewriter Norman wrote letters to most of
the newspapers in Massachusetts. He was
interested in landing a job with a newspaper.
(Probably for humane and understand-
ably kind reasons, Bannerman never
asked Sam if he knew that his son had not
received a diploma.)
  87. *L.A. Times*, Part VI, p. 8 (3/1/1987).
  88. Despite its name, Massachusetts
Agricultural College, a Land Grant college
founded in 1863 (with a co-ed dormitory
beginning 1920, when Em matriculated at
M.A.C.) offered arts and sciences studies and
degrees. It became the University of Massachusetts in name as well as in fact in 1947.
  89. Diane Corwin Okarski kindly
released her father's academic records to
the author's inspection; however, a 2015
search at Winthrop High School revealed
that 1925–26 student records had not survived. Norman wrote that he "flunked
Latin, was weak in French, and barely managed to stay afloat in math." *RE ME*, 19.
  90. Equally unanswered is the question
left begging why he (at 16, no less) did not
return to Winthrop High School and obtain
whatever course or credits he needed for
a diploma. From the record, Norman was
apparently doing nothing better than live
in the parental home in Winthrop between
June 1926 and September 1928.
  91. NC to Ruth Gersin (January 20,
1937), NCL 31–32.
  92. What Norman characterized as their
"strange and turbulent and delightful and

rueful friendship," some laughter and some quarrels, did not survive his departure from Winthrop. Long-lived Norman thus chanced to miss a lot of years with Ruth, the girl he spoke of meeting "with a kiss and a hug and a poem in his heart"—she lived to 102.

93. Without explaining why or the connection between Norman and McKenzie, Em said flatly, "Norman hated McKenzie." Em interview, January 22–23, 1977, transcript, 57, ARA.

94. The trips to New Hampshire were the family's summertime frolics to Lake Winnepesaukee, that he "visited many times in (his) first seventeen years of life in Boston and Winthrop. Letter Norman to John Tranghese (May 8, 2008). Author's copy, courtesy of Mr. Tranghese.

95. Norman Corwin letter to Em, about his surgery (April 1927 fragment), ARA.

96. For example, he early, famously, and successfully adapted Edgar Lee Master's *Spoon River Anthology*. "The Plot to Overthrow Christmas," his first hit, comically resurrected Nero and other residents of Hades. Other reviving programs include "To Tim at Twenty," "The Odyssey of Runyon Jones," and "Untitled," all three of which rank among his most effective dramas.

97. NCI/Columbia, 1. Norman described the foliage turning red and orange in Greenfield when he moved from Winthrop to western Massachusetts, but he also reported in his memoir handling the Recorder's phone in August 1927. Probably, he was in Greenfield after his birthday (May) in early summer, i.e., June or July.

98. Rejections were considered a moral duty by some Boston editors. When Norman's more experienced college graduate brother, Em, tried the *Boston Globe*, his reply came from a veritable legend in New England journalism, Louis M. Lyons. Lyons wrote, "The best thing any newspaper worker can do for any applicant is to try to discourage him. If he fails, he has at least tried to do his duty." COR03871, Folder 1, Louis M. Lyons to Em (10/7/27), ARA.

99. Haigis Correspondence, ARA. (NOTE: Norman's middle initial was not "H." His full name was Norman Lewis Corwin.) The recommendation from Young is enclosed with a June 17, 1935 cover letter from Haigis to Norman, congratulating him on his job (ultimately short-lived) with Station WLW in Cincinnati.

100. Norman loved Em, loved being with him, talking to him, fighting and arguing, sharing stories he wrote, getting feedback. Em was the audience of reviews of books he'd read. When Norman finished Huxley's novel, *Point Counter Point*, he wrote Em, "(I)f you haven't read it you have a tremendous kick in store for you. You will laugh aloud a dozen times although it is not a funny book. Its penetration of character is so skilled, its knowledge of human motives and its interpretation of actions is so searching, that it will amaze you. Withal, it is keen, trenchant, satiric." COR0875, NC to Em (in pencil: 8/1/1933), 2, ARA.

101. NC letter to Robert Young (February 7, 1993), NCL, 439. Norman's end of the conversation, spoken in an otherwise empty copy room, could have been recycled as the start of one of his radio plays. But it never was. He wrote no Sacco and Vanzetti drama, though issue-driven current events and historical figures often served as Norman's focus.

102. U.S. Census (1900); (1910); (1920). As of January 5, 1920. John W. Haigis Papers (Box 3), Scrapbook 1926–28, University of Massachusetts Amherst Special Collections. Haigis was, in 1927, in his third year in the State Senate. A shrewd evaluator of his possibilities, he had never lost an election, nor did he lose in 1928. Norman, in his first political campaign, likewise picked a winner.

103. *RE ME*, 30. Cigar smoke always reminded Norman of Pa, the scent of whose "malevolently odoriferous cigars" even clung to his letters to Norman. *RE ME*, 56.

104. The characters of his radio shows are typically adults. (One exception is the protagonist in "The Odyssey of Runyon Jones," which Norman treated on both radio and stage, and the children who sing and dance around Hitler's grave in "On a Note of Triumph.") The adults are caught up in struggles within the greater world, whether of economic stress, social justice or war. Even Norman's Christmas special, a hit, featured adults in Hell rather than Saint Nicholas visiting kiddies. He was never Dr. Seuss.

105. *RE ME*, 35–38.

106. NCL, 1–2.

107. *RE ME*, 36.

108. NC to Al (January 4, 1935), NCL 23.

109. *RE ME*, 49.

110. NC letter to Em (January 31, 1933), NCL, 10.

111. COR03864, Folder 1 (undated fragment, 1928? in pencil). President Coolidge, a dour Yankee, was widely known as emotionless. "Keep Cool with Coolidge" had been his 1924 campaign slogan. He did not choose to run in 1928.)

112. *RE ME*, 55. (Norman says 1930, clearly a misdating. Newspaper clippings of his articles in the *Springfield Union* from 1929 abound.)

113. *Ibid.*

114. Unpublished interview in 2008 of Norman by Ray Kelly of *The Springfield Republican*, courtesy of Ray Kelly. Norman asked Kelly if *The Republican* was "still the great newspaper he remembered from his youth." Although Norman covered the city at large, Norman recalled himself best as a reporter with a knack of getting "the off-beat story," such as one about "the man who had himself rolled down Main Street in a barrel."

115. In a January 1930 letter, ARA, Em gave even more specific advice: "What you should do is to breeze out of town at least once a week. Eat dinner at South Deerfield every Sunday, for example, or take more frequent trips home. Life in the town becomes monotonous without some change now and then. Read some fiction for a change. Get hold of 'Victory' by my friend Conrad and read it a couple of times.

"If I can inveigle Verstandig to take a run to your town a week from Sunday, prepare for a peppy time…we may pick up some mamas.

"Now for crissakes lay off'n the dumps. (signed) Em."

116. NC to Em (June 8, 1934), NCL 20–21.

117. *RE ME*, 52. NC to Hazel Cooley Spiller (March 19, 1970). NCL, 300–301. ("Of course you know that our collaboration on *So Say the Wise* was a thinly transparent device on my part to be *near* you.")

118. *Ibid.*

119. Em's letter, in COR 03871 (Folder 1), is ascribed to December 1928. If so, it indicates that Norman sometimes visited Springfield during his period as a Greenfield reporter and, further, that Hazel was one of the draws that perked his interest in applying to become a Springfield reporter.

120. *RE ME*, 13.

121. NC letter to Hazel Cooley Spiller (March 19, 1970). NCL, 300.

122. The episode is comically recounted in *RE ME*, 52–54.

123. COR 03871 (Folder 1). September 29, 1929, NC to Em.

124. *Ibid.* Norman described the book's "cheap paper, poor binding, unimpressive cover and typographical incongruities" as his major criticisms, not touching upon its content.

125. Letter from Betty McCausland to Norman (May 8, 1947) unearthed by David Okarski. Courtesy of David Okarski, who likewise inspired this much about Norman and the visual arts. "The best news" may have been that Norman was now married, to Kate Locke on March 17, 1947. McCausland never married.

126. One might additionally say that he left a mysterious, matronly sounding "fourth" or "final woman" behind in Springfield. In *RE ME* Norman noted someone with whom he had lunched but never dated or "had an arm around." When he took her to dinner as a sort of farewell, she seemed sad. He asked why and she told him, "Because I cannot be with you always. I would be happy just to take care of you. Always." Norman said that he covered her hands with his, saying nothing in reply. Then, when he took her home, he "kissed her long and hard and held her close, which was perhaps the wrong thing to do." *RE ME*, 99.

127. Facts concerning Jumbo's backstory are drawn from letter, John Tranghese to Norman (April 18, 2009). Author's copy, courtesy of Mr. Tranghese.

128. "Ash-Can-Rolling Sweepstakes Elevates New Sports Champion; Wearing Blue Shirt, Khaki Trousers and Nonchalant Air, Santiniello Wins Meet, Three Arguments and Acclaim of Spectators," (*Republican*, June 29, 1929, p. 1). Of its 105 lines, 18 were dedicated to Jumbo.

129. *Ibid.*

130. *Springfield Sunday Union and Republican* (January 31, 1931); *Springfield Daily Republican* (January 24, 1931); *New York Herald-Tribune* (January 27, 1931), *New York Evening Post* (February 11, 1931).

131. *The Boston Globe* (February 5, 1931).

132. *Springfield Daily Republican* (January 16, 1931).

133. NCI/Columbia, 2. Articles about Jumbo continued to run until spring, 1931. See *Springfield Daily Republican*, March 13, 1931. Norman's articles and interview validated, if they did not boost Jumbo's wavering confidence, and he went on to become a labor leader beginning 1942 as the long-time business agent of Laborers Union Local 999. Letters of John Tranghese to Norman (June 20, 2007, May 30, 2008, and July 27, 2011). Author's copies, courtesy of Mr. Tranghese.

134. *Ibid.*

135. And not only Ma and Pa. Norman got mail from Hawaii from a man in Honolulu who said that he heard Norman's broadcast over short-wave signal W-1XAC—a Boston rerouting world-wide—at 4:45 in the afternoon, just before the evening papers came out over there. Norman to Em (6/9/1932), ARA.

136. NCI/Columbia, 2.

137. *Ibid.*

138. Norman's acceptance, unpublished interview in 2008 of Norman by Ray Kelly, *The Springfield Republican*. Norman got a kick out of Bowles. He recalled him as, "a tall, powerfully built, lantern-jawed eccentric who drove a third-hand flivver." *RE ME*, 48.

Part Two

1. Norman did not date this judicial tirade, but it was probably 1932. Judge Thayer, who was the target of an unsuccessful bomb he received in 1932, became somewhat paranoid thereafter and required a bodyguard and police protection 24/7. He died in Boston of a brain hemorrhage in 1933.

2. By a five-minute drive or a twenty-minute walk Norman could be at either the Fort Street newsroom of the *Republican* or (as later mattered) the WBZ radio studios, then up the hill in the Hotel Belvedere.

3. Norman told Em little stories featuring Charlie as long-suffering and patient, Ida as cranky or marginally present. The Spicers formed an odd couple, Ida appearing mournful when not a harridan. To the 1930 Census taker Charles reported "Lodging House Keeper" as his job. Ida's occupation was noted to be "None." Why? Possibly, Ida suffered from depression and the couple lived together from habit or necessity. Charles, whom Em and Norman called "Charlie," was definitely their favorite Spicer, always exhibiting a mild-to-merry disposition.

4. U.S. Census, 1930. *RE ME*, When Norman "caught her," he admired her nonchalance. She exhibited no modesty, saying to Norman "Good evening" in reply to his "Good evening." She did not scurry to cover herself or shut her door. Norman was 20 at the time. He named no name. Of Donald Burt, he wrote in *RE ME*, 55, that he "was a dwarfed hunchback whose deformity affected his palate so that his speech came through his nose, and that with difficulty." (Norman must have thought of Eddy Torgussen.) "He was a cheerful, kindly man, as alone in this world as the last passenger pigeon, yet never bitter or self-pitying. I spent many hours entertaining him with the scuttlebutt of the courts and city government, and he listened with a raptness that always touched me."

5. Charles and Ida Spicer informed the census taker in 1930 that they were "Hebrew" and that both had been born in Poland to Polish Jews, Charles in Galicia and Ida in Vilna. Each came to the United States as children. Charles at 21 had married Ida, then 22, both having lived in the United States for about ten years. In 1930 Charles was 52 and Ida was 53. Norman knew that Charlie was European but thought that he was Austrian. Norman and Charlie both enjoyed music. Probably, Charlie shared stories about Vienna or some other cultural spot of Austro-Hungary from before his immigration to the United States.

6. *Springfield Union* (5/31/1931).

7. NC letter to Em April 1928, ARA. The typewriter "fell off a table on the train, victim of a nasty lurch" in Switzerland. NC to Ma and Pa (August 29, 1931), NCL, 5. He could not get it repaired. NC to Ma and Pa (September 9, 1931), NCL, 7.

8. NC to Em (1930?), ARA.

9. Ancestry.com, "New York, Passenger and Crew Lists, 1820–1957." The ship carrying Norman (and his brother and friend) departed for Hamburg out of New York. (The date of departure, October 1931, given on this list is discounted and omitted, as contradicted by the dates of Norman's letters home in August, 1931.)

10. Bannerman was the first to refer to Norman as an "innocent abroad." Bannerman, 23.

11. *RE ME*, 63.

12. *Ibid.*

13. NC to Em (5/8/1932), NC to Em (6/9/1932), ARA.

14. NC to Em (June 28, 1932), ARA.

15. COR03872, NC to Em (in pencil: "8/15/1932"), ARA.

16. *RE ME*, 72–77.

17. See "Requiem for Alfred Eisner," NC to Em (January 6, 1941), ARA.

18. *RE ME*, 74.

19. The winter of 1932–33, his midpoint at the sanatorium, may signify a high tide of self-concern and withdrawal. He wrote nothing when former President Calvin Coolidge died unexpectedly in nearby Northampton on January 5, 1933, although to Norman few public figures would have been more familiar. He was nine when Coolidge crushed the Boston police strike. Coolidge's son, John, had died in the White House, age 16, when Norman thrived during his amazing senior year at Winthrop High School. Coolidge was in the White House through most of Norman's adolescence, until Norman was just about to start working for the Springfield *Republican*.

20. COR03872, NC to Em (11/4/1932), ARA.

21. His several moves and new doctors are from the letters he wrote. His memoir is a blank on the moves and changes in doctors.

22. NC to Al (June 6, 1934), NCL 20.

23. COR03872, NC to Em (November 4, 1932), ARA. He talked the talk but did not walk the walk for over six months. To Mary Y. Munford, he wrote from Winthrop (June 3, 1933), NCL, 15–16, "Mary, it has been so long since I have fallen in love with a girl my age that the next one will seem like my first love." He sought from Mary, the head of a family welfare agency in Springfield, the address and telephone number of a Radcliffe girl "a good thinker and lovable" named Dorothy Kelly.

24. NC to Mary Y. Munford (June 3, 1933), NCL, 15.

25. Norman said of car "smashups," robberies, murders, suicides and bond issues that "[t]he variations are not without interest, but neither are they without a fundamental sameness." *RE ME*, 73, 75, 81, ARA.

Rutland was mistyped "Rotland" once, *RE ME*, 75, but this may be reading the draft with forced Freudian insight. COR03872, NC to Em (11/16/1932), ARA. The other time Norman composed something was late the following year when, back in Springfield, he composed "a theme and variations" for a local pianist. When Norman left Winthrop, the machine having served its function, he abandoned it. COR03877, Pa to Norman (3/28/1939), "You had an old dictaphone in the cellar, it's been there for years, felt like throwing it out many times. Little David, the boy upstairs, wants to know if he can have it to play with?"

26. NC to Em and Al Corwin (June 23, 1933), NCL, 16–17.

27. *Ibid.*

28. Esther Zelda Rubin, born in Connecticut in 1907 to a Russian Jewish couple who shortly afterwards moved to Springfield. "Miss Rubin," Norman's first flame in mature love, graduated from Springfield High School in 1923 and, after a time in Manhattan (U.S. Census of 1930), returned to Springfield, where she worked as a secretary to an unnamed magazine. In his letter to Em, Norman noted her as "a Miss Rubin from Springfield whom I invited to repay several dinners I have had at her house." COR03875, NC to Em and Al (in pencil: "Monday, 8/21/1933), ALA. In another letter, he spoke of girlfriends between "Esther and Kate." He likewise mentioned an "Esther" in interviews with Bannerman, when recounting his most serious relationship before Kate.

29. COR03875, NC to Em and Al (in pencil: "Monday, 8/21/1933), ALA.

30. *Ibid.*

31. *Ibid.* In the trip's final minutes, when they happen to hit a whole school of silver hake and everybody, but Pa was taking "one every 10 seconds," Norman added three or four silver hake as well.

32. COR03875, NC to Em and Al (in pencil: "Monday, 8/21/1933"), 2, ARA.

33. *Ibid.*

34. This was "the first time (Walsh) ever pulled in a fish on lake or sea." *Ibid.*

35. Springfield city directories for 1934 and 1935, author's observations of the buildings and neighborhood in 2012. That Norman planned on writing he demonstrated by buying a "new silent Corona portable" typewriter, splurging over $50 on a

machine "so silent that it can be used at the most ungodly hours of the morning without disturbing the neighbors." NC to Al (September 20, 1935), NCL, 27–28.

36. Supposedly, someone else (Rabelais). "You once sought my advice on marriage, which was like asking an Eskimo what brand of seersucker suit to buy, and I answered with my usual brashness, quoting counsel given by Rabelais to an undecided swain who asked the same question." NC to Em (February 27, 1994). NCL, 442.

37. NC to Em (in pencil "Dec. 1933"), ARA. Norman in his memoir affectionately recalled Walsh as "another splendid advertisement for the Irish-American" and a "thin man, bald as a melon, with an honest, big nose, a prominent Adam's apple, and thick lenses in his eyeglasses." *RE ME*, 49.

38. NC to Em (in pencil "Dec. 1933"), ARA.

39. NC to Al (June 6, 1934), NCL, 19. He added that he was applauded for "about two minutes" and that his formula was to give them "something they could understand, appreciate and find amusing."

40. NC to Em (March 14, 1934), ARA.

41. NC to Em (September 11, 1933), ARA.

42. *RE ME*, 68. (It probably ought to be mentioned that, before Norman, Em had been a reporter in Springfield. Because Em was an enthusiastic and accomplished classical pianist in his spare time—his college yearbook mentioned his "fiery" Chopin renditions and Norman reminded him that he could "make a pianny behave," (NC to Em, letter March 19, 1931),—it may be that Em introduced his kid brother to this pianist, or brought them together less directly but by some suggestion.)

43. *RE ME*, 68.

44. Norman fondly referred to Morton as "one of the last genuine Southern cavaliers. He could kiss the hand of your girl (something I had never seen done except in movies), and not look foolish or embarrass the girl." According to Norman, Morton also possessed "a knack for saying the kindest things in the kindest way." *RE ME*, 71.

45. NC to Em (June 1, 1934), ARA.

46. NC to Em (June 8, 1934), ARA.

47. NC to Em (June 18, 1934), ARA. (The coveted wholesale price was $ 43.)

48. NC to Em (September 12, 1934), ARA.

49. NC to Em (September 27, 1934), ARA.

50. NC to Em (October 25, 1934), ARA.

51. NC to Em (November 14, 1934), ARA.

52. NC to Em (November 22, 1934), ARA.

53. NC to Em (November 17, 1934), ARA.

54. *Ibid.*

55. Among other ideas Norman came up with, one sounds like he invented "the talk show." NC to John Holman (NBC network executive) (July 5, 1935), NCL, 24. ("I talked, without scripts and informally, to men and women outstanding in their crafts and professions—a prize-winning painter, a drama critic, an expert photographer, etc. The idea was old, the technique new. The informality of scriptless discussions, when the interviewer and his subject have their topic well in hand, creates an illusion of eavesdropping for the listener.")

56. *RE ME*, 83–84.

57. *RE ME*, 85, ARA.

58. *RE ME*, 86–87, ARA.

59. Walsh's send-off (with photo) was headlined "Norman Corwin Resigns His Post as Radio Editor of Republican." *Springfield Republican* (6/10/1935). The article said that Norman resigned "to take a position as junior executive of the Crosley Radio Corporation's giant station WLW."

60. *RE ME*, 89–90, 92, ARA. It amused Norman to read a WLW advertisement in *Variety* over ten years later in which his name was listed along with other radio celebrities who had started out at WLW. NCI/Columbia.

61. *RE ME*, 93–94. The trauma of 1933 remained lifelong. In sight of eligibility for retirement (not that he ever did retire), Norman read a book about joblessness, Allen R. Dodd's *The Job Hunter* (1965), and footnoted it in his memoir as an "excellent account" of that state. Bannerman, 23.

62. *RE ME*, 94.

63. NC to Em (February 19, 1935), ARA.

64. NC to Em (January 10, 1936), NCL, 29. He preceded the sentences quoted with, "Heard Jose Irubi at Smith College last Wednesday night. He sits cold as a dead herring at the pianny, and proceeds to watch the ceiling while his hands are traveling so fast that you can't see them."

65. Em to NC (May 22, 1936), ARA.

66. Oddly enough, although not enough

to suit him, Norman did handle occasional radio broadcasts for Fox. For example, at the lobby of a premiere, one Sunday over station WOR he led Darryl Zanuck, Jean Hersholt, Will Hays, Ethel Merman and others up to the microphone to speak. NC to Ma (January 10, 1938), NCL, 34.

67. COR03877, Pa to Norman (12/23/1936), ARA.

68. NBC was later deemed too big by the government, and it was broken up as monopoly in 1942, by the divestiture of NBC Blue (later renamed ABC) from NBC.

Em helped get Norman on the air. The file of correspondence, NC to Em, at the American Radio Archives, is topped by a cover document, an undated one-page typed "Note" prepared by BB (Beverly Brainard) under Norman's direction (COR03877, Folder One). It states that in 1938 Em contacted "various personnel within NBC to see if they could arrange for an audition for his brother on the program *The Magic Key of RCA*...Eventually, he was successful and Norman's first network broadcast (was) March, 1938." See also reference to interdepartmental correspondence to Em from William A. Hillpot (February 1, 1938), "I would suggest that we set this up some day in audition for the Magic Key Committee." *Ibid.*

69. NCI/Columbia, 10.

70. Elliott M. Sanger, *Rebel in Radio* (New York: Hastings House Publishers, Inc., 1973), esp. 16–17, 24, 50–51, and 76–77. Norman wrote Sanger when Sanger stepped down as WXQR's Chairman of the Board in 1967, "It is seldom that a man can put his finger on a moment of his life and say 'At that instant everything changed.' When our paths crossed thirty years ago, my life took another course. I choose to think it was for the better. God knows where I would be or what would have happened to me, had it not been for your generosity in giving what must have been the benefit of many doubts, to a brash young publicity flack from across town. I think of myself as Sanger's Folly." *Ibid.*, 77.

71. "Six-months contract" referred to in letter of NC to Ma and Pa (January 25, 1938), NCL, 35. Consciously high-brow, WQXR boasted of being "The Station for People Who Hate Radio." Bannerman, 27.

72. COR3877, Pa to Norman (3/14/1938), ARA.

73. Norman told his family years later that he picked his butcher for the man's "thick Russian accent." Anecdote courtesy of David and Diane Corwin Okarski.

74. Lewis was the network's initially accidental vice president. In charge of sustaining programing, he had been hired by a lucky fluke. He sent CBS a general inquiry about a job at the same time a "wanted" ad appeared in the *New York Times* in 1935 for "an important creative and executive post in radio broadcasting." The ad brought in over 600 applicants. Lewis was *not* one of them. By mistake, his inquiry about a job was dropped on top of the application letters of the six finalists chosen out of 600. Lewis had no high school diploma, but he made a favorable impression when interviewed and he was selected. He turned out to be a great choice. Lewis, an advertising man previously, was a natural when it came to identifying projects that the public would like. Barnouw, 63–64.

75. At American Radio Archives, a one-page typed "Note" prepared (probably by one Beverly Brainard, BB) under Norman's direction for his correspondence with Em (COR03877, Folder One), states that in 1938 Em contacted "various personnel within NBC to see if they could arrange for an audition for his brother on the program *The Magic Key of RCA*...Eventually, he was successful and Norman's first network broadcast (was) March 1938." However, NBC offered no contract.

76. NC to Ma and Pa (April 12, 1938). NCL, 37.

77. Michael Kacey, Norman Corwin Biography, http://www.normancorwin.com/Bio.html, 2.

78. COR03877, Pa to Norman (May 5, 1938), ARA. WHAI, a Greenfield station owned by one John W. Haigis. Haigis had struggled to find footing in a changing Massachusetts electorate. Haigis tried to balance his history of frugal fiscal policies by enthusiastic support for some New Deal programs. He appeared at mammoth rallies for FDR in both Springfield and Boston. When voters chose the Democrat over Haigis in both 1934 and 1936 races, he never ran for office again. He bought a radio station instead which he affiliated with CBS just in time (March 1938). Starting from Norman's first CBS show, Haigis noticed as Norman's star rose. He sent a fan

letter, keeping contact with the boy he had hired at seventeen for his first media job. COR03877, Pa to Norman (May 19, 1938), ARA.

79. NC to David Morton (May 21, 1938). NCL, 39.

80. COR03877, Pa to Norman (July 8, 1938), ARA; COR03877, Pa to Norman (August 22, 1938), ARA.

81. COR03877, Pa to Norman (October 16, 1938), ARA.

82. Norman Corwin interview, 8B, ARA. Transcribed by Kevin Soini.

83. Bannerman, 32. COR03877, Pa to Norman, only dated "Sunday afternoon," ARA.

84. COR03877, Pa to Norman (September 15, 1938), ARA.

85. COR03877, Pa to Norman (October 23, 1938), ARA. Dr. Abrams treated Pa without charge as Pa's "second opinion" man. Pa in turn brought him boxes of Christmas cards from "the factory" at no charge.

86. Bannerman, 32.

87. COR03877, Pa to Norman (December 7, 1938), ARA.

88. "Mid-1938" is a deduction. See Bannerman, 31–32, in which the Tuthill interaction was described but not dated.

89. Bannerman, 51, provides the list, and quotes Norman (in January 1940) in the hope that Coulter had not "permanently abandoned" his earlier idea of capturing the sounds of America.

90. NC letter to Charles R. Jackson (February 23, 1940), NCL, 45–46. Likewise, "by the end of 1938" reflects deduction.

91. NCI/Columbia, 11–12. (for 18th floor, see 24). Jackson's 1959 address to an Alcoholics Anonymous gathering is on youtube. He died in 1968.

92. NC letter to T. Wells Church (September 14, 1938), NCL, 39–41, evidences pure initiative on Norman's part. ("I knocked over Bill Lewis and Dave Taylor with an audition of a show I conceived and wrote. I asked Lewis to give me a budget of $100—script unseen—to audition a program of what I called 'orchestration and augmentation of verse.'...Lewis agreed." After Norman recorded an excellent show by a great cast, "the last I heard of the series idea was Lewis's opinion that the thing might be scheduled after the first of the year.")

93. John Dunning, *On the Air: The Encyclopedia of Old-Time Radio* (Oxford University Press, 1998) (hereafter "Dunning"), 82.

94. Lewis had a good, strong, deep voice—and quite a laugh. Norman appreciated it, noting that Lewis had "an explosive sense of humor. He would detonate with laughter, and his laugh would then trail off into a long wheeze and end up in a coughing fit." *RE ME*, 108.

95. Barnouw, 71.

96. *Ibid.*, 13.

97. *Ibid.*, 117.

98. Bannerman, 36.

99. NC interview, 8B, ARA. Transcribed by Kevin Soini.

100. NCI/Columbia, 14.

101. *Ibid.*, 14.

102. *RE ME*, 122.

103. Barnouw, 89.

104. *Ibid.*, 69.

105. *RE ME*, 238.

106. *Ibid.*, 123–24.

107. *Ibid.*, 122–23.

108. The inscription began with a rhyme to Al's wife, "There are few as pretty, and nobody sweeter,/Than C. de Cordoba, known as Sarita." "They Fly Through the Air," (June 8, 1939), ARA.

109. Barnouw, 16.

110. Barnouw, 17.

111. *RE ME*, 122; Bannerman, 60.

112. Bannerman, 44. Broadcast date from photographs inset in NCL, inset page 3, top image.

113. In his transcribed interview, Em acknowledged unequivocally, "Norman hated McKenzie." It seemed that on at least one occasion McKenzie referred to or told a (false) story about "pushy Jews." TR 57. On the other hand, Pa found that McKenzie—who lived in relatively affluent Winthrop long before the Corwins—"paid attention to (him) more than to anyone else." TR 58. Unquestionably, McKenzie had also helped the family when Pa was hospitalized and recovering from both a physical and mental breakdown in 1917–18. TR 60–63. McKenzie seems to have tended to just the type of bathetic displays of emotion that Norman crossed streets to avoid.

114. COR03877, Pa to Norman (January 4, 1939), ARA.

115. COR03877, Pa to Norman (June 11, 1939), ARA.

116. COR03877, Pa to Norman (July 1, 1939), ARA.

117. COR03877, Pa to Norman (September 27, 1939), ARA.

118. Bannerman, 46. See Corwin, *Thirteen by Corwin*, 46, 79. *New York Journal-American*, April 26, 1939.

119. NCI/Columbia, 14–15. The corresponding Peabody Awards were first awarded in 1940. Corwin, *Thirteen by Corwin*, 17.

120. NCI/Columbia, 17–18.

121. NC to Julian P. Boyd (January 21, 1942). NCL, 64.

122. Clipping in *Gandle Follows His Nose*, copy at ARA.

123. *RE ME*, 152–56.

124. *Ibid.*, 153.

125. *Ibid.*

126. *Ibid.*, 155.

127. Barnouw gave an example of Norman's courage and resistance to censorship. In 1939, Barnouw wanted to run with a Carl Sandburg poem in which a little girl predicts to her father, "Sometime they'll give a war and nobody will come." The line was censored as a potential promotion of draft resistance in some future war. Norman got Bill Lewis to overrule the censor, and the line stayed in the broadcast. He said, "The incident was typical of Corwin." Robert L. Hilliard and Michael C. Keith, *The Broadcast Century: A Biography of American Broadcasting* (Boston: Focal Press, 1992), 87.

128. Bannerman, 48.

129. Beulah Corwin to NC (10/25/1939), ARA.

130. Bannerman, 50–51.

131. *Ibid.*

132. *Ibid.*, 53–54 (including quote).

133. See Barnouw, 118–20.

134. The quote is from Norman's contemporary internal CBS memo, Bannerman, 50.

135. David Lodge, *The Art of Fiction* (New York: Penguin, 1992), 198.

136. *RE ME*, 221. "The Oracle of Philadelphi" was broadcast as part of the *Pursuit of Happiness* series on April 21, 1940. Bannerman, 234.

137. Bannerman, 54.

138. *Ibid.*, 113.

139. NC to Charles Kuralt (November 23, 1990). NCL, 421–23. ("My very first flight, my first time off the ground, was in an armada of six hundred U.S. Army planes: fighters, bombers, interceptors. All biplanes. All open cockpit. I wore a helmet, goggles, and felt-lined boots, and sat on a folded parachute. I was then a kid reporter in Springfield, Mass. It was the Spring of 1931. The Air Force, courtesy of Billy Mitchell, was out to familiarize America with its military flying machines…I had to sign a quitclaim, forgiving the Army any damages if the plane should crash.")

140. Five years earlier, Norman's employer, 20th Century Fox, had arranged for the purchaser of the first ticket on its inaugural flight to be America's most popular child actress, Shirley Temple. Now, Norman was making his own first flight. *LA Times*, Pt. VI, p. 8 (3/1/1987).

141. NC to Mary Ann Watson (March 2, 1985). NCL, 375. The car was a "nifty little Ford convertible." NC to Em (July 1, 1940). NCL, 47.

142. *RE ME*, 167.

143. Bannerman, 234.

Part Three

1. Norman never explained his preference for radio over Hollywood better than in a letter he wrote to a British officer, Lt. Col. Maxwell Setton (February 19, 1941). NCL, 58. ("I am best as a lone wolf, which radio permits me to be, and for this reason alone, I am returning to radio…")

2. "Ann Rutledge," broadcast in the *Cavalcade of America* series on October 23, 1940. Nothing he wrote was on the air for the next six months, until CBS (and Norman) took a big risk with *26 by Corwin* beginning on May 4, 1941. Bannerman, 234.

3. Nigel Simeone, ed., *The Leonard Bernstein Letters* (New Haven: Yale University Press, 2013) (hereafter, "LBL"), LBL, 40 ("that vaunted individualist, that brave soul, Eisner").

("Taking a course in the novel given by the League of American Writers school here, more as discipline to make me sit down more often to an already started novel, than in the hope of learning anything."). LBL, 56. Leonard Bernstein, *Findings* (New York: Simon and Schuster, 1982), 318.

4. LBL, 47, 62.

5. *Ibid.*, 33 ("$50 per" taken to mean $50 per day for a five-day workweek). 39 (?October 1939) ("And why the hell don't you write a guy? Too busy. Yeah, sure."). *Ibid.*, 320.

6. *RE ME*, 177.

7. A logical deduction. Although Norman did not name the sister at the time, in 1966 he asked for Eve Eisner's address to return a "hallowed file."

8. *RE ME*, 178.

9. *Ibid.*

10. LBL, 67.

11. *Ibid.*, 46. See 40, 47, 62. In an undated letter (?October 1940) Alfred wrote Leonard of Hemingway's latest novel, *For Whom the Bell Tolls*, which he read in galley proofs at the studio. It inspired Alfred artistically while its timing frustrated him politically: "Writing that positively *gooses* you! Hemingway saw Spain cameo-clear; and his book is just two years—two? Four!—too late and its anger will cause not a ripple in the hysteria of warmaking." LBL, 47. ("(A) producer wants to talk to me about a scene for Beery that even Beery can't play, and I am suddenly sick with the thought of talking about it. Weep for me among the lost and write."). LBL, 40. Alfred began to write a novel that summer of 1940. LBL, 55.

12. NC to Davidson Taylor (January 16, 1941), NCL, 54–57.

13. NCL, 54. Norman estimated that he and Eisner were some "three weeks" together at CBS. *RE ME*, 178–80. His guess seems correct, probably from early November to about Thanksgiving. Eisner was not in New York until after he read Hemingway's novel, *For Whom the Bell Tolls* (which came out October 21, 1940) in galley proofs in Hollywood. In "late November" Bernstein visited Eisner in the hospital. LBL, 68. Because Norman's only on-air radio production during October was *Ann Rutledge* (October 23), he was writing but not directing in November. Bannerman, 234.

14. *RE ME*, 181.

15. *Ibid.*, 182–83.

16. *Ibid.*

17. Norman knew Eisner only briefly. See Note 13 above. Twenty-five years after he last saw Eisner, Norman came upon his file. He quickly recognized it and recalled the young man and his sister. Norman wrote to ask Leonard Bernstein if he had Eve Eisner's address. He said that he wanted to give her "hallowed folder" back. NCL, 244. In the meantime, Leonard titled one of his compositions a requiem *In Memoriam: Alfred Eisner* (*January 4, 1941*).

18. Norman's January 16, 1941 memo revived an equally earnest but more succinct plea to Bill Lewis four months earlier. NC to Lewis (September 13, 1940). NCL, 51. ("I would be interested in any good 26-week setup…providing I could do a show that would make us all happy and self-respecting…I mean a whopper of a prestige show, in which I might be given resources and a free hand to write and produce the best goddam show on any air.")

19. LBL, 40. (Letter dated October 31, 1939).

20. Bannerman, 59.

21. Norman Corwin interview, Radio Pioneers Group IV, Columbia University Oral Archives (April 28, 1966), 21. Norman Corwin interview, 8B, ARA, transcribed by Kevin Soini. Norman was not entirely left alone. There were "all kinds of little hangnail things. I was asked to compose a singing telegram to Max Wyle (upon his) leaving CBS." In honor of the future author of "The Flying Nun," Norman composed, to the tune of "Auld Lang Syne," a telegram as follows: "When Wylie goes, we blow our nose/And wipe a weeping eye, /Because New York will sink/ when Maxie says goodbye. /So raise a drink to Maxie then, /So down a scotch or two. /We mean the real McCoy, sir,/ When We wish good luck to you." Oddly enough, he also kept what he called a "miserable little drop diary while I was working on that series." *Ibid.*

22. Barnouw, 105. By comparison, in 1945 only a half-million radios were purchased. By then, 89% of households had at least one.

23. Norman spelled phonetically. The correct spelling is "Sneden's Landing," known today as Palisades, New York.

24. *RE ME*, 189.

25. Although "Runyon" could just as easily have come to Norman from "Damon Runyon" or any other source, one in particular is tantalizing. On June 21, 1941 an Arch Oboler show entitled "Adolph and Mrs. Runyon" had aired on NBC. Starring Bette Davis as Mrs. Runyon and Hans Conried as Hitler, it was a fantasy journey. After Mrs. Runyon dropped her husband off to serve in the Army, driving along the road between New York and Massachusetts at night she wishes to God that she had Hitler in her power. Her wish was realized.

26. *Ibid.*

27. Norman described Pa's desk with its

surface area about the size of a spread-out newspaper as bearing "files, correspondence, stationery, postage stamps, clippings, a big pair of shears, a pot of paste, a ruler, an assortment of pens, pencils and markers, and a magnifying glass." *RE ME*, 56.

28. The large-sized, heavy scrapbooks are stored at ARA now, along with two scrapbooks that Norman kept himself. In this way, due to enormous coverage, Pa filled several of the scrapbooks just with 1946–47 "One World Flight" items.

29. *RE ME*, 236–38.

30. Lewis's official title was "Coordinator of Government Radio" for OFF. *RE ME*, 236. According to Erik Barnouw, Lewis "had little originality but quickly recognized it in others," often saying, "You've got an idea there!" Erik Barnouw, *The Golden Web: A History of Broadcasting in the United States, Vol. 2 (1933–53)* (New York: Oxford University Press, 1968), 65. The story of Lewis's hiring by CBS, told by Barnouw at pages 63–65 reads like a farcical comedy, with a happy ending.

31. Although there already was a Librarian of Congress, originally appointed by President McKinley, FDR persuaded the Republican Congress of the wisdom of funding two Librarians of Congress. The incumbent, George Herbert Putnam, took a side office and half-pay as the "Librarian Emeritus." The Emeritus actually outlasted MacLeish and kept regular office hours until 1954, when he retired at age 92.

32. Barnouw, 152. Norman Corwin biography, http://www.normancorwin.com/Bio.html.

33. *Ibid.*

34. This and other facts on origin of the program derive from *RE ME*, 238–39.

35. Norman Corwin, *Thirteen by Corwin* (New York: Henry Holt and Co., 1942), xi.

36. *Ibid.*, xii.

37. NCI/Columbia, 26. *Life* (April 27, 1942).

38. Bannerman, 41.

39. Arch Oboler, *Oboler Omnibus: Radio Plays and Personalities* (New York: Duell, Sloan & Pearce, 1945), 308.

40. Dunning, "Arch Oboler's Plays," 37–39.

41. *Ibid.*

42. NC letter to David O. Selznick (June 24, 1942), NCL, 65–67.

43. See also "Dorie Got a Medal," based on the "true incident of a black soldier who received the Congressional Medal of Honor after the bombing of Pearl Harbor." Bannerman, 133. Broadcast over CBS on April 25, 1944, he eighth show of the *Columbia Presents Corwin* series. *Ibid.*, 241.

44. See NC to Bill Lewis (September 13, 1940). NCL, 51. ("My plans for the fall, providing I am not indispensable to the armed might of the nation..."). Leon Edel, *The Visitable Past* (New York: University of Hawai'I Press, 200), 2. *RE ME*, 270. Although Norman did not specify in his memoir undergoing a physical, I infer this from what he said: "My medical history (scar on a lung, hospitalization for tuberculosis) kept me from serving in a military capacity." Norman did not state the year, but one guesses, given his age group, that Norman was greeted with a notice to appear for an exam in 1942 or 1943, and probably sooner rather than later.

45. *RE ME*, 331. Detroit shifted from producing automobiles to war production in 1942. A new Buick was like gold.

46. Norman Corwin, *Untitled and other Radio Dramas*, 163.

47. *Ibid.*, 192.

48. NC to Ma and Pa (July 2, 1942). NCL, 67–68.

49. *Ibid.*

50. "Sunspots, auroras, cosmic rays, faulty spark plugs, X-ray machines, vacuum cleaners, and power plants knocked one another down in their hurry to get into the act whenever we went on the air." *Ibid.*, 191.

51. Bannerman, 239, 241. December 1, 1943; May 9, 1944.

52. *RE ME*, 322. NC to Kate Locke (September 9, 1942). NCL, 69–71.

53. NC letter to David O. Selznick (June 24, 1942), NCL, 65–67.

54. Bannerman, 119.

55. *Ibid.*

56. Norman Corwin interview, Radio Pioneers Group IV, Columbia University Oral Archives (April 28, 1966), 29.

57. *Ibid.*

58. "In the spring and summer of 1944 I produced twenty-two broadcasts for CBS... All but five dealt with current issues and had to do, more or less, with the war." NC, *Untitled and Other Radio Dramas*, 428.

59. CBS wanted *half* of Norman's "subsidiary earnings." Bannerman, 201.

60. NCI/Columbia, 30.

61. As far back as 1943, an Allied invasion of the Continent was logically anticipated as the defeated Germans retreated before the Red Army after the brutal Battle of Kursk. Norman was buoyed up enough to act. In a telegram Norman sent to Davidson Taylor during contract negotiations, he mentioned that if "an extraordinary event requires a big, special show and CBS would like me to handle it," he was instructing his agent to insure his availability. Bannerman, 122. When executives did not signal back his selection to handle the "extraordinary event" that would require "a big, special show," Norman probably assumed that he was not in the running. Thus, Coulter's confidential comment may have been received as astonishing and unexpected.

62. NC, *Untitled and Other Radio Dramas*, 434. Bannerman, 242.

63. Bannerman, 30–32.

64. NC, *Untitled and Other Radio Dramas*, 489.

65. NCI/Columbia, 30.

66. NC, *Untitled and Other Radio Plays*, 489.

67. NCI/Columbia, 31.

68. *Ibid.*

69. Bannerman, 242. Broadcast November 5, 1944. See also Bannerman, 140–42. Norman did this project without charge. Not only the fourth term was unprecedented: as Norman recalled in the *Corwin* documentary film, the broadcast included a unique barbershop quartet comprised of Groucho Marx, James Cagney, Keenan Wynn and Danny Kaye.

70. NC, *Untitled and Other Radio Plays*, 490.

71. *Ibid.* The song went back to Norman's first wartime broadcasts, his *This Is War!* series.

72. See also NC to Bertha White Nason (January 26, 1945), NCL 84–85.

73. NC, *Untitled and Other Radio Plays*, 491.

74. E.g., Bannerman, 160.

75. *Ibid.*, 34.

76. NC to Mrs. Flora Schreiber (October 30, 1966). NCL, 254.

77. Jeff Porter's more extensive take is concise and definitive: "A landmark in radio, the hour-long program saluted America's GIs in high colloquial style and then went on to raise questions about the larger meaning of victory. As expressed by the Everyman character of the GI, these questions ("Who did we beat, how much did it cost, what have we learned, what do we know now, what do we do now, is it going to happen again?") are delivered in an earnest, humble voice that contrasts markedly with the booming accents of the narrator. The play is memorable for such opposition and mood swings, progressing by sudden turns that transformed the exhilaration of victory into something more emotionally fraught and intellectually challenging." Jeff Porter, *Lost Sound: The Forgotten Art of Radio Storytelling* (The University of North Carolina Press, 2016), 37.

78. How long was "On a Note of Triumph" memorable? The author recalls a panel game show, "What's My Line?" One of its frequent panelists was Martin Gabel. In the 1960s, when the panel successfully guessed the identity of the last contestant, the host, John Daly, said, "The show thus ends on a note of triumph," to applause and cheers of recognition by the studio audience. Any argument over whether Norman or Arch Oboler was the best wartime radio writer might be answered by comparing "On a Note of Triumph" (and its reception and endurance) against Oboler's play, likewise written in advance of V-E Day, titled "Strange Morning." Far different in tone, it was published as part of *Oboler Omnibus: Radio Plays and Personalities* (New York: Duell, Sloan & Pearce, 1945). "Strange Morning" begins with a "brassy, off-beat fanfare" intended to evoke trumpets sounding victory, followed by a narrator's opening, "This is a story of Victory."

79. "The Undecided Molecule" was broadcast July 17, 1945. Bannerman, 244.

80. See Michael James Kacey, *Memos to a New Millennium: The Final Plays of Norman Corwin* (Albany, GA: BearManor Media, 2015), 122. The 1945 play, revised and retitled "Fifty Years After 14 August" is included in this collection.

81. Norman Corwin, *Untitled and Other Radio Dramas* (New York: Henry Holt and Co., 1947), 506. The show, "L'Affaire Gumpert," starring Charles Laughton and Elsa Lanchester (and with Emil Corwin!) broadcast on August 21. It was the last of the *Columbia Presents Corwin* series. Bannerman, 244.

82. NC interview, ARA. Transcribed by Kevin Soini.

83. Norman does not say that he himself attended that premiere. By implication, the review led him to attend a later performance. It was Kate's first top billing but she debuted on Broadway in "Firebird" in 1932. John Mason Brown considered her interpretation of Ophelia in 1938–39 and 1939–40 productions of "Hamlet" to be definitive, "the greatest Ophelia in theater." See *Los Angeles Times*, September 17, 1995.

84. Taylor in 1941 was a twice-divorced man who would marry (and divorce) a third time, but not Giuliana Taberna and not until 1945. Twenty-something Taberna was pivotal. Corwin had used Taberna in small roles. She loved celebrities and was a great New York gadabout with many friends. From 1940 to 1945 Taberna—in pursuit of one celebrity in particular—was a presence at composer Deems Taylor's side at the Stork Club, "21" and other glitzy forums. (Taylor likewise enjoyed a large reputation as an on-air wit for his many appearances as a panelist on the popular NBC quiz show, *Information, Please.*) Taberna, who introduced Corwin to Katherine, also introduced Corwin to Taylor, whereupon Corwin hired him for several works for his radio programs. See James A. Pegolotti, *Deems Taylor: A Biography* (Boston: Northeastern University Press, 2003), 251–55, 287. With or without his wife's helpful memory, Norman identified Taberna definitely and expressly as the one who introduced them. It is intriguing to think that, in league with Kate or discreetly on her own, savvy Taberna at that corner was consciously match-making, given Locke's divorce—which was *either* imminent and pending or recently final.

85. Norman quoted Kate's phrase to Bannerman in an interview on how they first met. Bannerman, who may have spoken with Kate or reviewed documents after he spoke with Norman, wrote that they were introduced "only a few weeks" after her divorce from Maurice Helprin, a successful director's assistant with a huge estate in New Jersey. Divorce decrees were a two-step process at the time, requiring a waiting period after a divorce decree *nisi* before it became final.

86. NC interview, CD 12, ARA.

87. "It's in the Works," (broadcast March 24, 1942), Bannerman, 237.

88. NC interview, CD 12, ARA. Transcribed by Kevin Soini.

89. Bannerrman, 242. NC interview, CD 12, ARA. Transcribed by Kevin Soini.

90. In 1944, Norman did pen at the end of a letter, "I like to sit and gawk/ At Katherine Locke." NC to Kate Locke, January 18, 1944). NCL, 79–80. Also, near the end of a letter to Kate (March 8, 1946) Norman broke through his inhibitions and wrote, "As for you, you beautiful two-legged and blue-eyed creature who laughs at her own jokes, I hug you and kiss you with a sound approximating smack, smack." NCL, 93.

91. NC interview, 10A, ARA. Transcribed by Kevin Soini.

92. NC interview, 12, ARA. Transcribed by Kevin Soini.

93. NC interview, 12, ARA. Transcribed by Kevin Soini.

94. *Ibid.*

95. Bannerman, 195.

96. NC interview, 6, ARA. Transcribed by Kevin Soini.

97. *Ibid.*

98. NC interview, 6, ARA. Transcribed by Kevin Soini.

99. Bannerman, 245–47.

100. TR, 49.

101. *RE ME*, 1.

102. TR, 50. Their life-changing meeting occurred impromptu over dinner on moving train, an accidental encounter.

103. TR, 51.

104. Barnouw, 214.

105. Bannerman, 200–01.

106. *Ibid.*, 232. The one show he did in 1949 for the CBS Documentary Unit was "Citizen of the World," which Lee J. Cobb narrated. Bannerman, 247.

107. Other United Nations radio work followed, two shows in 1950. Bannerman, 210–11. According to Bannerman, NBC repeated "Could Be," and stations around the world (in Britain, Canada and Australia) did, too. After 1950, Norman also produced U.N. shows in 1951 and 1955. *Ibid.*, 247–48.

108. Michael James Kacey, ed., *Memos to a New Millennium: The Final Plays of Norman Corwin* (Albany, GA: BearManor Media, 2015), 71.

Epilogue

1. NC interview, 12, ARA. Transcribed by Kevin Soini.

2. *Ibid.*

3. See NC to Sally Bedell Smith (April 16, 1986), NCL, 385. The word "abandoned" for a book so nearly complete is striking. It might qualify as "unpublished" or even "unreleased." However, "abandoned" was nonetheless the adjective used in a prefatory note overseen by Norman. NCL, Editor's Introduction, xi. The emphasis of "abandonment" is upon the *incompleteness* of his exploration, its unfinished state. Gaps and omissions in the manuscript's coverage dominated his mind.

4. "Foreword by William Shatner," in Michael James Kacey, ed., *Memos to a New Millennium: The Final Radio Plays of Norman Corwin* (Albany, GA: BearManor Media, 2015), 6.

5. "William Shatner Talking About His Time with Norman Corwin," (posted September 5, 2011 by Audrey1700, with note, "This footage was taken at Dragon Con 2011."), at about 7:10. On youtube, Shatner was speaking about a PBS production. Another documentary shows Shatner playing in a Norman Corwin role, Les Guthman's *Corwin* (University of Southern California School of Journalism, 1996).

6. *RE ME*, 82.

7. NC to Esther Zieff (March 7, 1965). NCL, 229. "Katherine Locke" online obituary, *L.A. Times* (September 17, 1995). Norman had Em's presence up and into his own final year of life. "Emil Corwin, who worked for FDA until age 96, dies at 107," obituary by T. Rees Shapiro, *The Washington Post* (March 22, 2011).

8. John Tranghese interview with author, Springfield, MA. Mr. Tranghese kindly gave me a tour of relevant sites in Springfield, and shared copies of his correspondence with Norman.

9. *Ibid.*

10. *Ibid..*

11. Letter, Norman to John Tranghese (July 14, 2007). Author's copy, courtesy of Mr. Tranghese. See also NC letter to Esther Miller (April 22, 1938), NCL, 38. ("My last program on WQXR I gave on Wednesday. Albert Hirsch, a fine young man, played two compositions written by, guess who—me. One I laboriously set down as a musical supplement to James Weldon Johnson's ingratiating spiritual-poem 'Go Down, Death.' Several of my best friends and severest listeners thought it got across...") Note to this states that it was later arranged and sung by the Golden Gate Quartet on a CBS broadcast.

12. Copy of program courtesy of John Tranghese. (Norman was a good friend of Ray Bradbury. When Bradbury was twelve he was memorably startled by a circus performer. The performer, "Mr. Electrico," touched him with an electrified sword and shouted the words, "Live forever!" Within days, Bradbury began writing and he then wrote every day. In "Something Wicked This Way Comes," Bradbury mixed Mr. Electrico into the story.)

13. John Tranghese interview with author, Springfield, MA.

14. *Ibid.* John ebulliently told Norman in one letter that Italians toast people with the salute, "To a hundred years!" but, at Norman's age, he would toast him "To 200 years!" The last call John made to Norman was but three or four days before Norman died at age 101. Letter, John Tranghese to Norman (June 20, 2007). Author's copy, courtesy of Mr. Tranghese.

15. "A Note of Triumph: The Golden Age of Norman Corwin," (video, 2005).

16. Michael Kacey, phone interview with author. Also, see credit to Norman at the start of the documentary itself.

17. *Ibid.*

Bibliography

Collections

Norman Corwin Collection, American Radio Archives, Thousand Oaks Library, Thousand Oaks, CA

Books

Bannerman, R. LeRoy. *Norman Corwin and Radio: The Golden Years.* The University of Alabama Press, 1986.

Barnouw, Erik. *The Golden Web: A History of Broadcasting in the United States, 1933–53,* vol. 2. Oxford University Press, 1968.

Corwin, Norman. *More by Corwin.* New York: Henry Holt and Company, 1944.

Corwin, Norman. *Thirteen by Corwin: Radio Dramas by Norman Corwin.* New York: Henry Holt and Company, 1942.

Corwin, Norman. *Untitled and Other Radio Dramas.* New York: Henry Holt and Company, 1947.

Dunning, John. *On the Air: The Encyclopedia of Old-Time Radio.* Oxford University Press, 1998.

Kacey, Michael James, ed. *Memos to a New Millennium: The Final Plays of Norman Corwin.* Albany, GA: BearManor Media, 2015.

Keith, Michael C., and Mary Ann Watson, eds. *Norman Corwin's One World Flight: The Lost Journal of Radio's Greatest Writer.* New York: The Continuum International Publishing Group, Inc., 2009.

Langguth, A.J., ed. *Norman Corwin's Letters.* New York: Barricade Books, 1994.

Porter, Jeff. *Lost Sound: The Forgotten Art of Radio Storytelling.* The University of North Carolina Press, 2016.

Sanger, Elliot M. *Rebel in Radio.* New York: Hastings House Publishers, Inc., 1973.

Non-Print Media

Corwin, Norman. *Norman Corwin Centennial.* Radio Spirits, 2010.

Guthman, Les. *Corwin.* University of Southern California School of Journalism, 1996.

Kacey, Michael James, ed. *The Poet Laureate of Radio, An Interview with Norman Corwin.* Anthracite Films, 2006.

Simonson, Eric, ed. *A Note of Triumph: The Golden Age of Norman Corwin.* Direct Cinema Limited, 2005.

Index